Thomas Stafford

Pacata Hibernia

Or, a history of the wars in Ireland during the reign of Queen Elizabeth, especially within the province of Munster under the government of Sir George Carew, and compiled by his direction and appointment. Vol. 2

Thomas Stafford

Pacata Hibernia

Or, a history of the wars in Ireland during the reign of Queen Elizabeth, especially within the province of Munster under the government of Sir George Carew, and compiled by his direction and appointment. Vol. 2

ISBN/EAN: 9783337324421

Printed in Europe, USA, Canada, Australia, Japan

Cover: Foto ©ninafisch / pixelio.de

More available books at **www.hansebooks.com**

OR

A HISTORY OF

THE WARS IN IRELAND

DURING THE REIGN OF

Queen Elizabeth

ESPECIALLY WITHIN THE PROVINCE OF MUNSTER UNDER THE GOVERNMENT OF

SIR GEORGE CAREW

AND COMPILED BY HIS DIRECTION AND APPOINTMENT

EDITED AND WITH AN INTRODUCTION AND NOTES
BY
STANDISH O'GRADY

WITH PORTRAITS, MAPS AND PLANS

VOL. II.

DOWNEY & CO. LIMITED
12, YORK STREET, COVENT GARDEN, LONDON
1896

LONDON:
PRINTED BY GILBERT AND RIVINGTON, LD.,
ST. JOHN'S HOUSE, CLERKENWELL, E.C.

CONTENTS OF VOLUME II.

THE SECOND BOOK—(continued).

CHAPTER XIII.

PAGE

The Castle of Rincorran, guarded by the Spaniards, besieged; and the Spaniards repulsed—The Castle of Rincorran battered by the Lord President—A remarkable skirmish between us and the Spaniards that attempted to relieve Rincorran—The Lord Audley, Sir Oliver Saint-John, and Sir Garret Harvy hurt—A Spanish commander taken prisoner—The enemy demanded a parley, but the Lord President refused to treat with the messenger—The commander parleyed, but his offers were not accepted—The enemy endeavoured to make an escape, wherein many were slain and taken Prisoners—Sir Oliver Saint-John sent from the Lord Deputy with directions to the Lord President—The reasons that induced the Lord President to receive the Spaniards that were in Rincorran to mercy—The agreement between the Lord President and the Spanish commander that was in Rincorran 1

CHAPTER XIV.

Her Majesty's letter to the Lord President—A supply of munition and victuals—A resolution in Council that forces should be sent to encounter O'Donnell—The Lord President of a contrary opinion, and his reasons—The reasons why this service was imposed upon the Lord President—The Lord President marcheth towards O'Donnell—O'Donnell lodgeth near the Holy Cross, and the strength of his quarter—O'Donnell, by means of a great frost, passed over the mountain of Slieve Felim, whereby he escaped from fighting with the Lord President—O'Donnell's hasty march—The principal men that were in O'Donnell's army—The principal men in Tyrone's army 8

CHAPTER XV.

A part of Don Dermutio's examination concerning a practice for the taking or killing of the Lord President—A sally

made by the enemy in Kinsale—A Spanish captain slain—
Master Hopton died of a hurt—The Earl of Thomond
landed at Castlehaven with supplies of horse and foot—
Supplies of horse and foot landed at Waterford—The
Queen's fleet and supplies of foot with munitions, etc.,
arrived at Cork—Castle ny Park attempted to be taken by
us, but the enterprise failed—A council of war called by the
Lord Deputy 18

CHAPTER XVI.

The Earl of Thomond with his supplies came to the camp—
Castle ny Park surrendered by the Spaniards—A Spanish
captain wounded, whereof he died—A brave act of a private
soldier—Approaches made nearer to the town—The Lord
President with the Earls of Thomond and Clanricard
returned to the camp—A sally made by the Spaniards . 25

CHAPTER XVII.

The town of Kinsale summoned, and Don Juan's answer—The
Spaniards beaten out of their trenches—The Marshal went
to view the town to discover a fit place to batter—A skirmish
entertained for the viewing of the breach—An entrenchment
made on the west side of the town—A bold attempt of a
sergeant of ours, wherein he was slain—A soldier slain
standing between the Lord Deputy and Lord President—
The great sally made by the enemy with a furious charge,
both upon the platform where the battery was placed and
upon a new entrenchment on the west side of the town;
the enemy repulsed and beaten—The enemy gained our
entrenchment on the west side of the town—The entrenchment recovered from the enemy—The loss on the enemy's
part and on our part 30

CHAPTER XVIII.

A supply of Spaniards landed at Castlehaven—A Council of
War held—Good service done by a Scotsman—O'Donnell
joined with the Spaniards at Castlehaven—All the Irish in
the west of Munster and some of the English race revolted
and adhered to the Spaniards—Sundry castles rendered by
the Irish into the Spaniards' hands—Divers of the Irish
had companies in pay given them by Don Juan—The Castle
of Carrickfoyle taken and the ward murdered—Tyrone's
army discovered near our camp 38

CONTENTS.

CHAPTER XIX.

A brief report of the good service done by Sir Richard Levison upon the Spanish fleet at Castlehaven—A letter from Don Juan de Aguila to Tyrone and O'Donnell—A letter from Don Juan to Captain Juan de Abornoz y Andrada—A letter from Donnell O'Sulevan Beare to the King of Spain 43

CHAPTER XX.

Tyrone with his army approached within view of our camp, but could not be provoked to fight—The enemy sallied out of the town—The Irish army as before present themselves—The enemy from the town make another sally—Intelligence of the enemy's designs brought to Captain Taffe . . 50

CHAPTER XXI.

The means whereby Captain Taffe had his intelligence—The Battle of Kinsale, wherein the rebels were overthrown—The Lord President directed by the Lord Deputy to guard the camp against any attempt to be made by the Spaniards—A glorious victory—An old Irish prophecy proved true—Two sallies made by the Spaniards 54

CHAPTER XXII.

Zubiaur arrived at Castlehaven and immediately returned—O'Donnell, Redmund Burke, etc., embarked for Spain—The names of such of the Irish as fled into Spain—The loss which the rebels had in passing through Munster after the Battle of Kinsale 64

CHAPTER XXIII.

A parley desired by Don Juan, and granted by the Lord Deputy—Don Juan's propositions, with their answers and his reply—The reasons which moved the Lord Deputy and Council to yield to a composition—The articles of the composition 71

CHAPTER XXIV.

The names of the hostages delivered by Don Juan—Don Juan's demand of victuals for the transportation of his men—The victuals which were delivered to Don Juan and their rates—The number of Spaniards who were transported out of Ireland—The Lord Deputy broke up his siege and returned to Cork—Captain Harvey's commission for his government. 82

CONTENTS.

CHAPTER XXV.

Don Juan's request to the Lord Deputy—A resolution in Council to erect certain forts in Munster—The request of the inhabitants of Kinsale to the Lord President—Certain companies cashiered—A letter from the Lord President to Her Majesty—The examination of Richard Owen—Richard Owen's message from Tyrone to the Lord Deputy—Instructions for Captain George Blunt 90

CHAPTER XXVI.

The King of Spain's letters intercepted—A letter from the Duke of Lerma to Don Juan de Aguila—A letter from the Duke of Lerma to the Archbishop of Dublin—A letter from the Secretary Ybarra to Don Juan de Aguila—A letter from the Secretary Fragursa to Don Juan de Aguila—A letter from the King of Spain to Don Juan de Aguila . 101

CHAPTER XXVII.

The Spaniards embarked at Kinsale—The Spaniards dispossessed of Donboy by O'Sulevan Beare—A letter from O'Sulevan Beare to the King of Spain—A letter from O'Sulevan Beare to the Earl of Caraçena—A letter from O'Sulevan Beare to Don Pedro de Zubiare. 118

CHAPTER XXVIII.

An interlocutory discourse between Captain Roger Harvy and Pedro Lopez de Soto—Pedro Lopez de Soto's passport—Pedro Lopez de Soto's letter to Captain Roger Harvy . . 129

CHAPTER XXIX.

Don Juan embarked at Kinsale—The Lord Deputy departed from Cork towards Dublin—A letter from the Lord Deputy and Council to the Lords in England—The Lord Deputy sickened in his journey to Dublin—The Lord President surprised with a fever in his return to Munster . . . 136

THE THIRD BOOK OF THE WARS IN IRELAND.

CHAPTER I.

The estate of the province of Munster after the siege of Kinsale—The war of Ireland censured to be lawfully maintained

Contents.

by the rebels in the opinion of the learned men of Spain—The names of the doctors of Salamanca who censured the lawfulness of the rebellion in Ireland 141

CHAPTER II.

The Earl of Thomond directed to march with an army into Carberry, and his instructions—The Castle of Donboy fortified by the rebels—The Earl of Thomond having placed convenient garrisons in the west, returned to Cork—The Lord President resolved to besiege the Castle of Donboy—The list of the army in Munster—The Lord President advised not to enterprise the winning of the Castle of Donboy, and the reasons why—The Lord President perseveres in his resolution, and causeth the army to march towards Donboy 148

CHAPTER III.

Divers spoils done to the enemy—A letter from the Lord President to the Spanish cannoneers in Donboy—Captain Bostock and Captain Barry sent to Sir Charles Wilmot—A digression of Sir Charles Wilmot's proceedings in Kerry—Divers rebels slain—A traitorly soldier hanged—A ward put into Carrickfoyle—The Castle of Lixnaw taken by composition—The Castle of Ballihow taken and the Knight of Kerry defeated—Castle Gregory and Rahun taken . 160

CHAPTER IV.

The forces which the rebels had in Kerry in bonaght—The voluntary submission of Donnell MacCarty—Sir Charles Wilmot required by the Lord President to come to the camp at Carew Castle—A great prey taken from O'Sulevan More's sons—The Knight of Kerry upon humble suit protected—Sir Charles Wilmot with the forces of Kerry and the munitions and victuals from Cork arrived at the camp then at Carew Castle—Munition and victuals sent by the Lord President to the Lord Deputy—Dermond Moyle MacCarty, brother to Florence MacCarty, slain . . . 168

CHAPTER V.

A resolution in Council that the army should be transported by sea to the great island and thence to the main—The rebel Tirrell desirous to parley with the Lord President—All our horse sent from the camp to guard Kinsale, and likewise certain foot—Tirrell failed twice to parley with the Earl of Thomond, and the reason why 174

Contents.

CHAPTER VI.

The Army dislodged from Carew Castle—The regiments transported to the Great Island—Teg Reugh MacMaghon slain—The Castle of Donmanus surprised—A Spanish ship arrived—The conference between the Earl of Thomond and Richard MacGoghagan—The Lord President rides to the place where the forces were to land—The vigilant care of the Lord President—Two regiments directed to land in the Little Island, the other two to make to the main—The rebels deceived—The rebels defeated, and Captain Tirrell wounded 177

CHAPTER VII.

The Spanish ship which arrived near Ardea brought passengers, munition and money to the rebels—The distributors and distribution of some of the money—A letter from Owen MacEggan to Richard MacGoghagan at Donboy—A letter from James Archer, Jesuit, to Dominic Collins, Jesuit, at Donboy—A letter from John Anias to Dominic at Donboy—A letter from John Anias to the Baron of Lixnaw a little before his execution. 183

CHAPTER VIII.

The Lord President vieweth the castle of Donboy—The Lord President finds good ground to encamp in and to plant the battery, contrary to all men's opinions—Two spies of the rebels hanged—The artillery landed—The camp intrenched and the artillery drawn into the market place—Our approaches begun—The Island of the Dorseys taken, and in it divers rebels slain and taken prisoners, besides artillery, munition, and much other spoil—The rebels taken in Dorseys executed and the fort razed—Captain Kingsmill maimed with a shot—An attempt of the rebels given on our camp—Sir Samuel Bagnall brings letters to the Lord President from the Lord Deputy and from Don Juan de Aguila—A fair escape—The artillery planted before Donboy—Donboy battered and a breach made—The breach assaulted—Divers of the rebels slain in seeking to escape by a sally—Others slain in the water—The Lord President's colours placed on the top of the castle, but the vault still maintained by the rebels—Sundry rebels voluntarily yielded themselves—The remainder made election of a new captain, whose resolution was extraordinary—A battery made upon the vault—The rest surrendered themselves—A desperate resolution of Richard MacGoghagan—Eight and fifty rebels executed; the rest reserved for a time—The whole number of the ward in Donboy—The loss we received in the siege—Captains, men of quality, and others wounded—Artillery, munition, and spoils got in the castle . . 190

CHAPTER IX.

Tirrell's proffers for the redeeming of his men—Our ordnance (with those which were gained there) shipped—The services propounded to Tirrell he refuseth, and the reasons of his refusal—The castle of Donboy blown up with powder—Tirrell's men who were respited executed—The army shipped and transported into the Great Island—The Downings taken—Leamcon Castle taken—The castle of Lettertinless taken and burnt—The Lord President returned to Cork—The companies sent for by the Lord Deputy delivered over to Sir Samuel Bagnall—The confidence the Irish had of supplies from Spain made them obstinate . . . 206

CHAPTER X.

Supplies of a thousand foot sent out of England for Munster—Sir Charles Wilmot with his regiment sent into Kerry—James Archer and Connor O'Driscall fled into Spain—Sir Owen MacCarty's sons revolt—Divers castles taken in Carberry by the garrisons there—The description of Bearehaven—The description of Baltimore Haven—The description of Castlehaven—The Spanish hostages licensed to depart—A letter from the Lord President to Don Juan de Aguila 212

CHAPTER XI.

The taking of the Castle of Donboy was the cause that the army prepared in Spain for Ireland was stayed—Two thousand supplies of foot were sent out of England for Munster—John Fitz Thomas's practice to deceive the Lord President, but failed—A false rumour of a Spanish fleet on the coast of Munster—Sir Samuel Bagnall with his regiment commanded to stay in Munster 219

CHAPTER XII.

A letter from Teg MacCormock Carty to the Lord President, entreating the remission of his offences—Cormock Mac-Dermond Carty accused of sundry treasons—Cormock MacDermond committed—The Castle of Blarney in the custody of Captain Taffe—The Castle and Abbey of Killcrey rendered to the Lord President—Mocrumpe besieged—Cormock's wife and children imprisoned—Cormock MacDermond plotted his escape 224

VOL. II. a

CONTENTS.

CHAPTER XIII.

A letter from the Lords of the Council to the Lord President—Instructions for Captain Harvy to write to Spain—A letter written by Her Majesty's own hand to the Lord President—A letter from the Lord President to Her Majesty—A letter from Captain Harvy to Pedro Lopez de Soto, the Spanish Veador—A letter from O'Donnell to O'Connor Kerry—A letter from Don Juan de Aguila to the Lord President—A letter from the Lord President to Don Juan de Aguila—Captain Harvy's passport sent to the Veador—The Lord President's passport for Captain Edny into Spain—Spanish intelligence sent from Master Secretary Cecil to the Lord President—The Lord President's opinion sent to Master Secretary of a defensive war in Ireland . 234

CHAPTER XIV.

Cormock MacDermond escapes—The Castle of Mocrumpe taken and most of the ward put to the sword—O'Sulevan and Tirrell repair with their forces into Muskerry—Cormock MacDermond makes means to be received to Her Majesty's mercy—The reasons that moved the Lord President to accept Cormock's submission 258

CHAPTER XV.

The Lord President offers the Lord Deputy to send him of his list one or two regiments—O'Donnell's death—Tirrell's quarters assailed by Sir Samuel Bagnall—The loss on the rebels' part—Tirrell rageth in fury against the inhabitants of Muskerry and retireth into Beare and Desmond—The death of Captain Harvy—Captain Flower succeeded Captain Harvy in the government of Carberry—Cloghan summoned—The Constable's brother hanged, and the castle rendered. 266

CHAPTER XVI.

A branch of a letter from the Lords of the Council to the Lord President—The ensigns of magistracy re-delivered to the Corporation of Kinsale—Of Spaniards defeated at Kinsale in the time of King Richard the Second—The rising-out of the country committed to the charge of the Lord Barry—The Lord Deputy requires the Lord President to meet him at Galway—Sir George Thornton appointed to join the Lord Barry—A messenger from the rebel Tirrell to the Lord President, and his answer—The Knight of Kerry defeated—The Knight of Kerry, Thomas Oge, and O'Sulevan More's son make their submission—A foul murder committed by O'Sulevan More's son 273

CONTENTS. xi

CHAPTER XVII.

Sir Charles Wilmot Chief Commander of the forces in the absence of the Lord President—The rebels make three divisions of their forces—Tirrell, afraid, flies the province—The Lord Barry and Sir George Thornton join their forces with Sir Charles Wilmot—A skirmish entertained—A prey taken from the rebels out of the fastness—Divers rebels submitted themselves—William Burke, John O'Connor Kerry, and O'Sulevan Beare with the bonoghs fled out of the province—The rebels' loss in their passage through the County of Cork, and the hard shift they made over the Shannon—The good service done upon the rebels by the Sheriff of the County of Tipperary—Captain Henry Malby slain—Beare, Bantry, and Dorseys spoiled, and the Castles of Ardea and Carrigness rendered—Captain Taffe employed against the rebels in Carberry—The Pope's vicar slain and the rebels defeated—The Cartys of Carberry submit themselves to the Lord President 279

CHAPTER XVIII.

False rumours divulged of the state of Munster—The Lord President sent one thousand foot munitioned and victualled to the Lord Deputy—A letter from Her Majesty to the Lord President concerning the Earl of Clanricard—A letter from John Burke to the Lord President—A letter from John Burke to Sir George Thornton—A certificate from a Popish Bishop in behalf of John Burke 291

CHAPTER XIX.

The Lord Deputy sent to the Lord President for men and munition, and himself to repair to him—The list of Her Majesty's forces in Munster—Sir Edward Wingfield sent by the Lord President with five hundred foot into Connaught—The Lord of Lixnaw defeated by Captain Boys—The Castle of Kilco taken by Captain Flower—The Castle of Berengarry taken by Sir Charles Wilmot—Sir Charles Wilmot and Sir George Thornton left by the Lord President Joint Commissioners for the Government of Munster—A letter sent by the Lord President from the Lord Deputy to the Lords of the Council 299

APPENDIX 321

INDEX 353

LIST OF ILLUSTRATIONS TO VOLUME II.

	PAGE
Donnell O'Sulevan Beare	*Frontispiece*
Map of the Kingdom of Ireland divided into Four Provinces	*To face page* 1
Map of Castleny Park	,, 25
Map of the Fort of Haulbowlin	,, 91
Map of Cork	,, 137
Map of the Army on the Beare Country	,, 141
Map of the Siege of Dunboy	,, 191
Map of Muskerry	,, 267
Turlough Lynagh	,, 317

PACATA HIBERNIA.

CHAPTER XIII.

The Castle of Rincorran, guarded by the Spaniards, besieged; and the Spaniards repulsed—The Castle of Rincorran battered by the Lord President—A remarkable skirmish between us and the Spaniards that attempted to relieve Rincorran—The Lord Audley, Sir Oliver Saint-John, and Sir Garret Harvy hurt—A Spanish commander taken prisoner—The enemy demanded a parley, but the Lord President refused to treat with the messenger—The commander parleyed, but his offers were not accepted—The enemy endeavoured to make an escape, wherein many were slain and taken prisoners—Sir Oliver Saint-John sent from the Lord Deputy with directions to the Lord President—The reasons that induced the Lord President to receive the Spaniards that were in Rincorran to mercy—The agreement between the Lord President and the Spanish commander that was in Rincorran.

WE attended all that day for the landing of the artillery, and perfected the entrenchment about the army, which was left unperfected the day before through the extreme foulness of the weather; and at night Sir John Barkley, Sir William Godolphin, and Captain Bodly were sent to view the most commodious place to plant the artillery for the battering of the Castle of Rincorran, which was situated upon the River of Kinsale, something more than a quarter of a mile from the town, very convenient to forbid our shipping to ride near the same, wherein Don Juan de Aquila, the Spanish general, had placed a captain with one hundred and fifty soldiers, whom he promised to relieve if they were assailed, or bring them off in boats.

The two culverins were landed, and all means used to mount them; but it could not be done till the next day, so ill was everything fitted, by reason there had been no use of them for a long time.

These two pieces were mounted, and all things put in readiness to batter the next day. The Spaniards in the town, discovering our purpose, that night essayed to relieve the castle by boats, and were valiantly repelled by Captain Button with shot out of his ship.

The two culverins began to play upon the Castle of Rincorran, but within two or three shot the carriage of the better culverin broke, and about two o'clock in the afternoon the other developed a flaw, and by that means was made unserviceable, so all that could be done that day was to mount the whole culverin upon her carriage.

The same day they gave an alarm to our camp, drawing artillery out of the town, and with it played into our camp, killed two near the Lord Deputy's tent with a demi-cannon shot, and through the next tent to it broke two hogsheads of the Lord Deputy's beer, and every shot that was made fell still in the Lord Deputy's quarter near his own tent. Don Juan de Aquila, perceiving the castle would be distressed, attempted to relieve it by boats, but Sir Richard Percy beat them off, who had the command of the Lord President's regiment that this night was appointed to guard.

The culverin in the morning began to play, and about nine o'clock the demi-culverin was mounted, which after a few shots broke her axle-tree: before three she was remounted, and by that time a cannon likewise planted; and all the three pieces without intermission played. The Lord President, disliking the manner of the making of the battery, not being constantly made upon one place, but upon the spikes of the castle, requested the Lord Deputy to leave that service to his care, whereto he easily assented.

To show that he was well experienced in the profession of a cannoneer, wherein he had been, by reason of his employments,[1] long practised, he performed the office of a master-gunner, making some shot, and, that the artillery might play as well by night as day, himself did take and score out his ground marks, and with his quadrant took the true level, so that the want of daylight was no hindrance; but in doing thereof he fairly escaped two musket shot; for, as he was standing at the breech of a cannon busy about his work, the one lighted upon the muzzle of the piece, the other upon the carriage close to the trunnions. While we were busy attending the battery, five hundred of the principal men drew out of Kinsale, with show, to go to relieve Rincorran by land, towards a guard we kept between Rincorran and the town, leaving a great gross for the seconds under the walls, and under that colour to gain a safe passage for their boats thither; whereupon out of the regiments being then in arms in the camp divers broken companies drew that way, amongst which Sir Oliver Saint-John sent Captain Roe, his lieutenant-colonel, and Sir Arthur Savage's lieutenant, with one hundred men,

---

[1] Carew for a long time had been Master of the Ordnance in Ireland. He afterwards held the same post in England, and was an enthusiast in gunnery, a pleasing trait in such a character.

and, seeing them likely to draw on a round skirmish, took thirty shot of his own company and went up to them, where he found Captain Roe and Carberry,[1] lieutenant to Captain Thomas Butler, skirmishing with shot, the enemy being hard by them with some two hundred men, and another gross near towards the town to second them. The Lord Audley, who drew some of his regiment out of the camp, was then coming up. As soon as Sir Oliver Saint-John came where the skirmish was he saw the enemy drawing up to give a charge, coming close with their pikes, whom they presently encountered and beat them back towards their seconds, and made them retreat apace; notwithstanding they played upon them with their small shot out of every house in that quarter of the town, being full of towers and castles.

In this charge Sir Oliver received on his target and body divers thrusts with the pike, whereof one gave him a very small hurt in the thigh: he killed a leader and one other with his own hands. The Lord Audley coming up to the charge was shot through the thigh; Sir Garret Harvy hurt in the hand, and his horse killed under him; Captain Butler's lieutenant was slain, and four others; Sir Arthur[2] Savage's lieutenant was shot through the body, and thirty others were hurt. The enemy left ten or eleven dead in the place, besides those that were hurt, which in all likelihood were many, by reason of the nearness of the shot; and, as one reporteth that came the next day from Kinsale, and had been in the Guesthouse amongst

---

[1] Carberry MacEgan, *Gœlice* Cairbré. The MacEgans were hereditary standard-bearers to the House of Ormonde.

[2] The "Four Masters" commemorate in memorable terms the death of this young Royalist officer.

them, seventy were brought thither hurt, whereof eight died that night. In this skirmish was taken prisoner Juan Hortensio de Contreras, who had been sergeant-major of the forces in Brittany; and divers very good arms and rapiers were got from the Spaniards.

All this while the three pieces played upon the castle, until six o'clock at night, at which time they in the castle sounded the drum and prayed admission of parley, which the Lord President, whom the Lord Deputy had left there, himself returning to take care of the camp, accepted. There came with their drum an Irishman born in Cork, who prayed, in the name of the rest, that they might be licensed to depart to Kinsale with their arms, bag, and baggage: this being denied by the Lord President, who would not conclude with any but the commander of the place, he returned the messenger, willing him to tell the commander that no other but himself should be heard, and that he had no commission to grant them any other composition than to yield to Her Majesty's mercy. Then immediately they sent the drum again, and with him a sergeant, called Pedro de Herodiay Cuacola, whom the Lord President refused to speak with, upon whose return the commander himself, called Bartolomeo Paez de Clavijo an Alfero, came to the Lord President, but, not agreeing upon the conditions, for he still insisted upon departing with their arms to Kinsale, being put safe into the castle, the battery began afresh, and the defenders bestowed thicker volleys of shot than at any time before. At length, about two o'clock, when they found the weak state the castle was grown into by the fury of the battery, they sounded again their drum for another parley, which not being accepted, many of them endeavoured to escape under the rock close to the water-side, which being espied by us, our men ran presently close to the castle walls; and if the Lord President had not forbidden them (although the breach was not sufficiently assaultable), they would have entered the house of those who attempted to escape. There were three and twenty Spaniards taken; and of this country birth a great multitude of churls, women, and children: there were likewise slain of the Spaniards towards thirty. All this while the enemy shot not a shot, but as men amazed lay still. Of the Irish there was not a man taken that bore weapon; all of them being good guides escaped; only one, Dermond MacCarty, by them called Don Dermutio, was taken, who was then a pensioner to the King of Spain, and heretofore a servant to Florence MacCarty.

A good while before day the Lord Deputy sent Sir Oliver Saint-John to the President to signify his pleasure to him; which was, if they would render themselves he should accept their offer, excepting the Irish. Not long after Sir Oliver Saint-John was departed, that no error might be committed, towards the morning the Lord President went to the Lord Deputy to make relation of that night's proceeding, and upon deliberation it was thought convenient if the Spaniards would quit their arms and render the place, with promise of life only to be sent into Spain, that they should be received to mercy; the consideration whereof grew upon these reasons—the one because in forcing a breach it was likely many good men would be lost, and also to entice others that are in Kinsale to leave the place, wherein they felt misery, by the example of this merciful dealing with those of

Rincorran, but especially because expedition in the taking of this castle had many important consequences.

About one hour after day the commander sent word to the Lord President that he would render the place and quit all their arms, so that they might be sent to Kinsale, which being refused, he entreated that only himself might hold his arms and be sent to Kinsale, which also being denied, he resolutely determined to bury himself in the castle and not to yield. His company, seeing his obstinacy, threatened to cast him out of the breach, so that they might be received to mercy. In the end it was concluded that all his people should be disarmed in the house, which was done by Captain Roger Harvy, captain of the guards, that night, and himself to wear his sword until he came to the President, and then render it to him; which being performed upon his knees, they were brought prisoners into the camp, and thence immediately sent to Cork.[1]

The last of October the President received a gracious letter from Her Majesty, all written with her own hand. It was short, but yet therein is lively expressed in what a thankful sort his service was accepted, the true copy whereof ensueth :—

---

[1] We perceive something of the heroic Spanish temper in this story. Don Paez had rather bury himself in the ruins of Rincorran than come out without his sword. "The Spaniards," Carlyle asserts, "were incontestably the noblest European nation of the sixteenth century."

CHAPTER XIV.

Her Majesty's letter tothe Lord President—A supply of munition and victuals—A resolution in Council that forces should be sent to encounter O'Donnell—The Lord President of a contrary opinion, and his reasons—The reasons why this service was imposed upon the Lord President—The Lord President marcheth towards O'Donnell—O'Donnell lodgeth near the Holy Cross, and the strength of his quarter—O'Donnell, by means of a great frost, passed over the mountain of Slieve Felim, whereby he escaped from fighting with the Lord President—O'Donnell's hasty march—The principal men that were in O'Donnell's army—The principal men in Tyrone's army.

HER MAJESTY'S LETTER TO THE LORD PRESIDENT.

MY FAITHFUL GEORGE,—If ever more service of worth were performed in shorter space than you have done we are deceived. Among many eye-witnesses we have received the fruit thereof, and bid you faithfully credit, that what so wit, courage, or care may do, we truly find they have been all truly acted in all your charge; and for the same believe that it shall neither be unremembered nor unrewarded. And in meanwhile believe my help nor prayers shall never fail you,

Your sovereign that best regards you,
ELIZ. R.

The second of November the ordnance was drawn from Rincorran to the camp.

The third, the Spanish sergeant-major who had been taken prisoner upon the last of October, and the

Alferes, who rendered himself upon condition of life at Rincorran, obtained license to write to Don Juan, and one of our drums was sent to carry their letters.

The fifth, four barks, with munitions and victuals from Dublin, arrived in the haven of Kinsale.

The sixth, upon certain knowledge that Tyrone and O'Donnell were drawing towards Munster, the trenches of the camp were made deeper and higher.

The seventh, the Lord Deputy, having intelligence that O'Donnell, with a great part of the northern forces, was advanced near the province to join with the Spaniards, and that Tyrone was but a few days journey from him, it was debated in council whether it were necessary that forces should be sent towards him to divert his intention. It was agreed by the greater part that two or three regiments of foot and some horse should be employed in that service. The President was of a contrary opinion, alleging, for instance, that Tyrone, at his late being in Munster, at whose return the Earl of Ormond, having good espials, and very desirous to fight with him, yet could never have sight of him or of any of his company; "and the reasons (said he) are very apparent, for they are sure to have the country to friend, to give them hourly intelligence of our lodging and marches; and they are so light-footed, that if they once get the start of us, be it ever so little, we shall hardly or never overtake them." Notwithstanding these reasons it was concluded that forces should be sent; and for so much as the country would be more willing to give assistance to the Lord President than to any other, as also because he was best acquainted with the passages and places of advantage to give O'Donnell impediment, he was commanded with his own regiment, and Sir Charles Wilmot's, which were in list two thousand one hundred and fifty, but not by pole above one thousand, and three hundred and fifty horse in list, which were by pole two hundred and fifty, to undertake the service; and for his better strength Sir Christopher Saint-Lawrence,[1] who with his regiment was coming into Munster, and was to meet him upon the way, should join with him, and also the rising-out of the country. The President in obedience, though without hope to meet with an enemy that hath no will to hazard his troops in fight (for so he conceived of O'Donnell), the seventh of November left the camp, and never ceased travelling until with long and weary marches he came to Ardmail, in the county of Tipperary; O'Donnell, with his sharking troops[2] lodging not far from the Holy Cross, their

---

[1] Brother of Lord Howth. He accompanied Essex in that muddy ride to Windsor. A gentleman of the Court passed Essex without salutation. Sir Christopher laid his hand on his sword-hilt and said, "My lord, shall I kill him?" The first Irish Saint-Lawrence was the dear friend and comrade of the heroic John de Courcy, Earl of Ulster. The family never flung out a second conspicuous figure.

[2] "Sharking troops"? Carew, I think, set out on this journey with the resolution *not* to fight with O'Donnell. A battle with the young northern dynast, all the responsibility of which would rest undivided on his own shoulders, was like staking his whole fortunes on the cast of a single die. Moreover, Red Hugh and his "sharking troops" had an immense military reputation at this time. As Carew moved slowly northwards to meet Hugh Roe, a correspondence of a quite comical character went on between him and Mountjoy. "He is five, he is six, he is seven thousand strong," quoth Carew. "He is double and treble my force. Tyrone is very near him; I am undone. Why did the Council send me on this hopeless business?" etc., etc. A letter of some such purport Carew sent to Mountjoy almost every day. On the other hand Mountjoy, whose own fortunes were not involved, continued to assure Carew that Hugh Roe was only 1500 strong. "Even if you see 3000, don't believe your eyes; I know it," and to screw Carew's courage to the sticking-place sent after him every available man—Sir Christopher and his Leinster regiment, the young Earl of Clanricarde with the army of Connaught, the Earl of Thomond and his regiment—urging Carew, all he could, not to dally, but to go

camps not being distant the one from the other above four miles. But the country stood so partially affected to the traitors that by no promise of reward or other satisfaction could they be induced to draw any draught upon them; by reason whereof, but with great advantage, no probable attempt of good success could be made upon them; being lodged, as they were, in a strong fastness of bog and wood, which was on every quarter plashed.

For avoiding confusion I must ask some pardon of the reader to continue the discourse of the President's journey until I speak any more of the siege at Kinsale. O'Donnell, on the other hand, fearing our forces, which were increased by a regiment of foot and some horse which Sir Christopher Saint-Lawrence brought with him, durst not enter further into the country, because he could not avoid us, and at that time he had no other way to pass; for the mountain of Slieve Felim, which in summer time is a good ground to pass over, was, by reason of great rains, so wet and boggy that no carriage or horse could pass it.

This mountain is in the county of Tipperary, towards the Shannon; and from thence to come into the county of Limerick the passage is through a

in on Hugh Roe first, beat him, and then go for Tyrone. When Carew did eventually confront Hugh it was with an army of some three to one, yet even so he would not go in upon him, or even follow Hugh when the latter evaded him and slipped into West Munster. The Council could send Carew against Hugh Roe, but they could not make him risk all his fortunes on the issue of one battle with such a fighter as the northern chieftain. Carew's incapacity, prudence, or poltroonery on this occasion involved large consequences, for when Hugh Roe, unpursued, worked into West Munster, West Munster was at his mercy, and whether they liked it or not, all the West Munster lords were forced to join him. In fact Carew's behaviour on this occasion shook the provincial mind generally, and threw nigh half the province into the arms of Spain.

straight, near the Abbey of Ownhy, which Abbey, from the place where O'Donnell encamped in O'Magher's country, is at least twenty Irish miles. Having, as we thought by lodging where we did, prevented his passage, there happened a great frost, the like whereof hath been seldom seen in Ireland, and the enemy, being desirous to avoid us, taking advantage of the time, rose in the night and marched over the mountain aforesaid; whereof, as soon as we were advertised, we likewise rose from Cashell, whither we were drawn (mistrusting that they would take advantage of the frost), four hours before day, in hope to cross him before he should pass the Abbey of Ownhy, supposing that it had not been possible for him to have marched farther, with his carriage, without resting. The next morning, by eleven o'clock, we were hard by the Abbey, but then we understood that O'Donnell made no stay there, but hastened to a house of the Countess of Kildare's called Crome, twelve miles from the Abbey of Ownhy, so that his march from O'Magher's country to Crome, by the way, which he took without any rest, was above two and thirty Irish miles;[1] the greatest march with carriage (whereof he left much upon the way) that hath been heard of. To overtake him we marched the same day from Cashell to Kilmallock, more than twenty Irish miles; but our labour was lost. The morning following, O'Donnell, with all his forces, rose from Crome and lodged that night in the straight of Connelogh, where he rested a few days to refresh his tired and surbated troops. The President, seeing that this

---

[1] Equivalent to some forty English. Apparently an insurgent Irish army at this date knew at least how to march. Observe that Hugh Roe marched with "carriage."

light-footed general could not be overtaken, thought it meet to hasten to the camp at Kinsale to prevent his coming thither; wherein we used such expedition that if he had done his uttermost we were sure to be there before him, or force him to fight with us; for we took the next direct way, and he, for his safety, to avoid us, marched a farther way about through Dowalla and Muskerry, which was very troublesome to pass with horse and baggage. The time of our return to the camp was the five-and-twentieth of the same month. In our retreat towards Kinsale, between Kilmallock and Moyallo, we overtook the Earl of Clanricard with his regiment marching towards the camp, and also, between Moyallo and Cork, we met with the Earl of Thomond, who was sent by the Lord Deputy with his troop of horse to follow the President.

There came into Munster with O'Donnell these principal gentlemen of Ulster and Connaught, viz. O'Rwrke,[1] MacSwiny ne Doa,[2] O'Dogherty,[3] O'Boyle,[4] the two MacDonoghs,[5] MacDermond,[6] O'Kelly,[7]

[1] O'Rourke, Brian of the Battle-axes, referred to in the preface.

[2] *MacSweeney na Doe*, i.e. either of "the Districts" or of "the Battle-Axes," captain of a territory in the north of Donegal; nominated to that command by Hugh Roe.

[3] O'Dogherty, Lord of the Peninsula of Innishowen. Hugh brought this lord under his dominion in a singular fashion. At a parley he made a sudden charge on O'Dogherty and his gentlemen, overthrew them, took O'Dogherty captive, and only released him after he had given in hostages and sworn to obey him. This O'Dogherty was father of Sir Cahir, a chief who rebelled first against Hugh Roe and afterwards against the Government.

[4] O'Boyle, lord of West Tyr-Connall.

[5] The two MacDonoughs, lords respectively of Corran and of Tirerill, territories in the county of Sligo, over which Hugh exercised lordship.

[6] MacDermot, lord of the Curlew Mountains, hero of the battle of that name; an excellent soldier and gentleman. See Bog of Stars.

[7] O'Kelly, lord of a district in the east of the County of Galway.

O'Byrne, O'Connor Roe's two sons, O'Donnell's two brothers,[1] Donnell O'Connor Sligo's brother,[2] the two O'Flares,[3] William Burke, brother to Redmond,[4] and Hugh Mostian; besides of Munster men, the Lord of Lixnaw,[5] John FitzThomas, brother to the counterfeit Earl of Desmond, the Knight of the Valley,[6] Dermond Moyle MacCarty, brother to Florence, and many others. His whole number consisted of nearly four thousand foot and three hundred horse. This was related to the President by one, James Welsh, who was with O'Donnell when he fled the encountering of the President's forces; he also affirmed that Tyrone had in his army MacGenis, MacGuire, MacMaghon, Randell MacSorley, O'Neal, and all the chiefs of Ulster with their forces.

[1] O'Donnell's two brothers were Rory, afterwards first Earl of Tyrconnall, and Cathbarr (Top of Battle). The most interesting of Hugh Roe's brothers, Manus, was already slain in battle.

[2] O'Connor Sligo's brother. Hugh, having caught O'Connor Sligo intriguing with the Government, took him prisoner and advanced his brother Donal to his room.

[3] The two O'Flares? Probably O'Haras.

[4] Ricard Sassenagh, Earl of Clanricarde, had two sons, Ulick and Shane, surnamed of the Clover. Ulick succeeded his father as Earl. The two brothers quarrelled over the English and Irish aspects of their position, and fought out the quarrel with deadly animosity. According to the naïve "Four Masters," they "were at war with each other, but were both at peace with the Government." Eventually Ulick not only killed Shane, but took possession of his country, the Barony of Leitrim, in Galway. Shane was Baron of Leitrim. He left two sons, Redmund, Baron of Leitrim, and William, mentioned in text. Redmund was a very stout and brilliant warrior in the rebellion, though he repeatedly offered the Government his services if they would recognize his title, and compel the Earl of Clanricarde to restore him his patrimony. But the Government, then leaning strongly on the Earl, feared to alienate that great man.

[5] The lord of Lixnaw, Co. Kerry, was head of that branch of the Geraldines who called themselves MacMaurice or FitzMaurice, descendants of Raymond le Gros, the celebrated Norman Conquistador.

[6] The Knight of the Valley, also called the Knight of Glynn.

HUGH ROE O'DONNELL.

NOTE TO CHAPTER XIV.

Hugh Roe, or Red Hugh, whose characteristic appearance with his "sharking troops" we have seen, is one of the most interesting characters in Irish history. He was the son of Hugh, son of Manus, son of another Hugh Roe who was contemporary with Henry VII. This elder Hugh Roe was the most powerful Irish chieftain of his time. At one time he had all Ulster and nearly all Connaught under his control. He invaded the pale, and exacted tribute far and wide there, at which time he took into his pay and directed the action of the O'Moores of Leix (Queen's County), and of the O'Connors of Ifailey (King's County). So at this juncture he was lord of nigh half of Ireland. Finally, being opposed and rebelled against at many points, he made peace with Henry VII., swore himself as the King's "man," and surrendered to the latter a good deal of Connaught, over which his ancestors had exercised a certain hegemony.

I have often thought that the ambition and political and martial purposes of our Hugh Roe must have been stimulated by the thought of the great career of his father's grandfather, who had the same name as himself. Every chieftain at this time was intimately acquainted with his family history. Hence, to a great extent, the marvellous pluck and grit which many of them exhibited in their struggles with the Crown.

Manus, son of Hugh Roe, was taken prisoner by Shane O'Neill, who also conquered and governed Tyrconnall, or Donegal.

Manus was succeeded in the Chieftainship by his son Calvach. Calvach supported the Queen in the Shane O'Neill wars, and was, as a reward, presented by her with a patent for Tyrconnall, to himself and his heirs *in tail male*, a fact which I will beg the reader to remember.

Calvach, who was killed by falling accidentally from his horse, was succeeded in the chieftainship by Hugh, father of Hugh Roe. It was he who really broke Shane O'Neill's victorious career, beating him utterly in battle, after which Shane summoned the expulsed Mac-Donalds of Antrim to aid him, and was by them murdered in a drunken brawl. This Hugh's wife was the Ineen-Du, i.e. the Dark Daughter, of the house of the Cambells. All these northern lords, I may add, were closely connected in blood with the Scotch aristocracy. Before his marriage with the Ineen-Du, Hugh was father, by an Irish lady, of Donal O'Donnell, whom FitzWilliam made Sheriff of Donegal, and who, travelling beyond the bounds of his Shrievalty, made Hugh MacGuire lord of Fermanagh. This Donal, who aimed at the chieftainship, was shot with arrows by the Ineen-Du, mother of our Hugh Roe. Hugh, son of Manus, though he did beat Shane O'Neill in battle, was a feeble and unambitious man, governed by his wife and his principal chieftains.

In 1587, on the eve of the Armada, Sir John Perrott, Lord Deputy of Ireland, by a stratagem—and a very dishonourable one—took captive Hugh Roe, son of Hugh and the Incen-Du. Perrott, with the Armada about to sail, for it was announced for 1587, desiring to make his hold upon Ireland as strong as possible, stooped to this vileness. Hugh Roe was imprisoned in the Castle of Dublin. Thence in 1590 he made his escape, but was captured in the County of Wicklow and brought back. In the year 1591 he made his escape again, and was not recaptured; but, under romantic circumstances, made his way home.

At the time of his return his father, Hugh, son of Manus, was older and feebler than ever. In fact, he was never a strong man in any sense. Hugh Roe's mother, a very capable woman, resolved that her son should be the new O'Donnell, and induced her husband to resign in his favour. Most of his feudatories, however, determined to resist him. From this course they were diverted partly by the extraordinary energy of Hugh Roe, who was at the time only nineteen years of age, and partly by the fact that the Government, not knowing exactly what to do with him, sent orders that he should be obeyed as the O'Donnell. As the result of all this, Hugh Roe, accompanied by Tyrone, came before the Viceroy at Dundalk, prostrated himself in the usual style, swore oaths of allegiance, and returned to Donegal as the Queen's O'Donnell. So the boy, however famous as a rebel, commenced his career as the Queen's O'Donnell. This fact should never be forgotten by those who at the same time admire Hugh Roe as a patriot, and denounce the Queen's MacGuires, the Queen's O'Reillys, etc.

Eventually Hugh rebelled and joined the confederated lords of Ulster. For this rebellion no one can fairly blame him. It was certainly the purpose of the Government to drag down and destroy all the great northern lords, Hugh Roe amongst the number. Hugh and the rest determined to have a fight for it first; and I know of no law which forbade them. Most of the Plantagenet kings had sworn themselves as vassals of the King of France, yet none of them, who had occasion, hesitated to renounce his allegiance and draw sword against his suzerain.

Hugh Roe, having been proclaimed as the Queen's O'Donnell, speedily brought the recalcitrant lords of Tyrconnall under his dominion. Then he began to revive in Connaught the lapsed seignory, or overlordship of his ancestors. Possibly through the young chieftain's teeming brain passed thoughts of himself as King of Ireland. He was not afraid of O'Neill, i.e. Hugh, Earl of Tyrone, in spite of the latter's years and experience and great power. In a State paper signed by Tyrone, that lord writes, and with perfect truth, "Tyrconnall has been most times a match for Tir-Owen" (Tyrone), i.e. "the House of O'Donnell has been most times a match for my house, the House of O'Neill." And this was true.

Hugh Roe's military operations had been hitherto chiefly confined to Connaught. He had beaten Sir R. Bingham, and compelled the Queen to recall him in disgrace. He raided the Royalist territories of Connaught perpetually, and even made more than one victorious raid through Connaught against Munster. Eventually the Queen's people invaded Tyrconnall by sea. Hugh Roe beat the Queen's army into its fortifications at Derry, and leaving a sufficient force to hold it in check, resumed his operations on Munster. He was recalled by the news that his cousin Nial Garf, i.e. Nial the Rough, had made common cause with the invaders. Now who was Nial Garf? He was the grandson and heir of Calvach O'Donnell, to whom the Queen by Patent had granted all Tyrconnall, and to his heirs, in tail male. Nial Garf, if the Queen of Ireland's patent was good for anything, was rightful lord of all Tyrconnall. Nial seized this opportunity of asserting an indubitable right, and all his barons and gentlemen went with him enthusiastically in that business, maintaining that their lord was O'Donnell under the Queen's hand, Hugh Roe only by an order in Council and sheer force, having no just claim to the chieftainship either by English law or Irish. So Nial Garf rebelled, and in his rebellion, drew after him at the very start a third of Tyrconnall. Presently Cahir O'Dogherty, Lord of Innishowen according to patent, and divers others of Hugh's subject lords, joined the invaders, and Hugh Roe was obliged to fight at home for very existence. More than half of Tyrconnall was at this time opposed to him. I look upon this as the most brilliant period of his career. He fought and practically beat the Queen's forces and those of his revolted lords, and at the summons of Don Juan, marched at once and marched straight for Kinsale. We have met Hugh Roe upon his march. We find that he did not run away from Carew, but stiffly stood against him, that utilizing an opportunity he evaded him with great dexterity and marvellous dispatch, and succeeded in getting into West Munster without being attended or followed by any pursuing army.

Carew, who would not fight him when he met him, afterwards poisoned him at his leisure. See Preface.

CHAPTER XV.

A part of Don Dermutio's examination concerning a practice for the taking or killing of the Lord President—A sally made by the enemy in Kinsale—A Spanish captain slain—Master Hopton died of a hurt—The Earl of Thomond landed at Castlehaven with supplies of horse and foot—Supplies of horse and foot landed at Waterford—The Queen's fleet and supplies of foot with munitions, etc., arrived at Cork—Castle ny Park attempted to be taken by us, but the enterprise failed—A council of war called by the Lord Deputy.

THE dangerous hazard which the President was in this journey I may not omit to relate, as well for the peril he ran as for his temper in not seeming to see that which he perfectly knew and despising it; for Dermond MacCarty, called by the Spaniards Don Dermutio, taken as you have heard at the siege of Rincorran, being examined by the Council confessed to them that Cormock MacDermond, Lord of Muskerry, had intelligence with Don John, and certain presents had been mutually given and received, and that the said Cormock had undertaken, and faithfully promised, to deliver up the President to Don John alive or dead. The President was himself present at this examination, which notwithstanding, he took the said Cormock and ten horsemen, his followers, along with him, rode with him, ate and drank with him, and many times had private conference with him, not seeming to take notice of any treacherous intent; besides his army consisting of three thousand or thereabouts, what with country risings-out, and under captains in pay,[1] two thousand of these were of Irish birth, no less affected to the rebels than to themselves; and I can well assure the reader upon good grounds that if our forces had received any disaster they would all have turned Turks and cut the throats of their own commanders.

The eighth, certain ships to the number of thirteen were discovered, passing by Kinsale to the westward, but afterwards it proved to be the supplies sent out of England with the Earl of Thomond.

The Spaniards by that time had got knowledge of the departure of a good part of our forces, and thereupon supposing us to be much weakened (as it cannot be denied that we were) and inferior to them in town in bodies of men, they drew out about noon the

[1] Carew was plainly in no "dangerous hazard" during his abortive expedition against Hugh Roe, for though he brought Lord Muskerry with him, he only allowed him to be accompanied by ten of his followers. What Stafford surmises as to the attitude of his Irish troops in the event of Carew's being defeated by Hugh Roe, seems to be an unworthy slander. The Irish soldiers of the Queen were truer to their salt than her English soldiers.

The Queen's generals had sustained many defeats at the hands of the insurgent lords in this war, yet no such treachery as Carew apprehended ever occurred. When Hugh Roe, for example, in the battle of the Curlew Mountains utterly overthrew the President of Connaught, though the President's army was almost wholly Irish, nothing of the kind happened.

Certain it is that at least one other Irish lord, perhaps many, were playing a double game at this time. O'Sullivan Bere, while affecting to be a Queen's man, having just emerged into power as the Queen's O'Sullivan Bere, wrote to Don Juan offering to rise-out in his favour with 2000 men if the Spaniard would give him arms and pay for 1000. This is related by the chieftain's nephew, P. O'Sullivan, who, blinded by his devotion to the cause of Spain, does not seem to think that there was anything unworthy of a chieftain or a gentleman in his uncle's action.

most part of their forces, and anon after sent some threescore shot and pike to the foot of the hill close by our camp, leaving their trenches very well lined for their seconds. Some of ours were presently drawn out to entertain the skirmish with those that came up, and another strong party was sent out towards Rincorran, who from the bushy hill played in flank upon their trenches and beat them from the same; so that they that were first sent out close to our camp being beaten back by our shot, and thinking to find the seconds they left behind them, were disappointed by the quitting of their trenches, and by that means driven to follow the rest to the succour of the town. Our men, following them with much fury, hurt and killed divers, amongst whom they brought off the body of a sergeant, and possessed the enemy's trenches, which the enemy, being reinforced, made many attempts to regain, but were repulsed and beaten back into the town. We heard by divers that Don John committed the sergeant-major (who commanded then in chief) presently after the fight, and threatened to take off his head, commended highly the valour of our men, and cried shame upon the cowardice of his own, who, he said, had been the terror of all nations, but now had lost that reputation, and he gave straight commandment upon pain of death (which he caused to be set upon the town gates) that thenceforth no man should come off from any service until he should be fetched off by his officer, though his power were spent or his piece broken, but make good his place with his sword. Captain Soto, one of their best commanders, was that day slain, for whom they made very great moan, and some twenty more besides were hurt, which could not but be many. On our side only some ten were hurt and three killed, among whom Master Hopton, a gentleman of the Lord Deputy's, was sorely hurt, and since died thereof. If this skirmish had not been readily and resolutely answered on our part the Spaniards had then discovered the smallness of our numbers, and would no doubt have so plied us with continual sallies that we should hardly have been able to continue the siege.

The same day we had news of the Earl of Thomond's landing at Castlehaven with one hundred horse and one thousand foot of supplies out of England in thirteen ships, which by violence of foul weather had been driven to the westernmost part of Ireland, and with great difficulty recovered Castlehaven aforesaid, whence the fifth day following he came with horse and foot to the camp at Kinsale. The next day, being the eleventh, we were advertised that Sir Anthony Cooke and Patrick Arthur were landed at Waterford with two thousand foot and some horse.

The twelfth, Sir Richard Levison, admiral, and Sir Amias Preston, vice-admiral, of the Queen's fleet for Ireland, with ten ships of war, arrived at Cork with two thousand foot, besides munitions, cannoneers, carpenters, wheelwrights, smiths, etc. Presently the Lord Deputy sent them direction to come to Kinsale.

The thirteenth, nothing was done either by us or the enemy.

The Queen's ships with much difficulty recovered the harbour of Kinsale. The admiral, Sir Richard Levison, and the vice-admiral, Sir Amias Preston, came to the Lord Deputy's camp. That day and the next day the two thousand land forces were put on shore, and before that we had certain news of the arrival of the other forces from Barnstaple and Bristol at Waterford and Castlehaven; but they were not then come to the camp, nor in many days after.

The Lord Deputy, coming from aboard the ships, a great shot was made at him from the town, whence they might discern him in the head of a troop, and yet missed him very little.

Some of the Queen's ships, having direction, began to play upon a castle on the island, called Castle ny Park, held fit next to be taken, to invest the town on that side. They broke off some part of the top, but finding that they did it no greater hurt they left off shooting, and the rather because that day and the two next proved so extremely stormy and foul that as the ordnance could not be landed nor anything else well done; yet, out of an extraordinary desire to effect something, the seventeenth being the most happy day of Her Majesty's coronation, which we meant to have solemnized with some extraordinary adventure if the weather would have suffered us to look abroad, we sent at night, when the storm was somewhat appeased, the sergeant-major and Captain Bodley with some four hundred foot to discover the ground of Castle ny Park, and to see whether it might be carried with the pickaxe, which was accordingly attempted; but the engine[1] we had got to defend our men while they were

---

[1] This engine was called the *sow* in Ireland and Scotland, but elsewhere the mantelet. It was a strong wooden house, set on wheels and protected with raw hides. Being pushed close to a castle, the soldiers within it began to mine away at the castle walls. Meantime the defenders threw down upon it from the battlements great stones, hoping to smash it.

Clifford once brought such a sow against Sligo Castle. It was destroyed by the skill of a Scotch engineer called Crawford. Crawford had a contrivance on the battlements by which he alternately raised up and let fall upon the sow with devastating force an enormous beam of timber.

at work being not so strong as it should have been, they within the castle having store of very great stones on the top, tumbled them down so fast as to break it, so that they returned with the loss of two men and proceeded no further in that course.

The same day, the Lord Deputy called a council of war, wherein it was propounded that now that Her Majesty had plentifully furnished us with men, munition, and victuals, we were to consider our own strength, and the best way either to attempt the town or to continue the siege. We were also to consider the force of the enemy within Kinsale, and what aids they were likely to have out of the country, and of all other commodities or incommodities that were to happen on either side. The conclusion and resolution was that we should invest the town with all celerity to keep it short of relief, and before the making of a breach to break their houses that they might find no safety in them and thereby be exposed to the like incommodity of cold that we felt in the camp; in doing thereof it was conceived that many would be slain and endanger the destroying their magazines of powder and victuals; for if presently we should make a breach and attempt it by assault there was no difference between a weak place stored with bodies of men and a strong fortified town; besides the enemy had ground sufficient, if a breach were made, to cast up new earthworks which would put us to more toil and loss of men than an old stone wall; and, in the opinion of all the chiefest of the army, it was concluded that we could not do the enemy a greater pleasure, or unto ourselves a greater disadvantage, than to seek to carry it by breach before the forces in the town, either by sword or sickness, were weakened.

NOTE TO CHAPTER XV.

I don't know whether such will be the opinion of military men, but it seems to me that the Queen's commanders showed a great deal of incompetence throughout the whole of this business. It almost looks as if they wished to waste time and make the war-job as long as possible. Surely an active and resolute general would have burst a breach forthwith in those weak walls, and sent his men into it, and not wasted blood and time and opportunity over those small seaward-looking forts, or have sent half his force off into the middle of Ireland to meet O'Donnell, resultlessly, as it turned out.

Moreover time was very pressing, for another Spanish army was on the sea, and the two insurgent armies of Ulster were on the march.

Mountjoy in his dispatches always alleges want of men, yet at the time when he dispatched Carew against Hugh Roe he had at least 8000. Even now after the arrival of Thomond with his forces and the forces from Barstable, as well as the army of Connaught, he would not venture upon the breach-and-storm method, but commenced what turned out to be a quite useless bombardment.

I may add that though Stafford, writing for English readers, did not like to mention the fact, the only reliable portion of the Queen's army was the Irish portion. Mountjoy in his dispatches gives a deplorable account of the English. They could only fall sick and die, or run away in hope of getting back to England. Indeed, there must have been universal mismanagement. During the siege Mountjoy, according to the testimony of our author, lost "six thousand" men, and let it be remembered that, at this date, and in Ireland, even four thousand men constituted a great host. Mountjoy relates that the English soldiers were so stupid and lethargic that they would die rather than erect huts for themselves. Their huts were built for them by their Irish comrades, rude structures of sods or wattles. The Queen's soldiers apparently had to sleep on the dank earth, which killed off the Englishmen by thousands. Her Irish soldiers, warriors by trade, were constitutionally better able to rough it, and, no doubt, had many contrivances by which they rendered camp life in bad weather less deadly. We may therefore safely assume that most of the six thousand lost in the siege were English. Mountjoy succeeded in killing ten times more of his men than the Spaniard could ever have slain in the breach. All this time the lords of Munster were watching eagerly and endeavouring to guess which party would prove the stronger, all quite empty of enthusiasm or public principle, but all very intent upon the main chance.

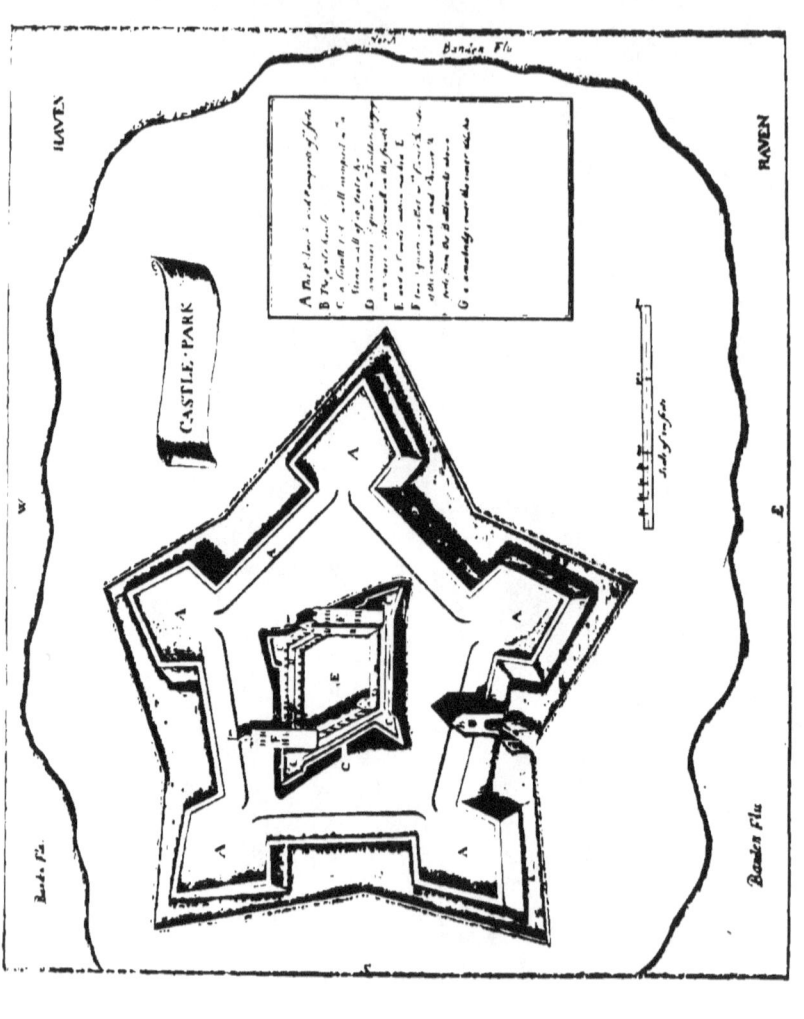

MAP OF CASTLENY PARK.

CHAPTER XVI.

The Earl of Thomond with his supplies came to the camp—Castle ny Parke surrendered by the Spaniards—A Spanish captain wounded, whereof he died—A brave act of a private soldier—Approaches made nearer to the town—The Lord President with the Earls of Thomond and Clanricard returned to the camp—A sally made by the Spaniards.

THE Earl of Thomond, also, with one thousand foot and one hundred horse, having been by force of weather driven far to the westward, and with much difficulty had recovered Castlehaven, came thence by sea to the port of Kinsale. The Lord Deputy, to refresh his men and horses, sent them to Cork, for in their healths they were impaired; and that evening some Spaniards fled from Kinsale and voluntarily came to our camp.

A demi-cannon was unshipped as soon as it was calm and placed on this side of the water, which played most part of that day upon that castle, and broke many places, but made no breach that was assaultable. In the night they of the town attempted to relieve the castle by boat, but were repelled by Captain Tolkern and Captain Ward, who lay with their pinnaces between the island and the town.

The demi-cannon played again, and a cannon then landed and placed by it, with some ordnance also out of the ship, though they served to small purpose. About noon one hundred men were sent with Captain York and Captain Smith to view if the breach were assaultable, and though they found it was not, yet the Spaniards within, being no longer able to endure the fury of the shot, hung out a sign for parley upon the first show of our men and yielded themselves and the castle upon the promise of their lives only; which being accepted, they brought them presently to the camp, being in number seventhen. Before the castle was yielded the Spaniards in the town made divers shot at Captain Tolkern's pinnace with a piece of ordnance which they mounted a day or two before close to the gate of the town, but did no hurt at all to her; the pinnace warping nearer to the other side under the hill, and at last riding safely without a shot. The same day a platform was made upon a ground of advantage, not far from the camp, that commanded one part of the town, that under the favour thereof we might the better make our nearer approaches, which at that time we could hardly have done by reason of the great frost, and a demi-cannon mounted upon it, with which some shot was made at the town, and a sentinel taken anon afterwards affirmed that the first shot went through the house that Don John was in and did otherwise great hurt.

Another cannon was brought up and planted by the demi-cannon, which the night before was brought from the ship, and this day the Lord Deputy went over into the island to view how thence the town might be best annoyed and invested.

Also the prisoners who were taken at Castle Park were sent to Cork with direction to the

Mayor to send them and all the former prisoners into England, the serjeant-major and the commanders of Rincorran and Castle ny Park excepted; and this day a great number of Irish women and children were put out of Kinsale to try their fortunes in the country.

Four other pieces were planted by the cannon and demi-cannon, which altogether played into the town; one of these shot killed four men in the market-place and struck off a captain's leg, called Don John de Saint-John, who is since dead of the hurt.

That evening one James Grace, an Irishman, ran out of Kinsale, assuring the Lord Deputy that Don John at his landing was five thousand men, and that he was yet three thousand strong; that he had four pieces of ordnance well mounted; that the Irish who were with him were so much affrighted with our artillery that Don John had much to do to hold them, whose departure, if it should happen, would be a great want to him, for by them he received ease and comfort; and that Don John's house, where he lodged, had been shot through with a great shot.

The six pieces began again about ten o'clock to batter upon the town, and so continued till night, in which time, and in all men's judgments, as by report of the prisoners we took, they did great hurt to the town. This day, while the Lord Deputy, the marshal, and the serjeant-major were viewing the ground where the approaches were intended, a private soldier of Sir Francis Barkley's, in the face of the Guards attempting to steal, as he had done divers times before, a Spanish sentinel, who was seconded with four that he saw not, fought with them all five, whereof one of them was the serjeant-major, whom he had almost taken, and when he found he could do no good upon them all he came off without other hurt than the cutting of his hand a little with the breaking of a thrust which one of them made at him, and hurt the serjeant-major. The Lord Deputy this night began to make his approaches nearer the town, and for that purpose caused some 1000 foot to be drawn out by Sir John Barkley, Sir Benjamin Berry, and Captain Bodley, who continued the work all night, and although the ground was extremely hard by reason of the frost, and the night very light, yet they brought the work to very good perfection. The enemy played all night upon them with great volleys, but hurt but three men neither in the trenches nor in divers sallies they made, in the one whereof a squadron of our new men beat them back to the gates. In the evening his Lordship sent directions to Sir Richard Levison to land three culverins this night and to plant them on the island, about Castle ny Parke, that thence they might likewise make battery upon the town, and Sir Richard drew in the admiral and vice-admiral between the town and the island, whence they did great hurt in the town next day.

All the artillery still played; but because the shot from the ships did but little hurt, save only upon the base town, the Lord Deputy gave directions to make very few shot unless it were at the high town. In the afternoon, the Lord President, the Earls of Thomond and Clanricard, Sir Thomas Burke, and divers others returned to the camp, O'Donnell with his force being stolen by them. This night direction was given to have a platform made for the artillery upon the trench which was made on Monday night. Somewhat after midnight the Spaniards made a sudden sally, with purpose to force that trench, but were quickly repelled by Sir Francis Barkley, who commanded there that night.

The companies that went with the Lord President returned, and with them two other regiments of the Earl of Clanricard and Sir Christopher Saint-Lawrence. The regiments were that night quartered by themselves upon the west side of Kinsale to invest the town and keep the Spaniards and O'Donnell from joining. This night the three culverins from the island were planted on the point of the hill, near the water, on this side behind the last trenches. This morning the Spaniards played with a demi-cannon from the town upon the admiral, which was twice shot, and the vice-admiral once, they riding both close by the town; and shot being made from those ships they dismounted the Spaniards' piece within and hurt their chief gunner, so that it played no more.

Betimes in the morning these three pieces from the point of the hill, near the water, played upon the town, doing great hurt by reason they were so near planted; but because the day fell out extremely windy and rainy they were forced to leave, and spend the rest of the day in drawing down some other pieces, that were planted upon the first platform.

CHAPTER XVII.

The town of Kinsale summoned, and Don Juan's answer—The Spaniards beaten out of their trenches—The Marshal went to view the town to discover a fit place to batter—A skirmish entertained for the viewing of the breach—An entrenchment made on the west side of the town—A bold attempt of a sergeant of ours, wherein he was slain—A soldier slain standing between the Lord Deputy and Lord President—The great sally made by the enemy with a furious charge, both upon the platform where the battery was placed and upon a new entrenchment on the west side of the town; the enemy repulsed and beaten—The enemy gained our entrenchment on the west side of the town—The entrenchment recovered from the enemy—The loss on the enemy's part and on our part.

IN the morning a trumpeter was sent to summon Kinsale, who was not suffered to enter into the town, but receiving his answer at the gate, viz. that they held the town first for Christ, and next for the King of Spain, and so would defend it *contra tutti inimici.* Upon his return with this answer the Lord Deputy gave directions to begin the battery with all the artillery, who continued shooting upon the gate till towards night, and broke a great part thereof. During the time the ordnance played Sir Christopher Saint-Lawrence drew out from the other camp some foot and gave upon the Spaniards' trenches, which they possessed with great numbers at the other end of the town, being forced to go there through the fury of the shot, which they could not endure in that part of the town where the ordnance played. At his first giving upon them he beat them out of the trenches, following them to the very gate of the town and killing some of them, returning without loss on our side save only some hurt.

All the artillery still played, and broke down most part of the gate and some part of a new work made before the gate.

The Marshal taking some fifty shot, went to the wall of the town to view which was the best place to make a breach, and found a wall close to the gate on the right hand to be the fittest. After he had taken view and made a slight skirmish with the Spaniards he returned without any loss saving some three hurt, and caused the artillery to beat upon that place, who played upon it without intermission and broke down before night a very great part of the wall, which the enemy attempted to make up in the night, but were beaten from it by our guards, who played upon them most part of the night. A Spaniard ran away this day from Kinsale, who reported to the Lord Deputy that our artillery had killed divers captains in the town, besides private soldiers.

Resolved in Council and by the Council of War that some foot should be drawn out of the camp to give the Spaniards a bravado and to view whether the breach was assaultable, and to cause the Spaniards to show themselves, that our artillery might the better play upon them; whereupon two thousand foot commanded by Sir John Barkley and Captain Blayny were presently put in arms and drawn near the walls of the town, who entertained a very hot skirmish with the Spaniards that had lodged themselves in a trench close to the breach without the town. During the continuance of this skirmish our artillery played upon those that showed themselves either on the breach or in the trench, and killed many of them, besides such as were killed and hurt by our small shot. After an hour's fight (or thereabouts), when full view was taken in what manner the breach was, and found not to be assaultable,[1] our men were drawn off with little or no hurt on our side saving some three hurt and Captain Guest's horse killed under him, who before killed two or three with his own hands. This night the Marshal, Sir John Barkley, Captain Blayny and Captain Bodley (the Lord Deputy leaving the President in the camp, being almost all night present) drew out five and twenty of every company and entrenched themselves on a hill on the west side of the town within less than half a caliver's shot of the same and cast up a small fort to lodge some foot to serve as seconds for the artillery that was to be planted not far from it. Our men, being at work, the Spaniards about midnight began to play upon them from the walls and from a trench they possessed close to the west gate, and so continued very hotly till the morning; our men, who guarded the pioneers, playing likewise upon them; and divers were hurt and killed on either side.

Our men continued still in that work, and brought

[1] The whole of this account of the siege is very viewy, one-sided, and, indeed, incredible. The Queen's soldiers seem almost never to have got killed, while they killed the Spaniards in vast numbers. This "bravado" now looks very like a full-blown attempt to storm. The two thousand foot sent upon the breach was the army of Ulster, the best fighting force in the camp. Yet only a horse seems to have been killed in the affair. Observe that though the breach was found not to be assaultable, the writer has previously informed us that at this point his artillery "brake down a great part of the wall," and that the enemy, attempting to make it up in the night, "were beaten from it by our guards." I don't think this part of Pacata could have been written by Stafford, it is so exceedingly ill-done.

the same before night to very good perfection, though the Spaniards, from their high castles and other places of the town, sought to annoy them what they could. While our men were thus at work, a sergeant of Captain Blayny's drew out some seven or eight shot, and suddenly fell into a trench that the Spaniards possessed close to the town wherein were some nine or ten Spaniards, of which the sergeant killed two with his own hands, and the rest every man one. Not being contented therewith he attempted to give upon another trench possessed by the Spaniards some good distance from it; but in going on the sergeant was shot through the body, and his company in bringing him off had two hurt.

The same day the Lord Deputy and the Lord President came to see the new work, and as they were discoursing very near together, a musket shot from the town passed between them and broke the backbone of a soldier who stood close by them, whereof he died.

This night, the trenches where the cannon were planted being manned with the Lord Deputy's company, commanded by Captain James Blunt, Sir Thomas Burke's, commanded by his Lieutenant, Sir Benjamin Berry's, commanded by his Lieutenant, Captain Rotheram himself, and Captain Hobby, Captain Ruse's, commanded by his Lieutenant, and Captain Roger Harvy, commanding in chief, being Captain of the Watch; and a fort on the west near the town between the two camps that was made the morning before, being manned by Captain Flower, with Sir Arthur Savage's company, Sir John Dowdall's company, Captain Dillon, Captain Spencer, Captain Masterson's Lieutenant, and Sir William Warren's

Lieutenant, with certain squadrons out of the Earl
of Thomond's quarter, who stood in guard without the
trenches.[1] The enemy sallied about eight o'clock
(the night being extremely dark and rainy), with
about two thousand men, and first gave slightly
towards the new trenches upon the west side, and
presently after, with a great gross upon the trench
of the cannon, continuing their resolution to force
it with exceeding fury, having brought with them
tools of divers sorts to pull down the gabions and
trenches, and spikes to cloy the artillery. The
alarm being taken in the camp, the Marshal, with
Sir John Barkley, Sir William Fortescue, Sir Francis
Rush, and Captain Roe, with some five or six hundred,
sallied presently towards the cannon for their seconds,
and Sir Benjamin Berry fell out with some hundred
directly towards the port of the town next to the
camp, to whose seconds the Lord Deputy sent Sir
Oliver Saint-John. Upon the arrival of the Marshal
with his forces the enemy broke, and our men did
execution upon them. Sir Benjamin Berry fell
directly upon the enemy's seconds, whom he
presently charged and broke, killed many of
them, and took the commander of that body, being
an old captain of chief account with the enemy.
At the same time the enemy gave upon our
new trenches, and continued the attempt a long
time with great fury, till Captain Flower sallying

---

[1] Though a considerable majority of the Queen's captains were
English, yet most of the officers appointed to this dangerous duty at
the works on the west side, away from the camp, were Irish. Sir
William Warren was Tyrone's best man when he eloped with Miss
Mabel Bagenal—described by Tyrone as "an honest English gentleman." He was in fact Irish of the Pale; but the Palesmen were
regarded as English.

out and beating back part of their forces the enemy entered before his return, and were possessed of the trenches, in which time Sir William Godolphin gave many charges for the seconding of our men, who continued fight in the field until the Earl of Clanricard, being sent for their second, with Captain Shipwith, Captain Slingsby, Captain Clare, Captain Boise, and Captain Thomas Burke, with some sixty men, for the rest of his regiment was not advanced so far, charged a gross of the enemy without the fort, broke them, and did execution upon them towards the town, and, returning, entered the fort again, which the enemy abandoned, with little resistance, and made it good till he was relieved. In this sally the enemy left behind them above six score dead bodies, besides such as were killed near the town, and we took nine prisoners, of whom there were a captain, a sergeant, and a drum; but since we heard out of the town, that they lost dead above two hundred of their best men, two captains, two Alferezes, the serjeant-major, being the second commander to Don John, Don Carlos Carty, and above two hundred hurt. On our side were hurt Captain Flower, Captain Shipwith (slightly in the face), the Earl of Clanricard's lieutenant, Captain Dillon killed, Captain Spencer, Captain Flower's lieutenant, and some five and twenty private soldiers. The enemy at the cannon cloyed a demi-culverin, which being a little crased was left without the fort, but the next morning it was made serviceable again. There were some of them killed upon the cannon, and upon the powder, and the trenches in some places were filled with their dead bodies, and in that attempt of the cannon only seventy-two dead bodies were left in the place of the best men the

Spaniards had, whereof many of them were found with spikes and hammers to cloy the cannon. The captains, officers, and soldiers that defended the cannon acquitted themselves singularly well.[1]

[1] This sally of the Spaniards, urged, as the writer admits, "with incredible fury," was, with perhaps the exception of the repulse of the storming party at the north port, the greatest event of the siege so far. The author, for once, abandons in describing it his customary manner, which is that of the *miles gloriosus*. Don Juan apparently put his whole force into the blow, and no matter what is said in the text, that blow was as completely successful as it was most bravely struck. A proof of this is that Mountjoy from this moment desisted from making any attempt to storm Kinsale, and that the Irish lords of Munster, who had been watching the duel so keenly, began now to revolt to the side that seemed to be winning. These facts establish the successful character of the Spaniards' sortie that night. The always fair and veracious "Four Masters," in their high-sounding but unilluminative style, give a picture of the night's doings more in harmony with the facts.

"At the same time the Spaniards made a sally by night on a quarter of the Lord Justice's camp, and having slain great numbers, they broke the stones and supporters (platform) of the great gun of the Queen's ordnance in order to prevent their enemy from firing out of it, and they would have slain more were it not for the Earl of Clanricarde; for it was he and those who happened to be with him who compelled the Spaniards to return back to Kinsale."

The Spaniards, in fact, damaged the battery before the north port, and ruined the platform and works on the west side, into which the great guns were to have been sent next day. But for the Earl of Clanricarde and the Connaught army, the Spanish force, which had occupied and destroyed the western battery, would then have marched to the assistance of their comrades fighting in the north battery, and the combined victorious force might afterwards have done anything. Clanricarde and the Connaught-Irish made history that night.

Clanricarde and his Connaught men were posted on the west of Kinsale, to prevent a junction between the Spaniards and Hugh Roe. He heard the firing, marched straight towards it through the night, and defeated and drove back to Kinsale that moiety of the Spanish force which was at the west works.

A little before Binghan was recalled from the Presidency of Connaught, he wrote in one of his dispatches, there is hardly an Englishman in the army of Connaught, and there is no reason for supposing that its composition had materially altered in the interim, especially as the President now was an Irishman, i.e. young Clanricarde, and by far the greatest nobleman in the west; a man who, out of his own warlike cousinry and vassals, could have furnished forth the Presidential army. Indeed, no commander who understood his business at this time, would have accepted English soldiers if Irish were procurable. This is no slur at all upon English valour, but only on Elizabethan administrative methods. The sweepings of the gaols and highways were considered good enough soldiers by the sheriffs, and Sir John Falstaff's recruits, with whom he would not march through Coventry, were no stage caricature, but a satirical stroke at fact. There was still in Ireland a military caste. In England it had ceased to exist, having been drawn into industrialism.

The reader will remember that Carew, while pacifying Munster, met with no warlike resistance, save from the bonoghs of Connaught. Here again Connaught turns up brilliantly, but this time on the other side, the Queen's side.

CHAPTER XVIII.

A supply of Spaniards landed at Castlehaven—A Council of War held—Good service done by a Scotsman—O'Donnell joined with the Spaniards at Castlehaven—All the Irish in the west of Munster and some of the English race revolted and adhered to the Spaniards—Sundry castles rendered by the Irish into the Spaniards' hands—Divers of the Irish had companies in pay given them by Don Juan—The Castle of Carrickfoyle taken and the ward murdered—Tyrone's army discovered near our camp.

INTELLIGENCE sent to the Lord Deputy that six Spanish ships were put into Castlehaven, and that six more were sent with them from the Groyne, but in coming were severed by tempest and no certainty what is become of them. In these were said to be two thousand Spaniards, come with great store of ordnance and munition, and that two thousand more were coming presently after.

A confirmation of Spaniards being at Castlehaven and that they were landed, whereupon it was resolved in Council that our camp should be strengthened and the artillery better entrenched and guarded, and to leave off battering;[1] the other camp to rise and lie

---

[1] The great Spanish sally which compelled the Queen's army to "leave battering;" the arrival of more Spaniards at Castlehaven; the presence of Hugh Roe, who sat down at Bandon and began to control the country; the approach of Tyrone, and the long and resultless siege of Kinsale, caused the Irish lords at this time to believe that the Queen's was the losing cause.

close by the town, between the north and the west
gate, adding one regiment more to it, and all the horse
to be drawn into our camp. A drum was sent to Don
John, to offer him to bury his dead bodies, which he
took thankfully, praying that we would bury them,
and saying that he would do the like for any of ours
if they happened in his power. And this day Sir
Charles Wilmot, with his regiment, was commanded,
for the better strengthening of the Earl of Thomond's
quarter, to rise out of the Lord Deputy's camp and
lodge there. Sir Richard Levison, with a good part
of the fleet, with towing got out of the harbour to
seek the Spanish fleet at Castlehaven, to take them if
he could, or otherwise to distress them as much as he
might.

A Scotsman, who had some eighty of these
Spaniards aboard, put into Kinsale harbour in the
morning, and, getting a boat, acquainted Sir Amias
Preston, the Vice-Admiral, therewith, and put them
into his hands; whereupon the said Scotsman and
four of the chief Spaniards (being officers) were
brought to the Lord Deputy and examined before
his Lordship, the Lord President, and divers others
of the Council. Their examinations were sent into
England. The ships were heard to be in fight that
day. This day our ordnance was drawn from the old
platforms into our camp, the better to control the
service of the field, and to place them more com-
modiously towards the west side of the town, if we
should see cause. News came this evening that
O'Donnell was joined with the Spaniards landed at
Castlehaven, and that Tyrone with his force was very
near us.

The same day, the ditches and trenches of the Lord

Deputy's camp, and the Earl of Thomond's quarter, were cast deeper and higher, and it was resolved that two small forts should be raised between the Earl of Thomond's quarter and the waterside, so that the town might be wholly invested, to forbid any access to or from it.

Until this time none of the provincials of Munster that had been either protected or pardoned, relapsed; but now, upon the coming of these seconds to Castlehaven, Sir Finnin O'Driscall and all the O'Driscalls, Sir Owen MacCarty's sons, and almost all the Cartys in Carberry, Donnell O'Sulevan Beare, O'Sulevan More's eldest son, Donnell MacCarty, the Earl of Clan-Cartie's base son, with all the Cartys of Desmond, John O'Connor Kerry, the Knight of Kerry, all the protected and pardoned men in Kerry and Desmond, and all else from Kinsale and Limerick westwards, joined with O'Donnell and the Spaniards—whereat little wonder is to be made considering what power religion and gold hath in the hearts of men; both which the Spaniards brought with them into Ireland. The supplies of Spaniards were but seven hundred, but more were promised to follow; which moved the wavering Irish to conceive that now the time was come for their deliverance from the English Government; whereupon they cast themselves into the Spaniards' arms, and, for testimony of their truths, Donogh O'Driscall delivered to them his castle[1] at

---

[1] Castlehaven was in possession of a minor sept of the O'Driscoll clan. The chief of this little sept, Donough, had four brothers, Dermot, Con, Teigue, and Dary. All five aided and abetted the Spaniard, and piloted him into harbour. Of the brothers, Dermot, "a man of culture and able to speak Latin," explained the political and military situation to Don Zubiaur. The brothers at once surrendered their castle to his use. Admiral Levison and the Queen's fleet

Castlehaven which commanded the harbour; Sir Finnin O'Driscall,[1] who never in the course of his whole life had been tainted with the least spot of disloyalty, rendered to him his Castle of Donneshed at Baltimore and his Castle of Donnelong in the island of Inisherkan, between which castles all entrances into that haven were debarred; and Donnell O'Sulevan surrendered to them his strong castle of Dunboy,[2] which absolutely commands Beare Haven; these three harbours being without all exception the best in the West of Munster. For the guard of these places Don John assigned that one hundred of the late supplies should remain at Castlehaven with a magazine of victuals and munition and eight pieces of ordnance; to Donneshed and Donnelong he sent one hundred foot, fifty for each of the castles, and two pieces of artillery; and to Dunboy he also sent one hundred foot and ten great pieces. And, to confirm these revolters by liberality to his master, the King of Spain, he bestowed

now followed the Spaniards into the harbour. Zubiaur, whose ships were only transports and hulks, was unable to fight Levison. He ran his ships close to shore, disembarked his cannon, and endeavoured to mount them. Levison was about to disembark his men to assault the Spaniards on shore, when O'Sullivan Bere with 500 infantry and troop of horse, having marched from Bantry to assist the Spaniard, arrived in the nick of time. Dermot, the man of culture, had advised Don Zubiaur to send to O'Sullivan Bere for assistance. So the tables were turned, and Levison, having been battered hugely by the Spanish guns, which were now, under O'Sullivan's protection, mounted and brought to bear, with difficulty made his escape from the haven.—*Historia Hiberniæ*, p. 225, by P. O'Sullivan.

[1] Sir Fineen was Lord of Baltimore and the surrounding country. The O'Driscolls had been at one time the leading family in West Munster, but had been long since reduced to their present condition by the Clan-Cartie.

[2] Philip O'Sullivan relates that his father Dermot conducted Vasco Sañavedro to Dunboy, and surrendered it to him by order of the chief. This is the first conspicuous appearance of Donal O'Sullivan, Prince of Bere, with whom we shall be so much concerned presently.

upon Donnell O'Sulevan two hundred foot in the King's pay; upon Donogh Moyle MacCarty, son to Sir Owen MacCarty Reugh,[1] one hundred; upon Finnin MacCarty, his brother, one hundred and twenty; upon Phelim MacCarty one hundred; and upon O'Donovan one hundred; in all, six hundred and twenty in the king's entertainment, and upon others he bestowed certain sums of money. About this time also (not many days after this defection) John O'Connor Kerry found the means to betray the Castle of Carrickfoyle,[2] which was his, and then guarded for Her Majesty by a sergeant and twelve soldiers of Captain Saxy's company.

The other camp strengthened their trenches and resolved to make two small forts beyond the camp westward, wholly to invest the town, the forts and the camp to flank one another.

The artillery was planted in several places of the camp for the best defence thereof, and a fort almost made near the town. A slight skirmish towards night, wherein Sir Francis Barkley's ancient and some others were hurt. In the evening the rebels' horse were descried about two miles off, and, after supper, all the army was drawn to arms upon notice, given us by the scout, that the rebels were discovered.

---

[1] It may interest the reader to be reminded that in the plate of the Battle of Kinsale, MacCarty Reagh, captain of all these Carties, is represented as with his forces besieging the Spaniards on the west side. Sir Owen, like all the rest, was now of opinion that it was all up with the Queen's cause, that he had best stick to the winning side, and make hay while the sun shone.

[2] See a plate of this fine castle.

CHAPTER XIX.

A brief report of the good service done by Sir Richard Levison upon the Spanish fleet at Castlehaven—A letter from Don Juan de Aquila to Tyrone and O'Donnell—A letter from Don Juan to Captain Juan de Abornoz y Andrada—A letter from Donnell O'Sulevan Beare to the King of Spain.

THIS night late, Sir Richard Levison returned to the harbour of Kinsale, and the next day came to the Lord Deputy, to whom he imparted that the sixth day, with the *Warspite*, the *Defiance*, the *Swiftsure*, the *Marlin*, one merchantman, and a caraval, he arrived at Castlehaven about ten o'clock in the forenoon. Before four o'clock the same day one ship of the enemy was sunk, the Spanish Admiral with nine feet of water in the hold drove ashore upon the rocks; the Vice-Admiral with two others drove likewise aground, most of the Spaniards quitting their ships. The seventh of December, the wind being extremely at south-east, he rode still at Castlehaven; the night following, the wind at west-south-west, he warped out with the ships; the eighth, at night, he returned as aforesaid.[1]

Since, we are informed by the Lord Courcy, that they are all sunk but one ship, and great harm was done both to their provisions and men.

[1] P. O'Sullivan says, that Levison lost 501 men in the engagement with Don Zubiaur: sixty knocked down by one shot as they sat at table. From the text one would suppose that Levison was brilliantly successful in this fight. We know now how much credence generally to attach to the narrative of the *miles gloriosus*. (*Vide* note to p. 40.)

The Spaniards, after their coming to Castlehaven, understanding the Queen's fleet was at Kinsale, expecting their coming thither, to make themselves as strong as they could, landed five pieces of ordnance, which they planted close by the water-side for securing the harbour; but Sir Richard Levison so plied the shipping that he sank and drove ashore as is related, and, having effected as much as might be done by sea, was willing to have left the harbour and return to Kinsale; but, the wind being contrary, he was not able to get forth, but was forced to ride four and twenty hours within the play of those five pieces of ordnance, and received in that time above three hundred shot through hulk, mast, and tackle; being by no industry able to avoid it until some calmer weather came, when by the help of some warps laid forth by their boats, not without great danger and some loss, he came to set sail and returned to Kinsale. All the shot were made particularly at his ship, except some few at a pinnace of the Queen's, whereof Captain Fleming was commander.

All the time spent upon the ninth, tenth, and eleventh, was in erecting the two forts formerly resolved upon, also in casting up trenches between the Earl of Thomond's quarter and the said forts, being more than thirty score in length, and making trenches near the Lord Deputy's camp. The Spaniards, as well to interrupt as to view our works, made certain light sallies, but they were easily beaten back without any hurt on our side.

The twelfth, the enemy sallied again, but altogether fruitlessly.

The thirteenth, the weather fell out to be extremely foul and stormy; and because of Tyrone's drawing near with all his forces it was thought meet not to attempt anything of great moment more than the removing of some pieces of orduance to a new platform, made on the west side of the town close to it, to play upon the castles which might most hinder our works when we should resolve to make a breach.

The fourteenth, foul weather, wherein nothing was performed.

The fifteenth, our artillery on the west side of the town much annoyed the enemy in breaking down the houses, wherein many were slain.

The sixteenth, the ordnance played into the town, as the day before.

The seventeenth, foul and stormy weather; nevertheless at night the enemy sallied and broke down the new platform which we had made.

The eighteenth, the cannon, as in former days, played into the town and annoyed the enemy very much. And the same day a letter was intercepted, written from Don John to Tyrone and O'Donnell, which is here inserted; and also a letter to Captain Juan de Abornoz y Andrada, both which were thus translated :—

A Letter from Don Juan de Aquila to Tyrone and O'Donnell.

I was confident your Excellencies would have come upon Don Ricardo's going to you, because he had order from you to say that upon the Spaniards joining with you (from Castlehaven) you would do me that favour. I beseech you so to do with as much celerity and as well furnished as you possibly may; for I do assure you the enemy are wearied, and but few, and they cannot furnish with guards the third part of their trenches, which shall little avail them; their first fury resisted all is ended. In what manner your Excellencies will come on is better known to you there than to me here. I will give them enough to do this way, being ever attending to give the blow in all that I can, and with some good resolution that, your Excellencies fighting as you are accustomed, I hope in God the victory shall be ours, for that the cause is His. I do as much desire the victory for the interest which your Excellencies have in it as for my own. There is nothing now to be done but that you would bring up your troops; come well appointed and in close order, and being once mingled with the enemy, their forts will do them as much harm as us. I salute Don Ricardo; the Lord preserve your Excellencies. From Kinsale the 28th of December, 1601.

Though you are not well prepared, yet I beseech your Excellencies to hasten towards the enemy, for it imports much. I think it needful to be all at once on horseback; the greater haste you make so much the better. Don Juan de Aquila.

A Letter from Don Juan to Captain Juan de Albornoz y Andrada.

I was extremely glad of your letter and of the health of your person. When Don Ricardo went, he brought for resolution that when the Earls had met with the Spaniards they would come. The ill passage for messengers is the cause that you have had no letters from me. Hasten their coming; they know there, better than we do, the ways and the news. I am ever in readiness; the enemy are few and wearied, and by good resolution from thence their trenches shall not avail them, nor can they maintain so much ground as they lodge in. I will give them their handsful from the town, and their first fury resisted all is ended. Commend me to Don Ricardo and to Captain Rius de Velasco, to whom I write not because the messenger should not carry too great a packet. I have written to the Earls to hasten hither before the enemy have bettered their quarter; it would profit much, and we being once mingled with them their forts will do them as much hurt as us. From Kinsale the eight-and-twentieth of December, 1601. DON JUAN DE AQUILA.

The nineteenth, by reason of stormy and foul weather, nothing on either side was performed; but the same day Donnell O'Sulevan Beare, in thankfulness to the King of Spain, and to endear himself the more into his favour, wrote to him this ensuing letter. The original was in Irish, and thus translated; but the reader may understand that it was long afterwards before it came to the Lord President's hands, yet here inserted in regard of the date thereof:—

A LETTER FROM DONNELL O'SULEVAN BEARE TO THE KING OF SPAIN.[1]

It hath been ever, most mighty and renowned Prince, and most gracious Catholic King, from time to time manifestly proved by daily experience among us the Irish that there is nothing worketh more forcibly in our hearts to win and to draw our love and affection than natural inclination to our progeny and offspring, and the memorial of the friendship which sticketh still in our minds; chiefly the same being

---

[1] In this letter O'Sullivan Bere recalls the Milesian legend of the Spanish origin of the Irish-Celtic race, i.e. the invasion of Ireland by the sons of Milesius, King of Spain.

renewed, cherished, and kept in use by mutual affection, and by showing like friendship to us also. We, the mere Irish, long since deriving our root and original from the famous and most noble race of the Spaniards, viz., from Milesius,[1] son to Bile, son to Breogwin, and from Lwighe, son to Lythy,[2] son to Breogwin, by the testimony of our old ancient books of antiquities, our pedigrees, our histories, and our chronicles. Though there were no other matter we came not as natural branches of the famous tree whereof we grew, but bear a hearty love, a natural affection, and an entire inclination of our hearts and minds to our ancient most loving kinsfolk and the most noble race whereof we descended. Besides this, my Sovereign, such is the abundance of your goodness and the bounty or greatness of your liberality, now every way undeserved of our parts, as tokens of love and affection by your Majesty showed to us, that it is not fit nor seemly for us but to bestow our persons, our men, and our goods in the service of a Prince that dealeth so graciously with us, that sendeth forces of men, great treasure, victuals, and munition for our aid against our enemies that seek to overwhelm and extinguish the Catholic faith diabolically, put to death our chieftains tyrannically, coveting our lands and livings unlawfully. For the aforesaid considerations, and for many other commendable causes me moving, I bequeath and offer in humbleness of mind, and with all my heart, my own person with all my forces, perpetually to serve

[1] Milesius, a mythical king of North Spain. His sons and kinsmen led the famed "Milesian invasion" of Ireland.

[2] *Recte* Ith. Ith led a still earlier but unsuccessful invasion, and was slain in Ireland. The O'Driscolls, once dominant in the south, claimed descent from him.

your Majesty, not only in Ireland, but in any other place where it shall please your Highness. I commit also my wife, my children, my manors, towns, country, and lands, and my haven of Dunboy, called Beare Haven, next under God, to the protection, keeping, and defence, or commerce of your Majesty, to be and remain in your hands and at your disposition. Also at your pleasure be it, my liege Lord, to send defence and strong keeping of the haven of Dunboy, first for yourself, my Sovereign, to receive your ships; and for me also as your loving servant, so that the Queen of England's ships may not possess the same before you, while I follow the wars in your Highness's behalf. I pray Almighty God to give your Majesty a long life, health of body and soul, with increase of grace and prosperity. So I betake you to the keeping of God. From the camp near Kinsale the nine-and-twentieth of December, 1601, *Stilo Novo*.

    Your most dutiful loving servant,
      DONNELL O'SULEVAN BEARE.

This morning being fair, the ordnance played oftener and broke down a good part of the wall; and to the end we might proceed the more roundly (if Tyrone's force came not the sooner upon us) another great trench was made beneath the platform, to hinder which the enemy made very many shot, but all would not serve; for by the next morning that work was brought to good perfection, though the night fell out stormy, with great abundance of thunder and lightning, to the wonder of all men, considering the season of the year. This night came certain intelligence that Tyrone would be the next night within a mile and a half of us.

CHAPTER XX.

Tyrone with his army approached within view of our camp, but could not be provoked to fight—The enemy sallied out of the town—The Irish army as before present themselves—The enemy from the town make another sally—Intelligence of the enemy's designs brought to Captain Taffe.

TOWARDS night Tyrone showed himself with the most part of his horse and foot upon a hill between our camp and Cork, about a mile from us, and on the other side of the hill encamped that night, where he had a fastness of wood and water.

Two regiments of our foot and some horse being drawn out of our camp made towards them; and, when they saw our men resolved to go forward, they fell back towards the place where they encamped. This night the Spaniards sallied again, and gave upon a new trench made a little beneath our camp, but were the sooner repelled, because that night we kept very strong guards, and every man was in readiness to be in arms by reason of Tyrone's being so near to us.

Tyrone's horse and foot kept still in sight in the place where they showed themselves the day before, and many intelligences affirmed to us that they had a purpose to force our camps. That night some of their horse and five hundred of their foot were discovered searching out a good way to the town, which was not made known to us until the next day. The Spaniards sallied this night hotly, and gave upon a trench, so that a sergeant, who had the guard thereof, quitted it. But Sir Christopher Saint-Laurence,[1] coming to his second, beat them back before they did any great hurt.

Our artillery still played upon the town, as it had done all that while, that they might see we went on with our business as if we cared not for Tyrone's coming; but it was withal carried on in such a fashion that we had no meaning to make a breach, because we thought it not fit to offer to enter, and so put all in a hazard, until we might better discover what Tyrone meant to do, whose strength was assured to be very great; and we found by letters of Don John's, which we had newly intercepted, that he had advised Tyrone to set upon our camps, telling him that it could not be chosen, but our men were much decayed by the winter's siege, so that we could hardly be able to maintain so much ground as we had taken when our strength was greater if we were well put too, on the one side by them and on the other side by him, which he would not fail for his part to do soundly.

Tyrone, accompanied by O'Donnell, O'Rwrke, MacGuire, MacMaghon, Randell MacSorly, Redmond Burke,[2] O'Connor Sligo's brothers, and Captain

[1] An Irish officer, brother of the Lord of Howth. It was he who made the revelation which afterwards led to "the flight of the Earls."
[2] Redmund Burke, Baron of Leitrim. We have met him several times before. The reader may remember him holding commerce with Carew. Redmund had certainly been badly used by his uncle. Reaching man's estate, he asked the said uncle, Ulick, father of our Earl, for his patrimony. The Earl replied that, "if he were to ask for only as much land as his cloak would cover, he would not get it." So Redmund came into Tyrone's league.

Tirrell, with the choice force, and, in effect, all the rebels of Ireland, being drawn into Munster and joined with the Spaniards that landed at Castlehaven, who brought to Tyrone's camp six ensigns of Spaniards and the greatest part of the Irish of Munster, who, being revolted, were joined with them, and entertained into the King's pay in several companies, and, under their own lords, resolved to relieve the town of Kinsale, and to that purpose lay, the one-and-twentieth of December, a mile and a half from the town, between the English camp and Cork, and, on that side of the army, kept from them all passages and means for forage;[1] the other side, over the River

[1] The Queen's army, while besieging the Spaniards, were now themselves in a manner besieged. Few in numbers, for sickness and desertion had almost abolished the English portion of the army, they were beleaguered by a host of some 10,000 insurgent Irish. Their forage was cut off, which meant that in a short time their cavalry would be useless, and they could now only get supplies by sea landed at Oyster Haven, and conveyed thence to the camp with great difficulty and danger. Meantime, the Spaniards in Kinsale had food enough to last a long time, while the confederate host had the whole of the open country at their disposal. Of the Queen's people, P. O'Sullivan writes: "*Ita eos primum inedia, mox fames, tandem pestilentia invasit.*"

Under these circumstances Tyrone was for playing a waiting game, but the headlong Hugh Roe overbore his authority. Don Juan, too, believed that by a simultaneous attack delivered by himself and the confederates, the Queen's army could be crushed with ease. He did not realize of what ill-assorted materials this great tumultuary Irish army was composed. It was an army of armies, each of its component parts commanded by a man who called himself *king*.

A greater danger threatened, though Carew seems to have been unaware of it. The fighting strength of the Queen's army consisted in the waged Irish soldiers, and the Irish lords of countries with their "risings-out." From many of these the confederates received promises that they would desert in a few days. O'Sullivan says that the promise was one to desert *en masse* within three days. I confess, however, I find a difficulty in believing that the senders of those promises were sincere. In the ensuing battle the Queen's Irish fought well, and were true to their salt if false to their promises. Possibly some of their chief men were hedging—wished to stand well with the insurgent lords and the Spaniards in the event of the Queen's power collapsing.

of Ownyboy, being wholly at their disposition, by reason of the general revolt of those parts. It seemed they were drawn so far by the importunity of Don Juan de Aquila, as we perceived by some of his letters intercepted, wherein he intimated his own necessity, their promise to succour him, and the facility of the enterprise ; our army being weak in numbers, and tired (as he termed us), with assurance from himself that whensoever he should advance to our quarter he would give the blow soundly from the town. During the abode of the rebels in that place we had continual intelligence of their purpose to give alarms from their party and sallies from the town, but to little other effect than to weary our men by keeping them continually in arms, the weather being extremely tempestuous, cold, and wet. On the three-and-twentieth of December, late in the night, Captain Taffe informed the Lord Deputy that one of the rebels sent him word (and confirmed it by a solemn oath) to the bearer that the resolution of the rebels was either that night, or between that and the next, to enterprise their uttermost for the relief of the town, with some particulars in what sort they intended to give upon our camp. The intelligence which Captain Taffe had was upon this occasion.

CHAPTER XXI.

The means whereby Captain Taffe had his intelligence—The Battle of Kinsale, wherein the rebels were overthrown—The Lord President directed by the Lord Deputy to guard the camp against any attempt to be made by the Spaniards—A glorious victory—An old Irish prophecy proved true—Two sallies made by the Spaniards.

TUESDAY, the two-and-twentieth of December, Brian MacHugh Oge MacMaghon,[1] a principal commander in the Irish army, whose eldest son, Brian, had many years before been a page in England with the Lord

[1] Lord of all Monaghan. The reader will probably be amazed at this act of duplicity and treachery on the part of such a high lord'; but I can assure him he would cease to be surprised if he were to read even one volume of the Calendar of State Papers for this period. Treachery was rife, because the insurgents were bound together by no principle in which they believed; and where there is no principle concerned, men who come together animated mainly by personal motives will not be true to each other, let their mutual oaths be what they may.

Let me try to diagnose MacMahon's state of mind when he sent this message. The beginning of the war found him a private gentleman and subject, but one who constantly said to himself, "If I had my rights I would be lord of all Monaghan and high chief of the MacMahon nation." Then came Tyrone's message, "Join me and I will make you the MacMahon." Brian Mac Hugh Ogue rose at once for Tyrone, cleared the county, and was nominated MacMahon. Such was Tyrone's policy. He aimed in the first instance at reviving all the lapsed seignories, and employing the new dynasts to support him against the Crown, he being the author of their being and their champion. But difficulties soon arose.

Brian was now the MacMahon. So far good, but as MacMahon he was also feudatory and vassal to O'Neill. In the commencement Tyrone treated all such men as Brian with scrupulous respect, spoke of them and used them only as his allies and confederates. But with the growth of his power all the old inherent regalities of his O'Neillship revived, with a certain inevitability, and Brian Mac Hugh Ogue began to feel himself pressed upon and tyrannized over. It was

President, sent a boy to Captain William Taffe, praying him to speak to the Lord President to bestow upon him a bottle of Aquavitæ, which the President, for old acquaintance, sent to him. The next night, being the three-and-twentieth, by the same messenger he sent him a letter praying him to recommend his love to the President, thanks for his Aquavitæ, and to wish him the next night following to stand well upon his guard, for himself was at the Council wherein it was resolved that on the night aforesaid, towards the break of day, the Lord Deputy's camp would be assaulted both by Tyrone's army, which lay at their backs, and by the Spaniards from the town, who upon the first alarm would be in readiness to sally. Whereupon the Lord Deputy gave order to strengthen the ordinary guards, to put the rest of the army in readiness, but not into arms, that about

a great thing indeed to be chief of the MacMahons, but a vile thing to be servant to O'Neill, ordered about by O'Neills, and subjected to tributes and requisitions. Brian liked being lord of Monaghan, but disliked extremely being subject to O'Neill, especially as the later MacMahons, owing to the weakness of the O'Neills and the growth of royal power, were practically liberated from that overlordship. He wished to rule Monaghan—and to be ruled over by no man.

When, as now, it seemed that the Queen's power was about to end, Brian looked forward to a state of hopeless subjection to O'Neill, and possibly did desire to see O'Neill and his party defeated in this battle, hoping afterwards to make such terms with the State that he could continue to be the MacMahon. Upon an Irish lord still tolerated by the State, the Queen's yoke did not press heavily, and assumed only the form of *rent*, about which she was very anxious. Yet the Queen's rent was light : at the utmost only 1*d.* an acre, or 10*s.* per plowland.

Again MacMahon, like so many others, may have been only hedging. What I wish to convey is that the high lord who sold his party for, apparently, a bottle of whiskey, was thinking at the time of more serious things, and that his treachery was anything but unique. His long name of course means only Brian son of Hugh (junior) MacMahon. I recall a passage in one of Burleigh's letters concerning Brian, written before his rebellion, and which seems to have a certain prophetic flavour : " Her Highness saith that Brian Mac Hugh Ogue is a *bad limb*."

the falling of the moon, the regiment volant, commanded by Sir Henry Power, and appointed only to answer the first occasion, without doing any other duties, should draw out beyond the west part of the camp, and there stand in arms, not far from the main guard of horse. A little before the break of day the Lord President went to the Lord Deputy's house, and as they two and the Marshal were in council, one of the Lord President's horsemen came to the door, and calling upon him, said, "My Lord, it is time to arm, for the enemy is near unto the camp;" and immediately Sir Richard Greame, who had the guard of horse that night, sent word to the Lord Deputy that the scouts had discovered the rebels' matches in great numbers; whereupon the Lord Deputy caused the army to draw presently into arms, sent a corporal of the field to cause the like to be done in the Earl of Thomond's quarter, and that thence they should draw out three hundred choice men, between that quarter and the fort built upon the west hill, near a barricade made across a highway, to stop the enemy's sudden passage in the night; and himself, accompanied with the President and the Marshal, advanced towards the scout, and having given directions to Sir Henry Davers, who commanded the horse under the Marshal, for the ordering of the troops, sent the Marshal to take view of the enemy, who brought him word that horse and foot of theirs were advanced; whereupon the Lord Deputy, with Sir Oliver Lambert, rode to view a piece of ground between that and the town, which had on the back of it a trench, drawn from the Earl of Thomond's quarter to the west fort; on the front a boggish glen, and passable with horse only at one ford, which he

had before entrenched. The ground whereupon the
enemy must have drawn in gross to force the passage,
was flanked from the Earl's quarter by the cannon.
It was resolved to make that ground good, being of
greater advantage for horse and foot, both to be
embattled and to fight; upon view whereof the Lord
Deputy sent the Marshal word that on that place he
was resolved to give the enemy battle, and sent the
Sergeant-Major (Sir John Barkley) to draw out Sir
Henry Folliot's and Sir Oliver Saint-John's regiments
to that place. O Campo, who commanded all the
Spaniards that came last out of Spain, desired Tyrone
that he might embattle his men and presently give on
to join that way with Don Juan; for their purpose
was at that time by that means to have put into the
town all the Spaniards with Tirrell and eight hundred
of their chief men, and the next night from the town
and their army to have forced both our quarters, of
the success whereof they were so confident that they
reckoned us already theirs, and were in contention
whose prisoner the Lord Deputy should be,
and whose the President, and so of the rest. But
Tyrone, discovering the Marshal and Sir Henry
Davers to be advanced with all the horse and Sir
Henry Power's squadron of foot, retired beyond a
ford at the foot of that hill with purpose, as he
feigned, till his whole army were drawn more close.
Instantly the Marshal sent the Lord Deputy word by
Sir Francis Rush that the enemy retired in some
disorder; whereupon the Lord Deputy came up to
him and gave order that all the foot should follow.
When we were advanced to the ford, but our
foot not only come to us, the enemy drew off in three
great bodies of foot and all their horse in the rear.

The Lord Deputy asked of some that understood the country whether beyond that ford there was near any ground of strength for the enemy to make advantage of; but being answered that there was none, but a fair champion,[1] he drew after the enemy, and then desired the Lord President to return thence and secure the camp and attend the sallies of Don Juan, which he did, with whom the Lord Deputy sent the Earl of Thomond's horse, Sir Anthony Cooke's, and Sir Oliver Lambert's, and only took with him between three or four hundred horse and under twelve hundred foot; but being drawn out some mile further we might perceive the enemy to stand firm upon a ground of very good advantage for them, having a bog between us, and a deep ford to pass, and in all appearance with resolution to fight. The Marshal, being advanced with the horse near the ford, sent to the Lord Deputy that he perceived the enemy in some disorder, and that if he would give him leave to charge he hoped to give a very good account of it. The Lord Deputy left it to his discretion to do as he should find present occasion out of the disposition of the enemy; whereupon the Earl of Clanricard,[2] who

---

[1] *Campus*—a plain.
[2] The chief credit for the ensuing victory would therefore seem to belong to the Earl of Clanricarde, who forced the fighting. The House of Clanricarde had made its terms with the State and had resolved to abide by that arrangement. They had indeed ceased to be sovereigns, chiefs of the High Burkes, but they were great subjects, and their quit-rent to the State was small, a penny an acre. All this was arranged under the famous "Composition of Connaught." By the composition the Clanricardes had stood loyally ever since the making of it, and were the chief instrument in the hands of the State for driving it over the rest of Connaught. Tyrone had indeed approached the late Earl, Ulick, with pleasant proposals, "Join me and I will make you MacWilliam, with all the old regalities, and restore to you all lands lost under the Composition." But the Earl, for many reasons best known to himself, had declined. Probably the strongest

was with the Marshal, importuned him exceedingly to fight, and the Lord Deputy sent to draw up the foot with all expedition close together, who marched as fast as it was possible for them to keep their orders. The Marshal, as soon as a wing of the foot of the vanguard was come up to him, and Sir Henry Power with his regiment drawn over the ford, advanced with some hundred horse, accompanied by the Earl of Clanricard, and gave occasion of skirmish upon the bog side with some hundred harquebuseers; the enemy thereupon put out some of their loose shot from their battle and entertained the fight, their three battalion standing firm on the other side of the bog. At first our shot were put close to the horse, but with a second they

of those reasons was his fear that the great and growing power of Hugh Roe in the West would eventually, should the confederates triumph, reduce him to a state of vassalage to the Northern chieftain. And yet before he had made his terms with the State that Earl had been a stout rebel.

In fact there was not a single great man in the island who had not been at some time a rebel, and also at some time in his career an instrument of the State for the chastising of rebels or the dragging down of some doomed chieftain. The embroiled, inextricably intertangled relations of the magnates with each other and with the State, were such as no pen, save perhaps that of a great historical novelist, can at all adequately portray. Tyrone himself had spent his youth and his prime in driving the Queen's power over Ireland. It was only his old age that he spent in rebellion.

Our young Earl, the hero of Kinsale, once narrowly escaped the edge of President Malby's sword. Malby, concerning one of the old Connaught wars, writes thus: "I invaded Ulick Burke's country and slew *old* and *young*." Ulick Burke was the father of our Earl.

And another curious fact is this. When the war was over in which he slew "old and young," the said Malby married the sister of Ulick Burke and got the town of Ballinasloe as her dowry. It was a very singular century, and the key to its mysteries not easy to find. One of Earl Ulick's sisters married Brian na Murtha O'Rourke, executed in London for rebellion, while another married this bloody man, Malby, a great officer of State. Again, our Earl, who as a child cowered in woods and caves before Malby's ruffians, and was described in State Papers as a wolf-cub, married the daughter of Sir Francis Walsingham, Secretary of State.

beat the enemy's loose shot into their battle; and withal the Marshal, with the Earl of Clanricard and Sir Richard Greame, offered a charge on a battle of one thousand foot, and, finding them to stand firm, wheeled a little about. By this time Sir William Godolphin, with the Lord Deputy's horse, and Captain Mynshall, with the Lord President's horse, who were appointed to keep still in gross, to answer all accidents, were come up, and Sir John Barkley, with two of our three bodies of foot; whereupon the Marshal and the Earl of Clanricard united themselves with Sir Henry Davers, Captain Taffe, and Captain Fleming, charged again the horse and the rear of the same battle, who presently thereupon, both horse and foot, fell into disorder and broke.

All this while the vanguard of the enemy, in which were Tirrell[1] and all the Spaniards, stood firm upon a bog on the right hand, unto whom, within caliver's shot, the Lord Deputy had drawn up our rear upon a small hill, and willed them to stand firm, till they received direction from him; but, perceiving the gross drawing between our men that were following the execution and the other bodies of foot, he drew up that squadron commanded by Captain Roe, to charge them in flank; whereupon they presently drew off, and in a great gross marched to the top of the next hill and there for a little time made a stand. The rear of

[1] Richard Tyrell, a famous captain of *condottieri*, whom we have met before. When the war was over he offered King James I. to collect all the swordmen of Ireland and bring them abroad in a body. Had King James closed with his offer there would have been no rising in 1641, and no Ulster massacre. The swordmen remained and lived upon their cousins the lords and great gentlemen, and begot more swordmen, till in 1641 the island teemed with valiant men who had no work to do.

the enemy being in retreat the van went off with few slain, but with the loss of many of their arms; their battle, being the greatest body, were all put to the sword, and not above some sixty escaped. The vanguard who went last off were broken on the top of the hill; the Irish for the most part quitted the Spaniards, who, making a stand, were broken by the Lord Deputy's troops, and most of them killed. O Campo, the chief commander, was taken prisoner by Cornet John Pykman; two captains, seven alferezes, and forty soldiers were taken prisoners by such as followed the execution, which continued a mile and a half, and left there, only tired with killing. There were, of the Irish rebels, twelve hundred dead bodies left in the place, and, as we heard from themselves, about eight hundred hurt, whereof many of them died that night. They lost above two thousand arms, their powder, drums, and nine ensigns, which were more than ever they had together before. Of captains, besides other men of mark, fourteen were slain, and on our side only Sir Richard Greame's Cornet was killed, Sir Henry Davers hurt with a sword slightly, Sir William Godolphin a little rased on the thigh with a halberd, Captain Crofts, the scout master, shot in the back, and not above five or six common soldiers hurt, many of our horses killed, and more hurt. The Earl of Clanricard had many fair escapes, being shot through his garments, and no man did bloody his sword more than his Lordship did that day, and he would not suffer any man to take any of the Irish prisoners, but bade them kill the rebels. After the retreat was sounded, the Lord Deputy gave the Order of Knighthood to the

Earl of Clanricard in the field in the midst of the dead bodies, and, returning to the camp, drew out the whole army, and gave God thanks for this victory with their prayers. At the ending whereof, and a volley of shot for joy discharged, Don Juan, who was attentive to hear of the Spaniards' approach, hearing the volley, and conceiving that his aids were in fight with us, made a sally out of the town; but when he perceived the Spanish colours to be carried by Englishmen in triumph, he made a speedy retreat. The enemy's army, as Alonso de o Campo doth assure us, was six thousand foot and five hundred horse. There were some of the Irish taken prisoners that offered great ransoms, but presently, upon their bringing to the camp, they were hanged.

Although no man is less credulous than myself of idle prophecies, the most whereof are coined after things are done, yet I make bold to relate this which succeeds, for a long time before the thing I speak of was brought to light myself was an eye-witness when it was reported. In concealing it I should wrong the truth, which makes me bold to remember it. Many times I heard the Earl of Thomond tell the Lord President that in an old book of Irish prophecies which he had seen, it was reported that towards the latter days there should be a battle fought between the English and the Irish in a place which the book nameth, near Kinsale. The Earl of Thomond, coming out of England and landing first at Castlehaven, and afterwards at Kinsale, as aforesaid, in the time of the siege, myself and divers others heard him again report the prophecy to the President, and named the place where, according to the prophecy, the field should be fought. The day whereupon the victory was obtained the Lord President and the Earl rode out to see the dead bodies of the vanquished, and the President asked some that were present by what name that ground was called; they, not knowing to what end he demanded it, told him the true name thereof, which was the same which the Earl so often before had reported to the President. I beseech the reader to believe me, for I deliver nothing but truth; but, as one swallow makes no summer, so shall not this one true prophecy increase my credulity in old predictions of that kind.

The five-and-twentieth, in the afternoon, the Spaniards made a sally, but they were forced to retreat into the town. At nine at night they sallied again to hinder our works in the trenches; the skirmish continued two hours; in the end they were repulsed. On our side the ensigns of Captain Roper and Captain Ghest were hurt; what harm they received we know not.

The six-and-twentieth, in the night, they gave again upon our trenches and forced a lieutenant with his guard to quit them; and thence they went to a little fort of ours on the west side of the town; but there they found so good a resistance that they were forced to retreat with the loss of four men slain and eight hurt.

The seven-and-twentieth nothing was done, and that whole day was, by the Lord Deputy, the Lord President, and the rest of the Council then in the camp, spent in making dispatches into England.

CHAPTER XXII.

Zubiaur arrived at Castlehaven and immediately returned—O'Donnell, Redmond Burke, etc., embarked for Spain—The names of such of the Irish as fled into Spain—The loss which the rebels had in passing through Munster after the Battle of Kinsale.

THE eight-and-twentieth, intelligence was brought to the Lord President, who related it to the Lord Deputy, that Pedro Zubiaur, who was, as is said, a great commander in the Spanish fleet that came to Kinsale, was lately landed at Castlehaven, and, hearing of Tyrone's overthrow, he made no stay but set sail for Spain, carrying with him O'Donnell, Redmond Burke, Hugh Mostian, with others of their train whose names I will omit; but for the better satisfaction of the reader I think it meet to set down the names of sundry other Munster men who not long afterwards fled into Spain, whose names ensue:—

A list of the names of such of the Irish as have shipped themselves for Spain out of Munster, besides divers others who attended these and whose names are not known, all which set sail since December, 1601.

FROM CASTLEHAVEN IN DECEMBER, 1601.

O'Donnell,
Redmond Burke, } and their train.
Hugh Mostian,

In a pinnace of advice that brought the King's letters, which were intercepted by the President in February, 1601.

O'Sulevan Beare's sons, and with them one Trant, of Dingle.

Donnell, son to Sir Finnin O'Driscall.

From Ardea in a Patache, the Seventh of June, 1602.

Donogh, bastard brother to Florence MacCarty.
Donogh MacMaghon O'Brien MacEnaspicke.
Brian O'Kelly.

From Kinsale with Don Juan de Aquila, in March, 1601.

Teg MacDonnell ne Conty.
William MacShane, the seneschal's son of Imokilly.
Dermond MacConoghor O'Driscall, of Castlehaven, together with his brother and sons.
Thomas O'Moroghoe, *alias* Thomas Keughe MacEdmond, of Muskery.
Richard Meagh, son and heir to James Meagh, of Kinsale.
Dominick White, of Kinsale, a carpenter's son.
Melaghlen Moore, of Kinsale, born in Connaught.
Conoghor O'Monowe, of Kinsale, and there born.
Edmond MacShane, of Kinsale.
Dermond MacShane, of Kinsale.
Donogh Deasogh, of Kinsale.
Andrew Butler, a kern, born at Galway, } brothers.
William Butler, a kern,
Maghan MacDonogh O'Lery, under Barry Oge.
Dermond MacOwen.

David FitzGarret Barry, and his wife and children dwelling at Rincorran.

Garrot Barry,
Nicholas Barry,
John Barry,
David Oge Barry,
} sons to David FitzGarrot aforesaid.

William Hartilige, of Rincorran.
John Hartilige, son to William aforesaid.
Dermond Oge O'Sulevan, of Rincorran.
Dermond O'Griffien, of Rincorran.
John MacDonell Kedie, of Rincorran,
Dermond MacDonell Kedie,
} brothers.
Maurice Roch FitzJohn, of Ellinfinchtown, in Kinaley,
John FitzJohn Roch,
} brothers.
Conoghor MacDonogh, of Rathmore, in Kinaley.
Donogh Gow, a Connaught man, dwelling at Rathmore, in Kinaley.
Hugo O'Hellie, a Connaught man.
Donogh Moel MacEnessis, Dermond Moel MacCarty's man,
Owen MacDonogh MacFinnin Carty, of Curowrane,
Donel Oge MacDonel Carty, brother to Don Carlos slain at Kinsale,
Finnin Oge Carty, another brother to Don Carlos,
} brothers.
Conogher O'Cullenan, of Rathmore, Kinaley.
Donell O'Griffien, of the same.
William MacCormock, a Connaught man.
Dermond MacShane, a Connaught man.
Edmond O'Lavien,
William MacRicard,
Cormock O'Lanahy,
} all Connaught men.

Dermond Deasergh, a Connaught man.
Dermond O'Longy, of Muskery.
Richard Cogan FitzPhilip, of Barnehelly, in Kerrywhery.
Finin MacDonogh Carty, a cousin to Don Carlos.
Dermond MacFinin Carty, of Skeagh, in Carbery.
Donnell MacFinin Carty, of the same.
Donnell MacTeg Carty, of the same.
David Skemnehan, of Rincorran.
John MacDermond MacShane, a Connaught man.
Cormock, the Lord President's footman, of the Birnes, in Leinster.
William MacShane, of Rathmore, in the county of Limerick.
Donnell MacShane O'Cullenan, of Rathmore, in Kinaley.
John Oge Olenssy, a Connaught man.
Teg Welsh, *alias* Teg Brenagh.
Cormock MacDonogh ne Mroen Oriardane,
Dermond MacDonogh ne Mroen Oriardane,
Owen MacDonogh ne Mroen Oriardane,
} of Muskery; brothers.

Donnell MacShane Oriardane, of Muskery.
John Feild FitzMaurice, of Tracten Abbey.
John Roe MacWilliam, of the county of Limerick.
Donnell O'Sissuane, of Kinsale.
Teg O'Sissuane, son to Donnell aforesaid.
Hugo Lacy,
Walter Ley, of Kilkenny,
Richard Stacboll,
One Master FitzJames, a pensioner.
} These came out of Spain with Don Juan, and returned with him.

From Ardea with Connor O'Driscall and Archer, the Seventh of July, 1602.

Connor O'Driscall, eldest son to Sir Finin O'Driscall.

James Archer, Jesuit.

Colly MacSwine MacEdmond, of the MacSwines of Carbery; his son was hanged at Donboy, in June, 1602.

Cormock MacDonogh, vic' Donnell Rabaghe, one of the Cartys.

Donogh MacConnor, of Castlehaven, and owner of it,
Donnell MacConnor, vic' Dermond O'Driscall, } brothers.

MacCon MacIffie O'Driscall,
Teg MacIffie O'Driscall, } brothers.
Morriertagh MacIffie O'Driscall,

Dermond MacConnor, of Kilkoe, } of the Cartys,
Dermond Oge, of the same,   } brothers.

Shane MacDermond Iholoughane, of Bantry.

Shane MacGillicuddy Iholoughane, of Beare.

Teg Oge ne Mocklogh,   } of the Cartys,
Owen MacTeg ne Mocklogh   } brothers.

Finnin MacBrown, of the O'Driscalls.

Connor O'Maghon, of Lemcon, one of the O'Maghons of Ivagh.

One of the sons of Gilliduff, of Cleere, and one of the O'Driscalls.

Dermond Oge MacDermond O'Driscall.

Connor MacFinnin Roe, of Bonnany, in Bantry.

Tirlogh, son to Teg Reugh MacMaghon, of Thomond, who slew his father when Donboy was besieged; his lands Her Majesty had given to the Earl of Thomond's brother.

Dowaltagh MacMorogh Incorromany, foster-brother to O'Donnell.

Elline ny Donogh, late wife to Dermond Moel Mac-Carty, brother to Florence.

Finnin Kearigh, of the Fioll, one of the Cartys.

Dermond MacShannagany, a rimer.

Gilliduff, a Thomond man.

Two soldiers of Thomond who served Connor O'Driscall.

David MacShane, of the Dingle, servant to James Archer, the Jesuit.

Shane MacDermond, vic' Donogh Oge O'Cullenan, Archer's boy.

Connor Oge O'Driscall, heir to Connor, Sir Finnin's son, nine years of age.

Thomas, son and heir to the Knight of the Valley, fourteen years old.

Donnell O'Maghon, a mariner who came in company with Owen MacEggan.

Five Frenchmen who were taken by Teg Reugh, when they took the ship and merchant of Galway.

The nine-and-twentieth, the Lord Deputy and the Lord President were advertised from sundry persons and divers ways, that Tyrone, in passing the broad water, lost many of his carriages and one hundred and forty of his men drowned. Those who took their way through Connologh (for they broke into many parts) had also loss of men and carriages in the River May, and the like at the Abbey of Ownhy in O'Mulryan's country; so that they lost of all sorts above two hundred. The footmen, wearied in the flight, to go the lighter, cast away their arms, and their hurt men, carried upon weak and tired garrans, were by their fellows left upon the way, where they died. Their tired horses were slain by their masters, and the country inhabitants, for spoil's sake, upon advantages would not spare to take some of their heads, but not in that proportion that they might have done if they had been sound subjects. Lastly, it was reported (but how true it is I am somewhat doubtful), that Tyrone himself and MacMahon were both hurt in the battle, and carried away on litters. To conclude, never men were more dismayed with extremity of fear than these light-footed traitors were.

> The " Four Masters " express great and natural amazement at such a victory obtained by a few men against many, and truly remark that many times the men here defeated had won victories against great odds. They add that few were slain, owing to the fact that those who pursued were few and those who ran many. In fact this great battle, the grand turning-point of the Nine-Years'-War, was won by a mere handful of determined men. The confederate host was full of traitors and trimmers, of men who had little love for the cause which they professed and little trust in each other. Upon this ill-combined host panic fell. P. O'Sullivan too, relates that a part of the insurgent cavalry, by accident or design, charged that portion which was under Hugh Roe's command.
>
> Irish writers as a rule feel a sense of national shame over this disgraceful defeat, believing, as they generally do, that the battle was won by Englishmen.
>
> Philip O'Sullivan, who had all his information at first hand, tells us that at this time the Queen's army consisted of seven thousand men, and that of these 2000 only were English, and 5000 Irish. Now the English, being the worse soldiers, would naturally have been kept in camp that day. The true way of regarding the battle is that the Royalist Irish, the Irish who adhered to the State and its fortunes, defeated the confederate Irish. It was but an incident in a great civil war, a war in which, for reasons best known to themselves, the far larger proportion of the Irish nation sided with the Queen. O'Sullivan relates that Hugh Roe at first defeated the Royalist cavalry, and drove them across a little river which flowed out of that boggy ground mentioned by Carew.

CHAPTER XXIII.

A parley desired by Don Juan, and granted by the Lord Deputy—Don Juan's propositions, with their answers and his reply—The reasons which moved the Lord Deputy and Council to yield to a composition—The articles of the composition.

THE last of December Don Juan offered a parley, sending the drum-major out of the town with a sealed letter to the Lord Deputy, by an Alferes, by which he required (as by the copy thereof conveyed in the dispatch by Sir Richard Morison into England may appear) that some gentleman of special trust and sufficiency might be sent into the town from his Lordship to confer with him, whom he would acquaint with such conditions as he then stood upon; which being granted by his Lordship, Sir William Godolphin was employed in that negotiation ; which in what sort it was carried, because it importeth much, in respect of many particularities of special moment to be considered, it is thought necessary it should be here more largely delivered. His first conference with Sir William Godolphin tendeth to this: That having found the Lord Deputy (whom he termeth the Viceroy) although a sharp and powerful opositor yet an honourable enemy, and the Irish not only weak and barbarous [1] but, as he feared, perfidious friends, he

---

[1] I do not know any authority for that saying so often attributed to Don Juan: "Surely Christ never died for this people." One of his officers did use that expression.

was so far in his affection reconciled to the one and distasted with the other as did invite him to make an overture of such a composition as might be safe and profitable for the State of England, with less prejudice to the Crown of Spain, by delivering into the Viceroy's power the town of Kinsale, with all other places in Ireland held by the Spanish, so that they might depart upon honourable terms, fitting such men of war, that are not by necessity forced to receive conditions, but willingly induced for just respects to disengage themselves and to relinquish a people by whom their king and master had been so notoriously abused, if not betrayed: that if the Viceroy liked to entertain further parley touching this point he would first be pleased to understand them rightly and to make his propositions such as might be suitable to men thoroughly resolved rather to bury themselves alive and to endure a thousand deaths than to give way to one article of accord that should taste of baseness or dishonour, being so confident of their present strength and the royal second of Spain that they should make no doubt of yielding good account of themselves and their interest in this kingdom; but that a just disdain and spleen conceived against the nation dissuaded them from being further engaged for it than of force they must. Sir William Godolphin, being commanded by the Lord Deputy only to receive Don Juan's propositions and demands, having made his Lordship and Council this relation was by them returned with the answer following. That howbeit the Lord Deputy, having lately defeated their succours, did so well understand his own strength and their weakness, as made him nothing doubt of forcing them within a very short time, whom he did know to be pressed with irresistible difficulties, how much soever they laboured to cover and conceal the same; yet knowing that her sacred Majesty, out of her gracious and merciful disposition, would esteem the glory of her victory to be blemished by a voluntary effusion and an obstinate expense of Christian blood, was content to entertain this offer of agreement so that it might be concluded under such honourable articles of her Highness as the advantage she had against them gave reason to demand, being the same which are sent with this dispatch signed by Don Juan, the leaving of his treasure, munition, artillery, and the Queen's natural subjects to her disposition only excepted: all which points he did peremptorily refuse, with constant asseveration that both he and all his would rather endure the last misery than be found guilty of so foul a treason against the honour of his prince and the reputation of his profession, though he should find himself unable to subsist, much more now when he might not only hope to sustain the burthen of the war for a time, but with patience and constancy in the end to overcome it: that he took it so ill to be understood in having articles of that nature propounded to him that were they but once again remembered in the capitulation the Viceroy should henceforth use the advantage of his sword and not the benefit of his former offers; adding that the Viceroy might rather think to have made a good and profitable purchase for the Crown of England if, with the expense of two hundred thousand ducats, he had procured Don Juan to quit his interest and footing but in Baltimore, to say nothing of Kinsale, Castlehaven, and Bearchaven; "for," said he, "suppose that all we, with the rest of our places here, had perished, yet would that peninsula, being strong in its own nature, bettered by our art and industry, provided, as it is, with victuals, munition, and good artillery, preserve to the King of Spain a safe and commodious port for the arrival of his fleet, and be able to maintain itself against a land army of ten thousand until Spain, being so deeply engaged, did in honour relieve them, which would draw on a more powerful invasion than the first, being undertaken upon false grounds, at the instance of a base and barbarous people, who in discovering their weakness and want of power have armed the King my master to rely upon his own strength, being tied in honour to relieve his people that are engaged and to cancel the memory of our former disaster; but this was spoken," said he, "in case the Viceroy were able to force this town, as I assure myself he cannot, having upon mine honour within these walls,[1] at this instant, above two thousand fighting men, who are strong and able, besides those who, having been sick and hurt, recover daily—the greatest part of these composed of old soldiers, who fall not but by the sword, and those who were new, being now both trained to their arms and grown acquainted with the climate, are more able to endure than at first. Our means are as good as they have been any time these two months, such as the Spaniards can well away withal, and thereof to suffice us for three months more; we lodge in good warm houses, have store of munition, and (which is best of all) stand well assured that our succours will be

---

[1] Carlyle says, "the Spaniards were incontestably the *noblest* nation of Europe in the sixteenth century." Every Spaniard who appeared in Ireland in this century supplies his quota of proof to that verdict. When Don Juan declares, as here, that he has 2000 fighting men, strong and able, within the walls, we know that he can be writing nothing but the truth. That he did so, we shall see later on.

shortly here. To be plain, we preserve our men and reserve our strength the best we may, hoping to front you in a breach, which, if our hearts fail us not, we have hands and breasts enough to stop against treble your forces; though I will give the Viceroy this right,[1] that his men are passing good, but spent and tired out with the misery of a winter siege, which he hath obstinately maintained beyond my expectation, but with such caution, and upon so good guard, that, having nicely watched all advantages, I could never fasten a sally yet upon him but with loss to myself, wherein I must acknowledge my hopes deceived that, grounding on some error in his approaches, promised myself the defeat of at least one thousand men at one blow; but when we meet on the breach I am confident, upon reason, to lay five hundred of your best men on the earth, and rest hopeful that the loss of those will make a great hole in an army that hath already suffered so much extremity; but, to conclude our business, the King, my master, sent me to assist the condees O'Neale and O'Donnell, presuming on their promise that I should have joined with them within a few days of the arrival of his forces. I expected long in vain, sustained the Viceroy's arms, saw them drawn to the greatest head they could possibly make, lodged within two miles of Kinsale, reinforced with certain companies of Spaniards, every hour promising to relieve us, and, being joined together to force your camps, saw them at last broken with a handful of men, blown asunder into divers parts of the world; O'Donnell into Spain, O'Neale to the furthest part of the north, so that now I find no such condees *in rerum*

---

[1] Observe that this high compliment, whatever Don Juan intended by it, is in fact addressed to the Irish, the Royalist Irish.

natura (for those were the very words he used) that I came to join withal; and therefore have moved this accord the rather to disengage the King, my master, from assisting a people so unable in themselves that the whole burthen of the war must lie upon him, and so perfidious that perhaps might be induced in requital of his favour [1] at last to betray him."

Upon relation made by Sir William Godolphin to the Lord Deputy and Council of these offers of Don Juan, which at several conferences had been brought to such heads that by the articles between them is more particularly specified, it was thought good, for divers important reasons, to proceed roundly to the agreement; for whereas in the propositions by him made there was not anything that admitted exceptions on our part, but only that he required to carry with him his ordnance, munition, and treasure, that being no way prejudicial to the main scope or drift of our treaty, which chiefly respected the common good and safety of the kingdom, deserved not almost to be thought upon. Besides that, the treasure being at first but one hundred thousand ducats, with four months' payment of so many men, and other necessary deductions, could not be but very nearly wasted, and that little remainder more fit for a prey to the poor soldiers, after this tedious travel, than for a clause in the composition. Furthermore, how needful it was to embrace this accord, may clearly be seen by whosoever considereth the state of our army, almost utterly tired; how full of danger and difficulty it was to attempt a breach

---

[1] I must again remind the reader that all nations in that stage of development to which the Irish had attained at this time, are and must be what is called perfidious. Atoms not compacted by force into an organism will follow each the law of its own nature.

defended by so many hands; how much time it might have cost us if we had lodged in the breach, before we could have carried the town, being full of strong castles; how Her Majesty's ships and others being in the harbour should have been forced speedily to forsake us for want of victuals; how ourselves were not provided for above six days at the time of this parley; that we had neither munition nor artillery but for one battery, in one place at once, five of our pieces being before crased; and, finally, that if we had missed of our purpose the whole country had been hazarded. Furthermore, that which seemed of greatest consequence to induce his Lordship to this agreement was that the Spaniards in Baltimore, Castlehaven, and Bearehaven, by virtue of this contract, were likewise to surrender those places and depart the country, which how hard a matter it would have proved, and how long and dangerous a war it would have drawn on, to root them out, they being strongly fortified and well stored with victuals, munition, and artillery, may easily be conjectured; for that of necessity the army for some space must have rested, and in the end have been constrained after a new supply of necessaries (to Her Majesty's intolerable charges) to transport themselves thither by sea, the way by land being impassable, in which time their succours out of Spain in all likelihood would have been come to them; the King being so far engaged in his honour to second his enterprise, and we barred of that prosecution of the rebels which now by this agreement we may wholly intend.

For which considerations the Lord Deputy and Council thought it in their wisdoms meet to condescend to more indifferent conditions, which being propounded and agreed upon by Don Juan, these articles ensuing were signed and sealed on both parts:—

THE ARTICLES OF COMPOSITION BETWEEN THE LORD DEPUTY AND COUNCIL AND DON JUAN DE AQUILA.

MOUNTJOY.

In the town of Kinsale, in the kingdom of Ireland, the second day of the month of January, 1601, between the noble lords the Lord Mountjoy, Lord Deputy and General in the kingdom of Ireland, and Don Juan de Aquila, Captain and Camp-master-General, and Governor of the army of His Majesty the King of Spain, the said Lord Deputy being encamped and besieging the said town and the said Don Juan within it, for just respects, and to avoid shedding of blood, these conditions following were made between the said lords general and their camps, with the articles that follow:—

First, that the said Don Juan de Aquila shall quit the places which he holds in this kingdom, as well of the town of Kinsale as those which are held by the soldiers under his command in Castlehaven, Baltimore, and the castle of Bearehaven, and other parts, to the said Lord Deputy, or to whom he shall appoint, giving him safe transportation (and sufficient) for the said people of ships and victuals, with which the said Don Juan with them may go to Spain, if he can at one time, if not in two shippings.

Item: That the soldiers at this present being under the command of Don Juan in this kingdom shall not bear arms against Her Majesty the Queen of England, wheresoever supplies shall come from Spain, till the said soldiers be unshipped in some of the ports of Spain, being despatched (as soon as may be) by the Lord Deputy, as he promiseth upon his faith and honour.

Item: For the accomplishing whereof the Lord Deputy offereth to give free passport to the said Don Juan and his army, as well Spaniards as other nations whatsoever, that are under his command, and that he may depart with all the things he hath, arms, munitions, money, ensigns displayed, artillery, and other whatsoever provisions of war, and any kind of stuff, as well that which is in Castlehaven as Kinsale and other parts.

Item: That they shall have ships and victuals, sufficient for their money, according and at the prices which here they use to give; that all the people and the said things may be shipped (if it be possible) at one time, if not at two, and that to be within the time above named.

Item: That if by contrary winds or by any other occasions there shall arrive at any port of these kingdoms of Ireland or England any ships of these (in which the said men may go) they be treated as friends, and may ride safely in the harbour, and be victualled for their money, and have moreover things which they shall need to furnish them for their voyage.

Item: During the time that they shall stay for shipping, victuals shall be given to Don Juan's people at just and reasonable rates.

Item: That of both parts shall be cessation of arms and security that no wrong be offered anyone.

Item: That the ships in which they shall go for Spain may pass safely by any other ships whatsoever of Her Majesty's the Queen of England; and so shall they of the said Queen and her subjects by those that shall go from hence, and the said ships being arrived in Spain shall return, as soon as they have unshipped their men, without any impediment given them by His Majesty, or any other person in his name, but rather they shall show them favour, and help them, if they need anything; and for security of this, they shall give into the Lord Deputy's hands, three captains such as he shall choose.

For the security of the performance of the articles, Don Juan offereth that he will confirm and swear to accomplish this agreement; and likewise some of the captains of his charge shall swear and confirm the same in a several writing.

Item: That he in person shall abide in this kingdom where the Lord Deputy shall appoint till the last shipping, upon his Lordship's word; and if it happen that his people be shipped all at once, the said Don Juan shall go in the same fleet without any impediment given him; but rather the Lord Deputy shall give a good ship in which he may go; and if his said men be sent in two shippings then he shall go in the last.

And in like sort the said Lord Deputy shall swear and confirm and give his word in behalf of Her Majesty the Queen and his own to keep and accomplish this agreement, and jointly the Lord President, the Lord Marshal of the Camp, and the others of the Council of State, and the Earls of Thomond and Clanricard shall swear and confirm the same in a several writing.

I do promise and swear to accomplish and keep these articles of agreement, and promise the same

likewise on the behalf of His Majesty Catholic,
the King, my master.
GEORGE CAREW.
THOMOND.[1]   DON JUAN DE AGUILA.
CLANRICARD.
RICHARD WINGFIELD.
ROBERT GARDINER.
GEORGE BOURCHIER.
RICHARD LEVISON.

[1] The Earl of Thomond, several times mentioned already, was, like young Clanricarde, son of an Earl who had been in rebellion. His House, too, had made terms with the State at a penny an acre rent, and was now zealous in warring down all other chieftains who stood upon regalities. Clare, the O'Brien country, was at this time a part of Connaught. The Earls of Thomond and Clanricarde, that is to say, the sept of the High Burkes and the sept of the O'Briens, were the chief pillars of the State in the west.

Nearly all the names appended to the treaty were those either of Irishmen or of men born in Ireland. Richard Wingfield is ancestor of our Viscounts Powerscourt.

CHAPTER XXIV.

The names of the hostages delivered by Don Juan—Don Juan's demand of victuals for the transportation of his men—The victuals which were delivered to Don Juan and their rates—The number of Spaniards who were transported out of Ireland—The Lord Deputy broke up his siege and returned to Cork—Captain Harvy's commission for his government.

THE day the articles were signed, Don Juan dined with the Lord Deputy, and the next day the Lord President (having Sir Richard Levison and Sir William Godolphin in his company) was sent into the town of Kinsale, where he dined with Don Juan, to treat with him about such shipping and victuals as he would demand for the transportation of his men, and at what rates, for which ready money was to be paid; and also to demand of him the three captains whom the Lord Deputy had made choice of, who were Don Pedro Morijon, Captain Pedro Cuaco, and Captain Diego Gonzales Sigler, to remain pledges until the return of the ships. The demands he made of victuals and tonnage for the victualling and transporting of three thousand two hundred men remaining in Kinsale, Castlehaven, Baltimore, and Donboy, whereof two thousand six hundred in Kinsale, and six hundred at the places aforesaid, were as followeth:—

First his demands were six weeks' victuals, in form following:

For every week four days flesh, three days fish.

For every flesh-day, bread four-and-twenty ounces for a man, and six of beef.

For every fish-day, four-and-twenty ounces of bread, six ounces of fish, and one ounce of butter.

For every hundred men, one pipe of wine, besides water.[1]

For shipping, for every three men, two tuns, and he to give forty shillings the tun, and his men to be landed at the first port they can touch in Spain.

For the expediting of these demands, the Lord Deputy gave present directions to all the ports within the province for the taking up of shipping, and warrant to Allen Apsley (the commissary for the victuals in Munster) to issue out of the Queen's store, according to the demands made, these quantities of victuals ensuing, for which he should receive money of Don Juan, whereby the magazine might be supplied:—

Towards the accomplishing whereof, the commis-

---

[1] All this is interesting as showing the diet of a Spanish soldier in this century. Scotch and Irish soldiers serving the insurgent lords at this time made no demand for meat, only for milk, butter, and oatmeal; no beer or whisky. Irish soldiers serving the Queen got beer, "the absence of which driveth them to drink large quantities of water which breedeth many diseases." Such at least was the opinion of Fenton, head of the fiscal department, who was very strong for beer as a good liquor for men marching and fighting. Sir Henry Sidney was called "Big Henry of the beer," he was so fond of serving out that beverage to his men. Possibly the Queen's beer attracted to her service many fighting men who would otherwise have served the insurgent lords, and if that be so, as doubtless it was, beer was a chief agent in the incorporation of Ireland in the Empire. A penny a day and diet was the pay of the lowest order of soldier, the Kerne or light foot. Tyrone and O'Donnell paid at this rate. Now as a penny then was more than equivalent to a shilling to-day, it follows that the Irish lords paid their soldiers as well, or even a good deal better, than the mighty British Empire pays the British soldier in our times. Shot and gallow-glasses were paid higher rates.

sary of the victuals delivered this ensuing proportion, viz. :—

	li.	£	s.	d.
Biscuit	186,052	2067	4	8
Butter	6,304	157	12	3
Flesh	47,394	789	18	0
Fish	18,339	305	13	0
Rice	1,235	30	17	6
Summa tot.		£3351	5	5

Which being with all possible convenience dispatched, haste was made for their embarking at two sundry times. There were shipped at Kinsale, the care whereof was committed to Captain Francis Slingsby, 2070; at Baltimore and at Castlehaven, by Captain Roger Harvy, 415; in all 3025, besides captains, inferior officers, priests, and religious men, and a great company of Irish.[1]

The fourth of January a Spanish ship appeared by the Old Head of Kinsale, hovering before the harbour mouth. The Lord Deputy, having concluded the composition with Don John for the rendering of the town of Kinsale, sent a boat with some men in her to let them know that Don John and he were good friends, and therefore he might safely come in without any danger (in which boat was one Thomas Foster, a nephew to Sir Anthony Cooke), which message, as soon as it was delivered, the captain of the ship took in all the men, hoisted sail, and stood away with all speed for Spain. This might seem to be an action performed with no good approbation, in putting those men into

---

[1] Don Juan seems to have altered his opinion of Irish fighting qualities when he brought off with him this great company of Irish. In fact his censures were applied only to the Confederate Irish.

their power; but, whether it be justifiable or not, the success proved it to be of very great consequence, for though the news of the defeat of the Irish army was come into Spain by O'Donnell and those with him, yet Don John stood firm in Kinsale, without danger to be much pressed by the Deputy, soliciting new forces, hoping thereby to repair their former losses, to reunite their dispersed companies, and to overthrow the English forces, being much spent and sorely weakened by their winter siege. Before the arrival of O'Donnell seconds were in preparing, and, after his arrival, both increased and much hastened, as may appear by the letters intercepted, which came out of Spain to Don John, when he was at Cork, from the King of Spain, the Duke of Lerma, the secretary Ibarra, and others; but when they understood by those men that Don John had compounded for the rendering of Kinsale and for their returning into Spain it put them to a stand for their proceedings, and they at last concluded to give over the attempt, finding so little assistance either in the power or courage of the Irish; and if this had not fallen out thus, and those seconds had come and landed in Ireland, it might have been much doubted, or rather positively believed the contrary, that those Spaniards would not have been bound by Don John's articles, but have taken the best opportunity of their force and power in kindling a new flame and making that kingdom again in as desperate a state as ever heretofore it had been, if not worse.

These things being thus ordered, and no cause appearing of longer stay in the camp, the ninth of January the Lord Deputy rose, and the same day he rode to Cork, having in his company Don Juan de

Aguila and many of the Spanish captains, the gross of his companies being left in Kinsale. The Lord Deputy lodged in the Bishop of Cork's house, Don Juan in the city, and the President at Shandon Castle. The day following the captains received directions to repair to sundry towns in Munster appointed for their garrisons; and the same day Captain Roger Harvy and Captain George Flower were dispatched with certain companies by sea, to receive the castles of Castlehaven, Donneshed, and Donnelong at Baltimore, and Dunboy at Bearehaven in the west, all of which were then in the possession of the Spaniards. Also the said Captain Harvy had a commission granted to him for the government of all the country between Rosse in Carberry and the Bay of Bantry, as followeth :—

A COMMISSION FROM THE LORD DEPUTY AND COUNCIL TO CAPTAIN ROGER HARVY FOR THE GOVERNMENT OF CARBERRY.

MOUNTJOY.

We greet you well. Whereas we have thought it very expedient for the furtherance of Her Majesty's service and the drawing and settling the inhabitants of the western parts of the province of Munster (which lately revolted) into Her Majesty's allegiance again, which in regard that divers the rebels which were united to Tyrone and the Spaniards, upon the overthrow given them made escape and are drawn to Baltimore, Castlehaven, and those other western parts: for the better prosecution, cutting off, and apprehension of those and of all other rebels, traitors, felons, and other capital offenders, by all the best and

speediest means that may be : we have thought it
good, in regard of the great knowledge and experience
we have had and found in your faith and valour, and
in respect of the special trust, confidence, and
sufficiency we repose in you, we have thought it good
to grant and commit unto you, during our pleasure,
the command and authority (by the power granted us
by Her Majesty) over the castles of Baltimore and
Castlehaven, and the whole country of Carberry, and
over all the countries, territories, or places of Colle-
more, Collibeg, Ivagh, Mounterbarry, Slewghteagi-
bane, Slewghteage, Roe, Cloncahill, Clondermot,
Clonloghen, and Coshmore, and over all the other
countries, territories, places by what name or names
soever they be called, from the town of Rosse to the
hither parts of the meres and bounds of Beere and
Bantry, and so in compass northwards to Muskerry :
and we do give you power and authority over the
Queen's people and her subjects and inhabitants in all
or any the said countries, appointing and authorizing
you hereby to prosecute with fire and sword all rebels,
traitors, or other capital offenders, and all their aiders,
relievers, maintainers, receivers, and abettors, or any
other offenders whatsoever that are not amenable
to Her Majesty's laws, or have combined or adhered
themselves to any Her Majesty's enemies, or to any
now in actual rebellion against her Highness, and to
make seizure of all their goods and chattels to Her
Majesty's use : and for the better affecting of this Her
Highness's service, and the special trust reposed in
you, we do hereby give unto you liberty to employ or
send among the enemies or rebels (now in action) such
messengers and espials as you shall think fit to use,
and to write, to parley, confer, or treat with them,

or any of them, and to receive messengers or letters from them, and to keep any of them in your company fourteen days, to procure the doing of service, or to gain intelligence from them; and upon assurance and good hopes that any of the said rebels will do service to Her Majesty; we do hereby authorize you to safe-conduct them, by warrant under your hand, for the like space of fourteen days, so as in the meantime you send them unto us or to the chief governor of the province (for the time being), which your safe conduct shall be duly observed to all those you grant it unto.

And for the better and speedier cleansing and purging the country from rebels and malefactors, we do hereby give and commit unto you full power and authority to execute by martial law all notable and apparent offenders and malefactors that can neither dispend forty shillings in lands per annum nor are worth ten pounds in goods, and as for such rebels and malefactors as are not within compass of martial law, them to apprehend and commit to the shire gaol, there to remain and attend their trials by due course of Her Majesty's common laws. And for the better advancement of Her Majesty's service we do hereby authorize you to go aboard any ship, bark or other vessel that shall be or arrive in those parts, and to make search in them for traitors, Jesuits, seminaries, letters, or prohibited wares, and to make stay of them if just occasion so require, and to press and take up any the boats or vessels that are or shall be within the compass of your command, and them to send and employ to such place or places as Her Majesty's service shall give you occasion, or otherwise to use and dispose of them as you in your discretion shall think meetest; and this our authority and commission to you granted, to have continuance during the pleasure of us the Lord Deputy; and if we shall not recall the same during our abode in this province, then the same to be in force during the pleasure of the Lord President, and no longer. And therefore we do hereby straightly charge and command all Her Majesty's officers, ministers, and loving subjects to be unto you (in the due execution of the premisses) aiding, obedient, and assisting at their utmost perils; and for such your whole doings herein. These shall be unto you sufficient warrant and discharge; given under Her Majesty's privy signet, at the camp before Kinsale, the seventh day of January, 1601.

GEORGE CAREW.
RICHARD WINGFIELD.
GEORGE BOURCHIER.

To our well-beloved captain, Roger Harvy.

The eleventh, the Lord President had intelligence from England that James, the late restored Earl of Desmond, was dead, and that eighteen hundred quarters of oats were sent into Munster for the relief of our horses.[1]

---

[1] The oats and the Earl are here curiously shoved together.

CHAPTER XXV.

Don Juan's request to the Lord Deputy—A resolution in council to erect certain forts in Munster—The request of the inhabitants of Kinsale to the Lord President—Certain companies cashiered—A letter from the Lord President to Her Majesty—The examination of Richard Owen—Richard Owen's message from Tyrone to the Lord Deputy—Instructions for Captain George Blunt.

THE fourteenth, Don Juan wrote to the Lord Deputy to pray his Lordship that expedition might be made in taking up of shipping for his transportation and that his Lordship would commiserate the poor Spanish prisoners in Cork, who were like to perish for want of food. During the siege there had been taken at Rincorran, Castle ny Parke, in sallies and in the overthrow of Tyrone, together with some runaways that voluntarily came to us, about two hundred, rather more than less, whereof some of them had been sent into England. About this time the Lord Deputy and the Lord President went by boat to an island in the river of Cork called Haulbowlin, six or seven miles from the city, which upon view they thought fit to be fortified, being so seated that no shipping of any burthen can pass the same but under the command thereof. Whereupon direction was given to Paul Ive, an engineer, to raise a fortification there, and also another at Castle ny Park to command the haven at

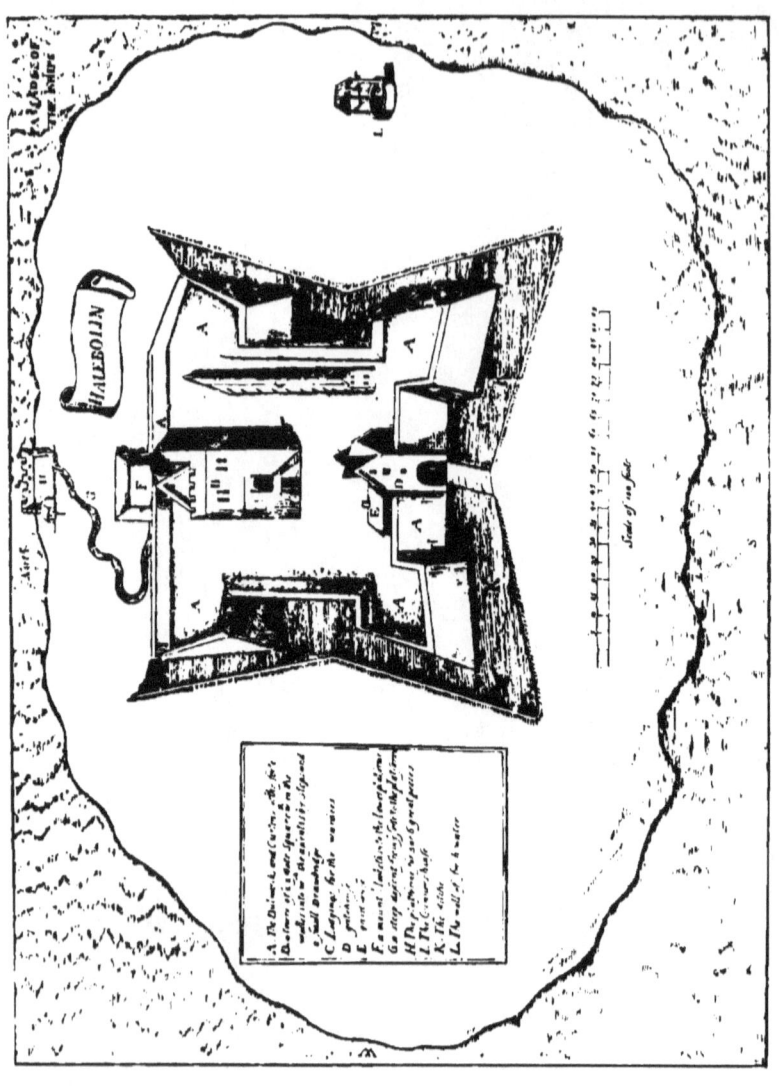

MAP OF THE FORT OF HAULBOWLIN.

Kinsale. Furthermore it was resolved in Council that forts should be erected at Baltimore and Bearehaven, as also citadels at Cork, Limerick, and Waterford,[1] to keep the citizens in some awe; but none of these works were performed save only the forts at Haulbowlin and Castle ny Parke aforesaid.

And the same day the better sort of burgesses of Kinsale came to the Lord President to beseech him to render unto them their charter, seal, mace, and standard, which some of them, upon the Spaniards' arrival at Kinsale, had delivered unto him to be safely kept until the Spanish storm was past; which they did not deliver unto him as a surrender, but to show and manifest their duties. The President acquainted the Lord Deputy with their petition, and by agreement the answer which the President made was that before he had received directions from England he might not restore their muniments to them, for he conceived that they were forfeited; but he would write in their behalf; and so he did; and not long after he had direction to deliver them, but with this caution, that they should at their own charge rebuild their walls and give help of labourers towards the finishing of Castle ny Pa ke, which they promised to perform.[2]

From the fourteenth of January unto the last of the same no matter of any consequence happened, all which time was spent in civil causes, in sending dispatches into England (as occasions did result), in discharging companies which were grown weak, whereof

[1] Observe the resuming of the intention to bridle the cities, now that by their aid the confederate lords had been overthrown.

[2] One would think that all this was essentially within the Imperial province of affairs, but the State at this time was always ready to screw out of every one as much as it could.

two thousand in list were cashiered;[1] in hastening away the Spaniards, and in settling garrisons in the eastern part of Munster. Among other private dispatches which the Lord President sent into England he wrote this letter to Her Majesty:—

A LETTER FROM THE LORD PRESIDENT TO HER MAJESTY.

SACRED MAJESTY,—Now that it hath pleased the omnipotent director of all things to bless you with a happy victory over the malicious traitors and foreign enemies which endeavoured with all their forces to draw from your imperial Crown this realm of Ireland, in the which, by your Majesty's express commandment, I have been, though far unworthy, employed in a charge wherein my weakness doth too much appear; yet since out of your princely favour your Majesty hath been pleased to accept of those poor services, which by your forces I have formerly performed, and with your royal hand (to my unspeakable comfort) unto myself have witnessed the same, I am emboldened (under the assurance of your gracious pardon) to present before your gracious eyes those unworthy lines, unworthy of your view as well in regard of him that writes them as the form wherein they are written. Since the victory aforesaid the face of this kingdom is strangely altered. The rebel (formerly proud) is now become a dismayed fugitive, the neutral subject, which stood at a gaze, better confirmed, and the Spaniard, which promised to

[1] Remark the cashiering of the companies the moment danger was at an end. The government, with a vile economy, hired its soldiers for the job. At the commencement of the Nine-Years'-War the Queen had only 750 soldiers in Ireland, an immense temptation to the discontented.

himself no less than a conquest, is glad to entreat a composition to depart; this wonderful work of God (for unto Him it is wholly to be ascribed) hath brought this realm (so far out of order) in a fairer way of reduction than ever I knew it. When your Majesty employed me in this service I then feared it was (as I now understand it to be) a secret punishment from God for my sins, for unto myself I had propounded that happiness (which others have) never to be far distant from the comfort of your royal eyes, which add fulness of joy with admiration to the beholders. Wherefore, gracious Sovereign, commiserate my exile, and let me, your poor servant, rich in faith and loyalty unto you, be partaker of others' happiness, that the remainder of my life therein may be blessed. But if I be not capable of such abundant grace in so great measure (which my soul desires), yet let my humble suit thus far prevail that in your princely favour you will be pleased to give me leave for a few months to behold that majesty which is envied but not equalled by any earthly prince. From your Majesty's city of Cork the nineteenth of January, 1601.

Your sacred Majesty's
vassal and creature,
GEORGE CAREW.

The fourth of February one Richard Owen, an old and intimate servant of Tyrone's, came to Cork with a message from his master to the Lord Deputy; but before I speak of his negotiation I think it convenient to fall back to the sixth of January, at which time he made means to have access to the President; for you must understand he had been with Don John in Kinsale. The President acquainting the Lord Deputy with it, he was called before them both, and was examined by them, whereunto he made an answer as followeth:—

He said he went out of Ireland with Sir William Stanley,[1] and was employed by him in the rendering of Deventer to Taxis.

He left Sir William upon a discontentment (about four years after, being then a lieutenant) because Sir William advanced the English and not the Irish to charges, and then put himself into the King's pay as a pensioner, and there remained in the Low Countries and France until about three years since. He came over into Ireland by way of Scotland, and landed at Dunluce, with purpose to serve O'Neale, whose kinsman he is by his mother, and remained with Tyrone, until by him he was employed to carry his son into Spain.

He had letters from Tyrone and O'Donnell to the King, and from Tyrone to Don Juan Idiaques, the Duke of Lerma, to Fray Gaspar de Cordova, the King's confessor, the secretary Prado, and to the secretary Estevan de Ybarra.

The contents of the letters were to pray aids to subsist the war, according to the promise made by the old king. If the aids were sent for Ulster, then Tyrone required but four or five thousand men; if the king purposed to send an army into Munster, then he should send strongly, because neither Tyrone nor O'Donnell could come to help them.

He said that Fray Matheo de Oviedo, the Archbishop of Dublin, out of an ancient knowledge which he had in this kingdom, having been before in this realm, in James FitzMaurice's rebellion, solicited the sending of

---

[1] Son of the Earl of Derby. He was a distinguished soldier in Ireland. Brought over an Irish regiment to the Netherlands to fight for the Queen, but deserted to Philip with most of his men.

forces hither, and came into the north purposely to see and understand the state of the country.

He also said that Tyrone sent his son into Spain to be there brought up, not being demanded of the king as a pledge.

He said that all the King's Council were very forward to thrust on the invasion, and for his own particular he advised that the Spanish forces should land at Carlingford, and if that Council did not like them, then he persuaded that the forces should land at Galway or Sligo.

He said that O'Neale's son hath two hundred ducats pension of the king *per mensem*.

He said that when the army came for Ireland, out of a desire to establish religion and to procure to the Irish lords some greater government in the realm, he came voluntarily hither, without pay, but protests that he never wished that the Crown of Ireland should be taken from the Queen. He said he never heard of any of Ireland that by letters solicited this invasion but James MacSorley,[1] who, as he heard, wrote to the King; that Florence wrote to the King he knows not, but Tyrone wrote to this examinate, that Florence would be in arms with him against Her Majesty.

He said that he thinketh that, if the Spaniards had prevailed in this enterprise, their meaning was not to possess themselves of Ireland, but from hence to have invaded England, and to have entertained the Irish nation in that enterprise.[2]

[1] Son of Sorley Boy MacDonald, Lord of South Antrim and ancestor of our Earls of Antrim.
[2] And the Irish nation under good discipline being led forth in this manner by Spanish captains under the authority of the King of Spain and supported by the Catholic party in England, always very strong, would probably have done what was expected. But all those possibilities were swept away by the Battle of Kinsale.

Being demanded if the English had been beaten out of Ireland what government should have been here established and who should have governed, he answered that therein he is wholly ignorant, but when Tyrone wrote for aid he said that he thinketh that, when the English were banished and expelled, then he would submit himself to be dealt withal as pleased the King.

He said that in March next he thinketh that supplies should have been sent to Don Juan, but now he is of opinion that never any more will be sent into Ireland.

He said that the reason that now he desired the Lord President to bring him to the Lord Deputy was because he was altogether weary to serve with the Irish, and also commanded so to do by Tyrone after his overthrow.

He was commanded by Tyrone, the next morning after the overthrow, to repair to the Lord Deputy and to tell his Lordship that he was willing and desirous to become a subject if he may be received and justly dealt withal; and to redeem his errors past he professed to do all possible service to Her Majesty,[1] but that he would not leave his son hostage for him.

He said that he thinketh upon his conscience that O'Donnell went into Spain without any advice of Tyrone's, and that Redmond Burke and Captain Mostian went likewise without his consent.[2]

---

[1] Why need we be surprised at the treachery so common amongst the insurgent lords when we find Tyrone himself promising secretly to come into Her Majesty's service and attack his own allies?

[2] The point of this will be evident when it is remembered that at the time it was considered a "horrible treason" to have anything to do with Spain. Rebellion was nothing to it. In Ireland no one regarded rebellion as high treason.

Which done, being sorry, as he protested, of his traitorly life, he humbly craved Her Majesty's gracious protection, promising to merit the same with future loyal service; which being granted, he departed. Upon the fourth of this month (as aforesaid), having been in the meantime with Tyrone, he made his second address to the President, the Lord Deputy then being in Cork, and being called before the Lord Deputy and the President, he delivered to them a message from Tyrone, the effect whereof was that he would be glad to be received into Her Majesty's mercy, being heartily sorry that he had given her so just a cause of offence, and likewise grieved in his soul that he had been the cause of the effusion of so much blood, the exhausting of Her Majesty's treasure, and the ruin of his native country. Nevertheless this pretended grief and humility was farced with some exorbitant conditions unmeet for him to demand from his sovereign, whom he had highly offended, or for a monarch to grant to a vassal. Notwithstanding it was thought good to take hold of the occasion; for although it should not work the end desired, which was to settle the kingdom in tranquillity, yet a motion only of submission, proceeding from the capital rebel, would work in the minds of the inferior traitors a mistrust of their estates, and seek, by his example, to sue for grace while there was time wherein they might hope to obtain it. Upon these considerations the Lord Deputy was willing, after he had shown his dislike to the conditions, to embrace the motion; and that he might be assured to have a true report returned, Captain George Blunt, who had been a familiar and intimate friend of Tyrone's when he was a subject, was employed in this business; and for his manner of treating with him he had these instructions following, subscribed by the Lord Deputy and the Lord President:—

"When you speak with Tyrone you shall tell him that you understand that Richard Owen came from him to the Lord Deputy with commission from him to tell his Lordship that he desired to be received into the Queen's mercy if his life might be secured.

"Whereupon you finding in him such conformity out of your ancient love, which in former times you bore him, were glad of the alteration, and therefore as his friend did now undertake this long journey to persuade him to those courses which might best answer his duty to his Prince and repair his estate, which in your opinion is desperate.

"If you find him desirous to be received to mercy you shall give him hope of it and promise him furtherance for the effecting of it upon these conditions: That he shall in token of his penitence, and according to the duty of a subject to his natural Prince, first under his hand write a letter of submission to the Lord Deputy humbly craving in the same Her Majesty's mercy, with promise to redeem his errors past by his future service; that likewise he shall write a public submission to Her Majesty, imploring at her hands forgiveness of his faults, and likewise promise amendment of his life, with a willing desire to do her some acceptable service in recompense of his transgression, in the same protesting to serve Her Majesty against all men, either of Ireland or foreigners that shall endeavour the disturbance of this country.

"That he shall put into Her Majesty's hands his eldest son for the assurance of his future loyalty, and four principal gentlemen of his blood, as he formerly promised.

" That he shall at his charge find workmen to build such forts in the county of Tyrone, and in such places as the Lord Deputy shall think fit.

" That he shall permit throughout Tyrone Her Majesty's Officers of Justice, as the Sheriffs and others, to have free liberty to execute their offices, as is accustomed in other provinces and counties of the realm, and answer all other duties formerly promised.

" That he shall only undertake for himself and his pledges to lie for no more than those that dwell upon that land only that is contained in his letters-patents, not any way undertaking for the rest of Tyrone, as Tirlogh Brassiloe's sons, MacMaghon, O'Cane MacGuire, MacGenis, the two Clandeboyes, and all of the east side of Ban. That if any of his neighbours shall continue in rebellion, none of their people shall be harboured in Tyrone, and likewise that none of Tyrone shall, by his consent or knowledge, succour any rebel or give assistance to them; and if any such offender shall happen to be discovered, either by himself or any other of Her Majesty's officers, upon knowledge thereof that he shall do his best endeavour to prosecute the parties offending, and either take them, whereby they may be tried by the laws of the realm, or kill them if they may not otherwise be had, and shall assist Her Majesty's officers in taking to her use the goods and chattels of the offenders and their retinues; that he shall not only truly pay all Her Majesty's rents and duties from this time forward due to her out of Tyrone, but also pay the arrears that for many years have been by him detained.

" That in respect of the great charges that he hath put Her Majesty to (although it be not the thousandth part of her disbursements), *in nomine pœnæ* (which in all such great offences is accustomed) towards the victualling of Her Majesty's garrisons he shall pay two thousand cows within six months; that the country of Tyrone may be limited, and no more by him to be possessed than is contained in his letters-patents; that the territory of Tyrone might be divided into shires and have gaols as he hath formerly desired; that he put at liberty the sons of Shane O'Neale and all other prisoners, English and Irish. These things you shall only propound as from yourself, yet as conceiving that they will be demanded at his hands if he be received, and to draw as large an overture from him of what he will agree to as you can persuade him, telling him that the greater assurance he doth give the estate of his loyalty the greater will be his safety, for we shall construe his good meaning by his free offer thereof, and after we shall have the less reason to be jealous of him.

"MOUNTJOY.
"GEORGE CAREW."

CHAPTER XXVI.

The King of Spain's letters intercepted—A letter from the Duke of Lerma to Don Juan de Aguila—A letter from the Duke of Lerma to the Archbishop of Dublin—A letter from the Secretary Ybarra to Don Juan de Aguila—A letter from the Secretary Fragursa to Don Juan de Aguila—A letter from the King of Spain to Don Juan de Aguila.

ABOUT the tenth of February Don Juan de Aguila was residing in Cork, whilst his troops were preparing to be embarked for Spain. In this interim a Spanish pinnace landed in the westernmost part of the province, and in her was a messenger sent from the King to Don Juan de Aguila with a packet of letters. The President, having knowledge thereof, told the Lord Deputy that if he had a desire to know the King of Spain's intentions, there was a good occasion offered. The Lord Deputy's heart itching to have the letters in his hands, he prayed the President to intercept them if he could handsomely do it. The President undertook it, and having notice that the next morning the messenger would come from Kinsale to Cork, and, knowing that there were but two ways by which he might pass, called Captain William Nuce to him (who commanded his foot company) to make choice of such men as he could trust to lie upon those passages, and when they saw such a Spaniard, whom he had described to him, to seize upon him and as thieves to rob him both of his letters, horses, and money;[1] not to hurt his person, but to leave him and his guide bound, that they might make no swift pursuit after them, and when they had delivered him the letters to run away. Captain Nuce so well followed his instructions that the Spaniard was taken in a little wood and the letters were brought at dinner-time; Don Juan, if I do not mistake, that very day dining with the President, who instantly carried them to the Lord Deputy, where at good leisure the packets were opened and read, which done, the President went to his house, leaving the letters with the Lord Deputy. The same evening the Spanish messenger, having been unbound by passengers, came to Don Juan de Aguila relating his misfortune in being robbed not five miles from the town. Don Juan de Aguila went immediately to the Lord Deputy, grievously complaining that the messenger was robbed by soldiers (as he alleged). The Lord Deputy seemed no less sorry, "but," said he, "it is a common thing in all armies to have debauched soldiers," and he thought it to be rather done by some of the country thieves; but if the fact was committed by soldiers, it was most likely done by some Irishmen, who thought it to be a good purchase (as well as the money) to get the letters, to show them to their friends in rebellion that they might the better understand in what estate they were in. Don Juan, not being satisfied with this answer, desired the Lord Deputy to inquire of the Lord President (for of his intercepting of them he had a vehement suspicion) whether he had

---

[1] This was a pretty trick for such high officials to play. It will involve them in more vileness before it ends.

any knowledge of the matter, and so they departed. The next morning the Lord Deputy related to the President the complaint and his answers. Don Juan, eager in the pursuit of his letters, came to know of the Lord Deputy what the President answered. The Lord Deputy answered him upon his faith that he was sure that the President had them not; which he might well do, for they were in his own possession. In conclusion, a proclamation was made, and a reward in the same promised for him that could discover the thieves, and a pardon for their lives granted to those that committed the deed if they would come in and confess it; with this Don Juan rested satisfied. How much the intercepting of these letters imported Her Majesty's service (not one Spaniard being then embarked, but remaining in a body at Kinsale) may appear by these ensuing letters (Englished) taken at that time :—

A LETTER FROM THE DUKE OF LERMA TO DON JUAN DE AGUILA.

Not many days past I wrote to you, and now I make answer to those which I received from you the thirteenth of the last October, assuring you that His Majesty puts great confidence in your care and valour. As touching the men and other things which you demand, there is despatched a good quantity and more is in preparing, and make you no doubt but still more shall be in sending, as much as may be; for His Majesty hath it before his eyes, and I have taken in hand the soliciting thereof; wherefore you may be assured that you shall not want anything which may be sent that is needful. There are now in readiness one hundred and fifty lances, which shall be presently embarked, and more men are in levying with expedition, with whom money shall be sent. And so, referring myself, for the rest, to His Majesty's dispatch, I will say no more but to assure you that in all things which may concern you esteem me ever to be your solicitor. God keep you. Valladolid, the fourth of December, 1601.

   EL DUQUE DE LERMA, MARQUES DE DENIA.

To Don Juan de Aguila, Master of the
 Camp, General of the men of war in
 Ireland.

A LETTER FROM THE DUKE OF LERMA TO THE ARCHBISHOP OF DUBLIN.

I have received your Lordship's letters, giving thanks to God for the success of your journey, for by it it appears that there is a way and door open for many good purposes for His service, and His Majesty hath much care of the confidence and zeal which your Lordship hath for the progression in the same. Now we send you a good body of men, with such things as are necessary, and more shall be prepared, and so continue sending as much as we may, whereof you need not doubt; for His Majesty (whom God preserve) holds it before his eyes. Forasmuch as the most important thing appertaining to this business is the joining of the Earls with Don Juan de Aguila, His Majesty commandeth your Lordship to do in it your utmost endeavour, according to the confidence he hath in your zeal. God preserve your Lordship. From Valladolid, the fifth of December, 1601.

EL DUQUE DE LERMA, MARQES DE DENIA.

Let not your Lordship be wearied with your travails; I hope in God they will be full of good successes.

Al Arcobispo de Dublin.

A LETTER FROM THE SECRETARY YBARRA TO DON JUAN DE AGUILA.

By Captain Albornoz I wrote to your Lordship, and I wish that this dispatch may overtake him at the Groyne according to the desire I hold, that it and that which goes with it were with your Lordship, certifying you that as much is done as may be for your supply in all things. I wrote to your Lordship that there were two companies of horse ready to be sent unto you, but now I say there are three, and in them two hundred and twenty soldiers well armed and horsed. And it please God they shall be all embarked in this month; God in His divine mercy guide them. There are men levied in all Castile and Portugal, and shipping engaged to transport them, victuals, and other necessaries in providing; and now at this instant there are embarked in Lisbon, in the Groyne, and Saint Andera more than six thousand hanegas of wheat, three hundred pipes of wine, some beans and rice, and six hundred arrobas of oil; and, moreover, besides this which I say is embarked, there are commissaries taking more up, and no care shall be wanting to hasten them away. I have spoken with Captain Morcles, and of that which he hath told me of the seat of the place, and of the small number of men your Lordship hath, I feel myself grieved; but when I call to mind what a person Don Juan de Aguila is, the way is open to me to expect great matters, and I hope God will grant the same, according to the worth of your Lordship, against your wicked enemies. Let your Lordship hasten the joining of the Earls with you, for of all things that is most important, which, being done before the Queen can reinforce her army, all is accomplished. I am desirous to hear that the very good horsemen were with your Lordship, that with them your Lordship may win honour in the field, etc. From Valladolid, this seventh of December, 1601.

ESTEVAN DE YBARRA.

To Don Juan de Aguila,
General Master of the Camp.

A Letter from the Secretary Franquesa to Don Juan de Aguila.

His Majesty is much satisfied with the good government in these occasions of your army, and I hope in God, that with the succours which now shall be sent to you, it will be bettered in such sort that you will not only be able to defend yourself from the enemy, but also to chastise them. The means to effect the same is for you to hold yourself as you are, until the succours aforesaid do come. In the meantime the more you are pressed upon, the more will be your reward and recompense which His Majesty will confer upon you, which I will thrust on as occasion shall offer itself, and be always vigilant in those things which shall concern your Lordship as I have

been. God preseve your Lordship according to my
desire. From Mansilla, the thirteenth of January,
1602.

    To Don Juan de Aguila, Master of the
       Camp, General of His Majesty's
       Army in Ireland.

A LETTER FROM THE DUKE OF LERMA TO DON JUAN
DE AGUILA.

By that which Zubiare and Pedro Lopez de Soto have written, and by the coming of the Earl O'Donnell, who is now in the Groyne, we have learned of the overthrow of the Earls, and from this is gathered that all the forces are now bent against you, and that only your valour and wisdom have been able to resist them; and let the great estimation His Majesty holdeth of you mitigate the care which this business may bring you. His Majesty hath commanded me speedily to prepare gallant succours, both by land and sea, which is done, and shall be presently dispatched; and this ship is only sent to advertise you thereof, to the end that you may with the more courage defend yourself, and to bring a true report in what state you stand, which may more particularly appear unto you by His Majesty's letter, which with this you shall receive, whereunto he hath commanded me to add this, that he hath in his favour made you one of his councillors of his Council of War, upon which I congratulate you; assuring you on his part that, God willing, he will confer greater favours upon you, wherefore proceed cheerfully, as both now and heretofore in the course of your life you have done, taking every occasion to strengthen yourself in this siege, and to harm the enemy that he may not hinder you, and to assure the army. No man living hath received greater rewards from His Majesty than you shall receive. I take upon myself the care of it, and I pray you to write me such good news as I desire, whereof I hope in God. In Mansilla, the thirtieth of January, 1602.

EL DUQUE DE LERMA, MARQUES DE DENIA.

God is my witness that I neither eat nor sleep with less care than any one of them that are with you, and I would willingly be in the peril of every one of you, and, if the shedding of my blood might be advantageous, I would readily give it for you all that have such need. Do your endeavours, for presently succours shall be sent unto you.

To Don Juan de Aguila, Master of the
    Camp, General of the men of war in
    Ireland.

A LETTER FROM THE KING OF SPAIN TO DON JUAN
DE AGUILA.

EL REY.

Don Juan de Aguila, Master of the Camp, General of my army in Ireland; by that which Pedro de Zubiare and Pedro Lopez de Soto have written to me I have learned of the defeat of the Earls O'Neale and O'Donnell, and likewise I now see that all your hopes remain in your valour and wisdom, wherein I have such confidence that I hope, in the midst of so many dangers and labours wherewith you are environed, that you will preserve the army until more succours of shipping, men, arms, and munitions be sent unto you, which are with all possible expedition in preparing, and shall be speedily dispatched. You may make use of them and take revenge of the enemy, and until they come, which shall be, as I have said, with celerity, preserve yourself. I do not advise you of any particulars, because I assure myself of your judgment and experience, which knows how to take advantage of such occasions as the enemy shall give for the benefit of the siege. And yourself and the army which is with you shall have good testimony of my bounty, thankfulness, and honour I will do unto you all; and so much do you signify to the army from me. The Duke of Lerma shall write more unto you. From Mansilla, the one-and-thirtieth of January, 1602.

Yo, El Rey.

To Don Juan de Aguila, Master of the
Camp, General of our army in Ireland.
Don Pedro Franquesa.

Not long after most of the Spaniards were embarked in Kinsale, only a few remaining who were to pass with Don John, the day before his departure, the Lord Deputy showed him the copy of the letters, saying that they were sent to him out of Ulster by a priest, who was his spy about Tyrone, to whom the letters had been carried. Don Juan, taking this for good payment, thanked the Lord Deputy for his favourable care. All the while Don Juan was at Cork, every day the President and he had familiar discourse together, but for the most part their passages in speech were between jest and earnest, somewhat sharp, and especially when they spoke of religion, their sovereigns, or the nations. But it seems that he carried a good respect of the President, as by writing and presents sent which shall in due place appear.

The fifteenth, the Lord Deputy and the President, having acquainted the rest of the Council with the effect of the Spanish letters intercepted as aforesaid, though not with the manner that they were got, thought it meet to write to the Lords of the Council in England this ensuing letter, whereby they might understand how things stood for the present, as also to provide for the future, since by the intercepted letters it appeared that the King of Spain had set his heart upon the war of Ireland.

A Letter from the Lord Deputy and Council to the Lords in England.

May it please your Lordships: The fourteenth of this month we dispatched Sir Richard Morison with our letters to your Lordships from this place, and the nine-and-twentieth we wrote again by Captain Butler, yet to this day the wind hath continued still so westerly that since the departure of Sir Richard no shipping is come to us either out of England from your Lordships, as we desired, or from Waterford, Wexford, and those parts, as we directed, to carry the Spaniards hence; nor yet until Sunday, the seventh hereof, could those ships stir that lay ready at Kinsale to be sent to Baltimore, Castlehaven, and Bearehaven; but now they are gone, we hope that the service to be done by them (which is the possessing of the castles and sending away of the Spaniards in them) will be presently accomplished, although the wind hath served them so scantily that we fear they will hardly recover all the places whereto they are directed. There is only one Scottish ship gone from Kinsale to Spain, which carried one hundred and sixty Spaniards, with part of the artillery, but there lies now ready at the harbour for the first wind so much shipping as will carry away fifteen hundred more; so that there will be yet remaining in Kinsale above one thousand more, which with the first shipping that comes from the other ports shall be embarked. Don Juan stays to go last. It appeareth by some letters intercepted, which we send herewithal to your Lordships, that the King of Spain purposeth to send a larger supply hither with all expedition. Don Juan assures us to do the best he can to stay them, and if he arrive first in Spain he makes no doubt to dissuade their coming; but if they should come before his departure he promiseth to return them according to his covenant in the contract, if they do not come under the command of some other that hath a commission apart from his from the King. The Irish have of late received letters from O'Donnell to encourage the rebels to persevere in their rebellion, assuring them of present aid from Spain; in the meantime, the best of them all do but temporize, being ready to assist them when they come, especially if they come in any strength, as it is to be thought in all reason they will, having found their first error. Her Majesty must therefore be pleased to be at some charge to erect fortifications at Bearehaven, Kinsale, and this place, the commodities and weakness of these places being as well known to the Spaniards as to us, and further withal to erect citadels at Limerick, Cork, and Waterford, though it be only to assure the towns from revolt. It appeareth by the King of Spain's letter, and so by the Duke of Lerma's, that his heart is very much set upon the enterprise of Ireland, and it is not unlikely that he may send more supplies, after or before Don Juan's arrival in Spain, either under him or some other commander; which, if he do, it is also likely the same will be sent shortly. For prevention thereof, if in your Lordships' wisdom it shall be thought meet, we do humbly beseech that the four thousand supplies heretofore desired, and by your Lordships intended, may be presently sent hither, whereof two thousand to be erected in companies, and their captains to be named here, and the other two thousand for the supplies of the army, which is exceeding weak; for our men die daily in greater numbers than they died in the camp, the infection being greater, and by some thought a kind of plague (for the people in the towns die in far greater numbers than the soldiers), though we hope the contrary. And we do further desire that Her Majesty will be pleased to hasten her fleet to the coast of Spain, which, coming timely, will in our opinions hinder any enterprise for Ireland; but lest that should fail, we renew our former motion that the *Tremontania* and the *Moone* may be returned to serve upon the coast of Munster, that the proportions of munition and victuals desired in our former letters may speedily be dispatched hither, and that victuals without impediment may come for all places to relieve us; for already a very great dearth is begun, and a famine must ensue, the rates of all things being incredible, and the new money[1] much repined at, which

---

[1] Now for the first time in her reign Queen Elizabeth issued base coin. Hugh O'Neill had in fact beaten the State to bankruptcy.

notwithstanding we do our utmost endeavours to advance it. But in a matter of so great importance we humbly desire your Lordships to give us leave to deliver our opinions freely, having so assured ground for it that if the King of Spain continue his war in this country it will be hard to preserve Her Majesty's army and kingdom without the altering of the current money, so general is the dislike thereof, and so insolently do they begin already to refuse it; but if there come no other foreign aid, Her Majesty, as we think, may securely continue it as it is; for all we that are of the army, whom it most concerneth, in regard we live wholly upon our entertainment, will, God willing, endure it for the advancement of the service, though we are sensible of our loss by the excessive enhancing of the prices of all things that we are to live upon, which cannot be helped so long as this new coin continues current. Of Tyrone, since his overthrow and departure, we hitherto have heard little, neither do we think he will be able to do any great harm, without the aid of new supplies from Spain. And so we humbly take leave, etc.

From Cork, 15 February, 1601.

Among many letters and papers which were found in the Castle of Dunboy (of the winning whereof you shall afterwards hear) there was one written, bearing date the fourth of February, 1602, *stilo novo*, by Patrick Sinnet,[1] an Irish priest, remaining in the Groyne with the Earl of Caraçena, to Dominick Collins, a Jesuit, who was taken at Dunboy and executed. Amongst sundry other things he related of

[1] This Patrick Sinnett was tutor to Philip O'Sullivan, the historian who gratefully commemorates him in a Latin poem.

O'Donnell's landing in the Asturias, who, with the General Pedro de Zubiare, embarked at Castlehaven the —— January; the next day after he came to the Groyne, where he was nobly received by the Earl of Caraçena, who invited O'Donnell to lodge in his house; but he, being sea-sick,[1] in good manner refused his courtesy; wherefore the Earl lodged him in a very fair house, not far from his; but when his sea-sickness was past he lodged in the Earl's house; and upon the twenty-seventh of January O'Donnell departed from the Groyne, accompanied by the Earl and many captains and gentlemen of quality, who evermore gave O'Donnell the right hand, which within his government he would not have done to the greatest duke in Spain; and, at his departure, he presented O'Donnell with one thousand ducats, and that night he lay at Santa Lucia. The Earl of Caraçena being returned, the next day he went to Saint James of Compostella, where he was received with magnificence by the prelates, citizens, and religious persons, and his lodging was made ready for him at Saint Martin's, but before he saw it he visited the Archbishop, who instantly prayed him to lodge in his house; but O'Donnell excused it. The nine-and-twentieth the Archbishop, saying Mass with pontifical solemnity, ministered the sacrament to O'Donnell, which done he feasted him at dinner in his house; and at his departure he gave him one thousand ducats. The King, hearing of O'Donnell's arrival, wrote to the Earl of Caraçena concerning

---

[1] It is singular that hardly any of the Irish lords, even those who, like Hugh Roe, had maritime countries, ever sought to do anything upon the sea. So when Hugh Roe had been taken prisoner by Perrott, there was not a ship in Tyrconnell which could be sent in pursuit of the kidnappers.

the reception of him and the affairs of Ireland, which was one of the most gracious letters that ever king directed; for by it it plainly appeared that he would endanger his kingdom to succour the Catholics of Ireland to their content, and not fail therein; for the perfecting whereof great preparations were in hand. O'Donnell carried with him to the court Redmond Burke, Father Florence, Captain Mostian, and nine gentlemen more, where they were nobly received. Although the knowledge of the reception of O'Donnell in Spain was not well known by me until after the taking of Dunboy, yet I thought it requisite to insert it in its due place, according to the time of his being at the Groyne. But now let us return to the affairs of Munster.

Captain Roger Harvy, according to his directions being come to Castlehaven, Pedro Lopez de Soto, the Veador, who had the chief command thereof, after the receipt of Don Juan de Aguila's letters and messages entertained him with great humanity, and upon the twelfth of February rendered the castle to him, receiving an acknowledgment under his and his brother's, Captain Gawen Harvy's, hands in writing for the receipt thereof, which done they embarked their victuals, baggage and ordnance; lastly their men, to the number of one hundred and forty by poll, and four Spanish captains. Captain Roger Harvy delivered the charge of the castle to his brother Captain Gawen Harvy, there to remain in garrison with his company of one hundred foot. The same day that Captain Harvy came to Castlehaven, the O'Driscalls, who had the inheritance of the same, by a sleight got into the castle, and had made themselves masters of it. The Spaniards, to recover it again, assaulted it, and were undermining the same when Captain Harvy was entering the haven; but upon the sight of his ships the Irish, by composition, to depart in safety, rendered it to the Spaniards, who had lost two of their soldiers in the attempt. The one-and-twentieth Captain Harvy, having in his company the Veador and some other Spaniards, set sail for Baltimore, whereupon the three-and-twentieth they went on land and were feasted in the castle of Donnelong by the governor thereof, called Andreas do Aervy, and the next day, by the direction of the Veador, their ordnance (being seven in number in the castle) were shipped. And the six-and-twentieth the said castle, and the castle of Donneshed, were with Spanish gravity rendered to Her Majesty's use. The second of March following they were all embarked, and set sail for Spain. While these things were in doing Captain Roger Harvy sent a party of men to Cape Clear,[1] the castle whereof was guarded by Captain Tirrell's men, which they could not gain, but they pillaged the island and brought thence three boats; and the second day following, the rebels, not liking the neighbourhood of the English, quitted the castle, wherein Captain Harvy placed a guard. At this time Sir Finnin O'Driscall came to Captain Harvy and submitted himself. The tenth of the same month, the Lord Barry, Captain Taffe, and Captain John Barry, chanced to light upon Donogh Moyle MacCarty's men, and slew eighteen of the best of them.

---

[1] A good deal of this castle still stands. It is situated on a rock separate from the mainland of the island. There is a pretty strand and little harbour close beside it. It was one of the O'Driscoll castles.

From Baltimore, Captain George Flower was shipped in a hoy of one hundred and twenty tons, with two companies of two hundred in list, but weak by pole, to receive from the Spaniards the castle of Dunboy, but do all he could, by reason of foul weather and contrary winds he could never, although he was at the mouth of the Haven of Beare, recover the land, and so was forced to return, effecting nothing. In this short navigation fifty of his best soldiers by infection died, and but seven of the sailors living.

CHAPTER XXVII.

The Spaniards embarked at Kinsale—The Spaniards dispossessed of Donboy by O'Sulevan Beare—A letter from O'Sulevan Beare to the King of Spain—A letter from O'Sulevan Beare to the Earl of Caraçena—A letter from O'Sulevan Beare to Don Pedro de Zubiare.

The twentieth of February, twenty Spanish captains, with one thousand three hundred and seventy-four soldiers, set sail from Kinsale for Spain.

The composition which Don Juan made when he surrendered Kinsale infinitely grieved and offended the Irish, and especially those who had voluntarily delivered into his hands their castles, but especially Donnell O'Sulevan, who, considering that if his castle of Dunboy should be in the possession of the English he was likely to be banished his country, not having any hope of favour from Her Majesty, unto whose crown and dignity he had manifested himself to be a malicious traitor, resolved to set up his rest in regaining it out of the Spaniards' hands, and afterwards to defend it against Her Majesty's forces as well as he might. For accomplishing whereof they watched a fit opportunity, and surprised it in this sort. Although the Spaniards were the masters of the castle, yet he had recourse into it, and lodged therein with such of his men as he thought good. In the dead of the night, when the Spaniards were soundly sleeping, and the key of the castle in the captain's custody, O'Sulevan caused his men, amongst whom there were some masons, to break a hole in the wall, wherein four-score of his men entered, for by appointment he had drawn that night close to the castle Archer,[1] the Jesuit, with another priest, Thomas FitzMaurice the Lord of Lixnaw, Donnell MacCarty, Captain Richard Tirrill, and Captain William Burke,[2] with a thousand men. When day appeared, Archer prayed Francesco de Saavedra, the Spanish captain, to go with him to O'Sulevan's chamber, unto whom he made relation that his men had entered the castle, that he meant no personal hurt, either to him or to any of his, and that he would keep the same for the King of Spain's use, and also told him that he had one thousand foot within harquebuss-shot of the castle. The captain, seeing himself surprised, made no resistance, and willed his men to do the like; but the Spaniards in fury discharged a few musket shot amongst the Irish and slew three of them and hurt one; but by the mediation of O'Sulevan and Francesco de Saavedra, the captain, all was pacified, O'Sulevan being very careful that no hurt might be done to the Spaniards. Afterwards O'Sulevan disarmed them all, kept the captain, and a few of the better sort, with three or four gunners, in the nature of prisoners,

---

[1] He was with Owny O'Moore at the taking of the Earl of Ormonde.

[2] Brother of Redmund, Baron of Leitrim. A captain of Condottieri now in the employment of O'Sullivan Bere. We have met him frequently before.

Tyrone, before leaving Munster, appointed O'Sullivan as his representative in the south, and captain of the confederate Irish there. These, however, laughed at his authority. The notion of obeying a mere follower and vassal of M'Carty Mare was ridiculous to their high and mighty minds.

and the rest he sent to Baltimore, to be embarked for Spain. He also seized all the Spanish ordnance, munitions, and victuals which were there in store. The captain not long after was set at liberty, and returned with the Veador from Baltimore into Spain, and with him the other soldiers who were detained, but the cannoneers O'Sulevan reserved.

When report was brought to Don John de Aguila, then in Cork, of the surprise of Dunboy, he took it for a great affront, and would presently have drawn from Kinsale the Spanish companies there yet remaining and march to Dunboy to regain it by force, and to deliver it according to the composition into Her Majesty's hands. But the Lord Deputy and the President, who were desirous to see his heels towards Ireland, wished him not to trouble himself with that business; and when he was gone the President should take order for the reducing of it into his hands. The Castle of Dunboy was surprised (as before said) in this month of February, 1601, and held by O'Sulevan to the use of the King of Spain; but yet to excuse himself to the King, and to make it appear to him how much he was his servant, he wrote to him, to the Earl of Caraçena and to Pedro de Zubiare, there being then in Bearehaven the Spanish pinnace which brought the packet from Spain, intercepted between Kinsale and Cork as aforesaid.

A LETTER FROM O'SULEVAN BEARE TO THE KING OF SPAIN.

MY LORD AND MY KING,—Out of his love to your kingly greatness, your humble steadfast servant Donnell O'Sulevan Beare, enforced through peril and constraint, doth make bold to inform your Greatness, that upon the landing in Castlehaven, in the West of Ireland, of your General Pedro de Zubiar, and Pedro Lopez de Soto, with a fleet and men from your Greatness, according to the inward conceit of mind I always held, which I manifested in my young years, and would have still followed unless disability had constrained me to the contrary; finding a happy and good opportunity (as I imagined) I came to their presence, tendering my obeisance to them in the name of your Highness, and, being with four hundred men at my own cost towards your service, I yielded out of my mere love and goodwill, without compulsion or composition, into their hands, in the name of your Majesty, not only my castle and haven called Bearehaven, but also my wife, my children, my country, lordships, and all my possessions for ever to be disposed of at your pleasure. They received me in that manner, and promised, as from your Highness, to keep and save the said castle and haven during the service of your Grace. Notwithstanding, my gracious Lord, conclusions of peace were assuredly agreed upon betwixt Don Juan de Aguila and the English, a fact pitiful and, according to my judgment, against all right and human conscience. Among other places whereof your Greatness was dispossessed in that manner, which were neither yielded nor taken to the end they should be delivered to the English, Don Juan tied himself to deliver my castle and haven, the only key of mine inheritance, whereupon the living of many thousand persons doth rest, that live some twenty leagues upon the sea coast, into the hands of my cruel, cursed, misbelieving enemies, a thing, I fear, in respect of the execrableness, inhumanity, and ungratefulness of the fact if it take effect as it was plotted, that will give cause to other men not to trust any Spaniard hereafter with their bodies or goods upon these causes. My Lord, in that I judge this dishonourable act to be against your honour and pleasure (as I understand by your last letters that came into Ireland), considering the harm that might ensue to the service of your Majesty and the everlasting overthrow that might happen to me and my poor people, such as might escape the sword of our enemy (if any should), I have taken upon me, with the help of God, to offer to keep my castle and haven from the hands of mine enemies until further news and order come from your Highness. I have sent my son and heir, being of the age of five years, as a pledge for accomplishing your will in this behalf and for the performing of my promise passed unto your Greatness. I would not omit myself in person to come and visit your Highness, but that I fear our wars here would grow weak in respect of my absence, for which cause myself and the rest of our men of worth have sent in haste, with intelligence unto your Greatness, our loving friend Dermond O'Driscall, in respect of our confidence in him, our knowledge of him, and the continual endeavours we see in him towards this Catholic war, as from us all. And forasmuch as we could not conveniently write all that we wish unto you, we humbly beseech that he may be heard as from us all, as if ourselves were present, and to hasten helping news that shall rejoice us and our people, and afterwards to speed your gracious help unto us, for the sooner the better, whilst our enemies are not in readiness; and until the coming of news from your Grace unto us I will have in readiness, where the service shall require, the number of one thousand men! and I will upon my knees pray the merciful God to give unto your Grace long life, with health of body and soul and all happiness, and so do commit you to the safeguard of the Omnipotent. Donboy, viz., Bearehaven, the twentieth day of February, 1602.

DONNELL O'SULEVAN BEARE.

A LETTER FROM O'SULEVAN BEARE TO THE EARL OF CARAÇENA.

My duty remembered: It may please your Lordship to understand that, according to my former letters, it hath manifestly appeared here the resolution of Don Juan de Aguila to have been by his composition with the English to yield to the enemy's hands all the forts and havens voluntarily delivered by the lords and gentlemen of this land for His Majesty's service, which will be to the dishonour of the King, the prevention of his most godly attempt, and the utter ruin and destruction of thousands of this country gentlemen and Catholics, who without compulsion entered into this action. All which having considered, I have, of mere affection to my religion, his Highness's service, and love to my people and country, so endeavoured the recovery of my castle that I drew into the same some hundred of my followers, whom although the Spaniards have attempted to resist, and killed three of my best gentlemen, yet durst none of my people kill any of them, but without harm forced them out of my said castle, saving their captain, with five or six to whom I have allowed certain rooms in my house, to look to the King's munition and artillery; which castle and haven I do detain, and will evermore, for His Majesty's service, to defend until his Highness's pleasure and your Lordship's resolution unto me shall be further known. And for manifestation of my loyalty and faithfulness to His Majesty I have sent my son and heir thither, whom I hope ere this time is present before your Lordship, and have cessed all the Captain's company upon my own people and charges, humbly beseeching it may please your Honour to be a mean to his most Catholic Majesty that he may vouchsafe speedily to relieve this place, where many of his royal ships in time of service may be kept in safety; or otherwise to send some small ship towards this coast to receive me and the rest of my family and children, to be carried into Spain, for the saving of our lives out of the hands of these merciless, heretical enemies, making choice rather to forsake my ancient inheritance, friends, followers, and goods, than any way to trust to their most graceless pardon or promise. Thus much I hope your godly charitable nature will draw you to do for such a one as I am, who hazarded life, lands, goods, and followers [1] for the Catholic faith and the King's Majesty's service. All which, leaving to your honourable discretion, through whose virtuous means I chiefly hope to receive com-

---

[1] All very fine, but it must be remembered that all these lands, goods, and followers he had secured for himself by petition to the Imperial Council and by grant from the Queen, so ousting the reigning O'Sullivan, Sir Owen. In one of those petitions he advances divers reasons why it was probable that he would be a faithful servant to the Queen, e.q., he was educated at a school in the loyal city of Waterford, he could speak English, he had helped the Queen in the Desmond wars, etc.

fort, I humbly take leave. From Bearehaven Castle, the last of February, 1602.

Your most faithful and bounden

DONNELL O'SULEVAN BEARE.

To the Earl of Caraçena, Governor and Captain-General for His Majesty in the Kingdom of Galicia.

A LETTER FROM O'SULEVAN BEARE TO DON PEDRO ZUBIAUR.

MY HONOURABLE GOOD FRIEND,—Your kind letters I have of late received, and for your careful furtherance I cannot but rest beholden and thankful as before. Our state since your departing, notwithstanding many crosses, was reasonably well, partly because of the weakness of the English forces, until a bruit came to us credibly that Don Juan de Aguila did not only agree and compound to yield the town of Kinsale, but also the other castles and havens delivered voluntarily by the owners to you and the Veador to the King's use during the occasion of service; which notwithstanding, being delivered to the enemy's hands, would mightily discourage and weaken all the King's friends in Ireland; namely myself, who by keeping my possessions belonging to my castle and Haven of Bearehaven, and able (God be thanked) and ready at all times to find at all times for His Majesty's service, upon warning and necessity, one thousand men, besides the ward of my own castle, whose losing the same so unexpectedly, and surrendered to the hands of most heretical enemies, I am not only disappointed of all power, but also driven to run to the mountains, there to live like wolves, for the of Spanish ordnance to be conveyed to the island, with a certain quantity of powder and shot, and having sixty choice men, fortified the same as he thought against the most potent enemy; but we leave these rebels busying their brains and wearying their bodies about these fortifications, and return to Captain Harvy. While the Veador, Pedro Lopez de Soto, remained at Baltimore, many courtesies and familiar conferences passed between them, wherein he showed himself to be a man of great humanity and a good statesman, able to relate many things concerning the State of England, and particularly the nobility in the same, as well as some that had spent their whole lives in that realm; but the end of all his conference still tended towards a peace between our sovereign and his master, whereby it may be gathered that the King of Spain was weary of the war which himself had injuriously begun. The substance of their discourse Captain Harvy related to the President, and also showed him a passport of the Veador's, and a letter which he sent to him after his arrival in Spain, all which are thus Englished :—

CHAPTER XXVIII.

An interlocutory discourse between Captain Roger Harvy and Pedro Lopez de Soto—Pedro Lopez de Soto's passport—Pedro Lopez de Soto's letter to Captain Roger Harvy.

A DISCOURSE THAT PASSED BETWIXT CAPTAIN ROGER HARVY AND PEDRO LOPEZ DE SOTO, THE SPANISH VEADOR, THE SIX-AND-TWENTIETH OF FEBRUARY, 1601, IN THE ISLAND OF INNYSHARKIN, WHILST THE SPANIARDS WERE EMBARKING THEIR MUNITIONS AND ARTILLERY THENCE; THE EFFECT AS FOLLOWETH :—

SOTO. Sir, is it not a miserable and lamentable thing, in any honest man's conscience, to see the daily effusion of blood and infinite expense of treasure that this war betwixt Spain and England doth daily bring forth and consume?

HARVY. I told him it was too high a mystery for me to censure, but I thought it to be the judgment of God, for we must understand that princes are God's ministers and agents upon earth, and what they do is beyond our limits to look into. Notwithstanding I thought the pride of his master's gold so puffed him up, that either he must have all the world or nothing can content him, or else his king would never have sought out such a place as Ireland is to have buried so many crowns in, besides the loss of no small number of his subjects; but it may be of Spanish ordnance to be conveyed to the island, with a certain quantity of powder and shot, and having sixty choice men, fortified the same as he thought against the most potent enemy; but we leave these rebels busying their brains and wearying their bodies about these fortifications, and return to Captain Harvy. While the Veador, Pedro Lopez de Soto, remained at Baltimore, many courtesies and familiar conferences passed between them, wherein he showed himself to be a man of great humanity and a good statesman, able to relate many things concerning the State of England, and particularly the nobility in the same, as well as some that had spent their whole lives in that realm; but the end of all his conference still tended towards a peace between our sovereign and his master, whereby it may be gathered that the King of Spain was weary of the war which himself had injuriously begun. The substance of their discourse Captain Harvy related to the President, and also showed him a passport of the Veador's, and a letter which he sent to him after his arrival in Spain, all which are thus Englished :—

CHAPTER XXVIII.

An interlocutory discourse between Captain Roger Harvy and Pedro Lopez de Soto—Pedro Lopez de Soto's passport—Pedro Lopez de Soto's letter to Captain Roger Harvy.

A DISCOURSE THAT PASSED BETWIXT CAPTAIN ROGER HARVY AND PEDRO LOPEZ DE SOTO, THE SPANISH VEADOR, THE SIX-AND-TWENTIETH OF FEBRUARY, 1601, IN THE ISLAND OF INNYSHARKIN, WHILST THE SPANIARDS WERE EMBARKING THEIR MUNITIONS AND ARTILLERY THENCE; THE EFFECT AS FOLLOWETH :—

SOTO. Sir, is it not a miserable and lamentable thing, in any honest man's conscience, to see the daily effusion of blood and infinite expense of treasure that this war betwixt Spain and England doth daily bring forth and consume?

HARVY. I told him it was too high a mystery for me to censure, but I thought it to be the judgment of God, for we must understand that princes are God's ministers and agents upon earth, and what they do is beyond our limits to look into. Notwithstanding I thought the pride of his master's gold so puffed him up, that either he must have all the world or nothing can content him, or else his king would never have sought out such a place as Ireland is to have buried so many crowns in, besides the loss of no small number of his subjects; but it may be hereafter he will know us better, and perchance think our nation fitter to conquer than to lose what we have.

Soto. But do you think that gold is so abundant with us?

Har. The Indian world which you possess makes us believe so.

Soto. Well, be not deceived, for myself have been a dealer these many years in great affairs for the King, and by that I do somewhat understand his hacienda, which I must confess to be very great, and yet not so exceeding as the world thinks. But if it were far greater than it is, I assure you the infinite number of garrisons which he is daily forced to maintain would devour other such Indies if he had them; for do but look into how many several branches his treasure is divided, and then you will believe me; but yet of all the rest his expenses in the wars of the Low Countries are most chargeable and of greatest import to him, and for which he may thank your Queen of England, for had not she assisted those traitors they long since had borne the yoke of their deserts, and neither Ireland nor England had ever been looked into, or offended by us.

Har. Why, then I perceive it is not religion or conscience that hath brought you hither to relieve the Irish, but only revenge for our aiding the States of the Low Countries against the Cardinal.

Soto. But did you ever think otherwise? I know you did not; and if you say so, I know you dissemble with me, for the place where you have been brought up in hath better discipline.

Har. Why, where have I been brought up?

Soto. I hear that you are near in blood to the President, and that from a child you have followed him, and I know that you are better instructed than you make show of.

Har. I must thank you for your good opinion of me; but have you ever seen the face of the President?

Soto. I assure you no, and which I am very sorry for; for I hear that he is a worthy gentleman, and one of the wisest men in Ireland; and if I would take the Irish opinions for my belief of him, they confidently believe that he hath a familiar, for they say he knows all things and that nothing can be hidden from him; besides he is so intimate with the Secretary of England that his power thereby is the greater, which strengtheneth much my belief of his worth, but I pray you, sir, is it so?

Har. Truly I must confess that I am nearly allied to him, and that I am wholly his creature from my childhood; but for your better satisfaction of what you have heard of him, unless in modesty I should wrong him, I cannot do less than maintain the same opinion which the world holds of his worth and sufficiency; but for any familiar that he hath, more than a noble spirit and judgment, and than the long experience of this nation may sufficiently give him understanding, I assure you he hath not any, and therefore the Irish in that wrong him. And as for the greatness with the Secretary of England, I know in his affections he hath been very near him these many years, and to his uttermost hath wholly devoted himself to him; and in any reasonable matter I think Master Secretary will as soon hearken to his counsel as to any if he were in England.

Soto. But why would not the secretary keep him still with him, but suffer him to spend his time among this barbarous nation, for which, I think, Christ never died?[1]

Har. I cannot say but you object well; but I assure you the necessity of his coming hither was such that for the public good he was forced to it; besides Her Majesty's opinion of his experience is such that she knew he was able to end all the wars in these parts with expedition, which in four months myself can testify he had finished; and had not your armies coming hither caused a new rupture he had good hopes to have been called home again long since, which I know nothing under heaven he desireth more.

Soto. That makes me think that he is weary of the wars and would be contented now to live in peace.

Har. I think not so unless it were a very happy peace, otherwise wars are far more welcome to him (although I think not the Irish wars); but I think a Spanish journey, royally undertaken, would please him as much almost as to be seven years younger.

Soto. Since your President loves a hot climate so well, I would to God he would be a means to make a peace betwixt the two kingdoms, and then he might take his choice in which of them he would live, and be a welcome man unto both; but was not he in France with Master Secretary when that business was treating?

Har. Yes.

Soto. And were you there likewise?

Har. No.

Soto. I assure you there was excellent juggling on your side, and will be still where great personages

---

[1] This saying is usually attributed to Don Juan.

are the actors, otherwise I imagine there had fallen out better success; but we have some spirits in Spain as that of Essex's was in England, and will never rest until they have either ruined the kingdom or themselves; but dare you, sir, impart this conference to the President?

HAR. I promise you if I live I will.

SOTO. It may be out of this may proceed some good effect, for from less beginnings than this have greater matters risen.

HAR. I believe you, although I have small hopes of this.

SOTO. And why? Cannot England stand without the Low Countries?

HAR. Yes, against all the earth, but not so quiet if they were yours.

SOTO. Why? We will not ask any assistance from the Queen, but only have her stand a neuter, and for her safety and the kingdom's we will put in pledge twenty of the best houses in Spain; such as your State will choose; and if the State of England will but look judicially into it they shall find the offer honest, and fit to be accepted; considering that the Queen of England is by nature as mortal as others of less quality; and if she were dead, I know the next that shall succeed will afford it and be glad of it upon less conditions, or else I am deceived.

HAR. But God be thanked we have no cause in England to dream of succession, but hope she shall be eternal to us.

SOTO. That were ill news to him who looks to succeed.

HAR. But, sir, to the matter; because I have promised you to impart this conference to the President, let me entreat you to have something under your hand to justify it.

SOTO. You shall have a pass (either for yourself or any other) from me to come into Spain touching this business. The effect whereof I most humbly refer unto God, and so bid you farewell.

. . . . . .

Pedro Lopez de Soto, Overseer-general of the army of my Sovereign the Catholic King, etc. For certain due respects, behooful for His Majesty's service, this free passport, in his royal name, is assured for any England ship which shall bring any dispatch from Roger Harvy, Governor of the garrisons at Castlehaven and Baltimore, directed and superscribed to me, which shall happen to arrive in any port in Spain from the date hereof to the end of July next; by virtue whereof His Majesty's chief officer that shall govern the province or port where the said ships shall arrive shall give commandment for the service of His Majesty that both it, the seafaring men, and all other persons with their goods, shall be freely received and entertained, and accommodated to their liking and content, until the dispatch in the said ship, directed to me, be sent to Don Pedro Franquesa. The said ship, with her men and goods, may not only freely return to these northern parts without any impediment, but rather to be treated with all possible courtesies. And if any of His Majesty's ships of war, or any of his subjects' ships, shall meet with this English ship, either outward or homeward bound, they shall permit her to pass without any detention, it being convenient for His Majesty's service so to do. Written at Baltimore, the ninth of March, 1602.

PEDRO LOPEZ DE SOTO.

Pedro Lopez de Soto's Letter to Captain Roger Harvy.

Although you be an Englishman and myself a Spaniard, nevertheless, finding you to be, as it appears to me, a man of honour in all your actions, I cannot but assure you that I am extremely affectioned unto you, and the cause that moves me to desire your friendship and correspondence is the just respect I have to the good proceedings of the Lord Deputy, and the Lord President, and their ministers towards the King my master, as also of you and the rest in the service of your Prince, which hath obliged us to a good correspondence. The passport which I left with you shall be always faithfully accomplished when occasion shall serve, and of the same you may be confident, for we will fully observe it. And so God keep you. From the Groyne, the ninth of April, 1602.

Pedro Lopez de Soto.

To Captain Roger Harvy, Governor of Castlehaven and Baltimore.

CHAPTER XXIX.

Don Juan embarked at Kinsale—The Lord Deputy departed from Cork towards Dublin—A letter from the Lord Deputy and Council to the Lords in England—The Lord Deputy sickened in his journey to Dublin—The Lord President surprised with a fever in his return to Munster.

THE eighth of March, Don Juan was at Kinsale, hourly expecting a wind to be gone, and finding a flattering gale went aboard. The Lord Deputy, on the other hand, desirous to be at his work in Ulster, for the prosecution of Tyrone, the day following began his journey towards Dublin, on whom the Lord President attended, until he had brought him out of the province. But Don John, for want of a fair wind, departed not from Kinsale until the sixteenth of the same month. The day before the Lord Deputy's departure, or the same day, I know not which, his Lordship, being mindful of the sufficiency, blood, and valour of Sir Richard Percy, caused him to be sworn a Councillor of the province of Munster, and the night that he left Cork he lodged at Cloyne, a town and manor-house sometime belonging to the bishop of that see, but now passed in fee farm to Master John Fitz-Edmonds, who gave cheerful and plentiful entertainment to his Lordship and all such of the nobility, captains, gentlemen, and others that attended upon him. The Deputy, as well to requite his perpetual

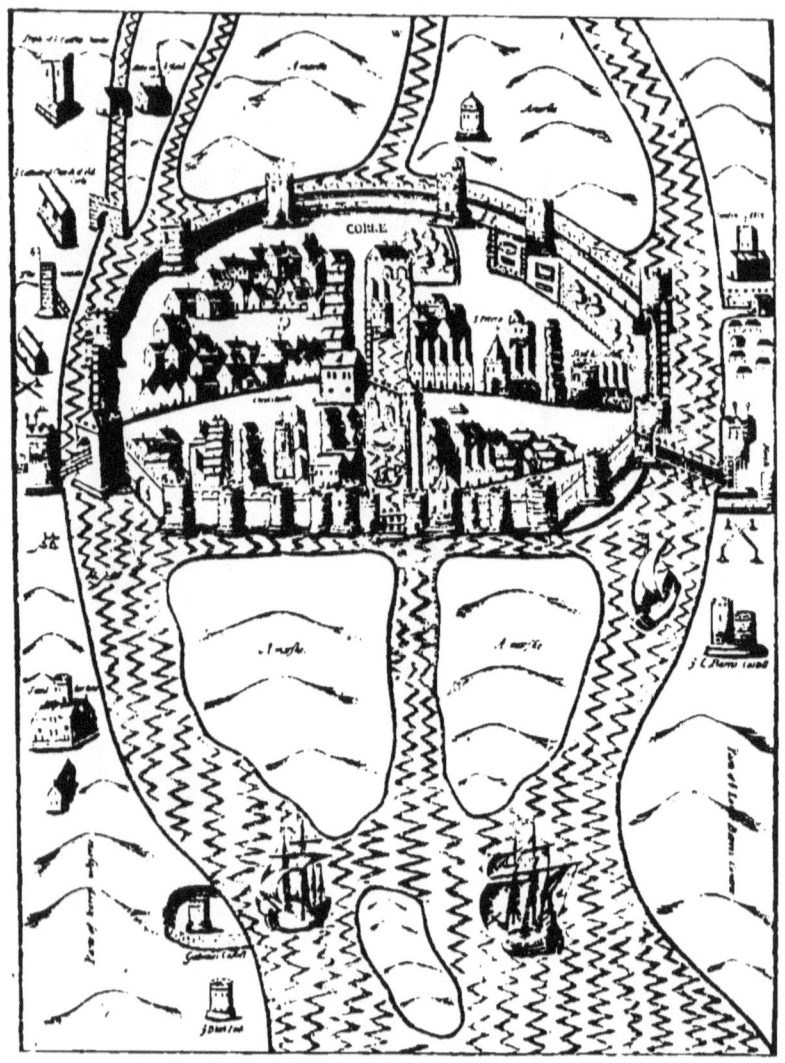

MAP OF CORK.

loyalty to the Crown of England, as also to encourage others in the like, at his departure honoured him with the order of knighthood, and then continued his journey towards Waterford, where he bestowed the like honour upon Edward Gough and Richard Aylward,[1] two old and well-deserving citizens.

The President, having attended the Lord Deputy to Kilkenny, where they lodged in the Earl of Ormond's house, and all things considered which concerned the state of the kingdom, upon the four-and-twentieth of March, the last day of the year 1601, the Lord Deputy and Council made a dispatch into England, which here ensues :—

A LETTER FROM THE LORD DEPUTY AND COUNCIL TO THE LORDS IN ENGLAND.

It may please your Lordships, having certain intelligence since our coming to this place, that Don Juan and all the rest of the Spaniards departed from Kinsale on Tuesday the sixteenth hereof, and that the wind since that time hath served them so well that we assure ourselves by this they are near the coast of Spain ; we thought fit hereby to give your Lordships notice thereof that you may know that we are free now of them all. Since our being here there hath been brought in a notorious rebel, one William Mac-Hubbard, lately taken in Upperossery, who of late hath done great spoils and murders in these parts, more than any other, so that we have caused him to be executed in this town to the great terror of many. About the same time that he was executed a son of

[1] I think this is the first example of a knighthood in Ireland conferred on a citizen.

Garret MacMortagh's, named Morris MacGarret, died of a hurt lately given him in fight, who was a most dangerous young man, likely to trouble all the country. The death of these two rebels, as also of a notorious rebel, by birth of Munster, lately slain, called Dermot MacAwley, who was an intimate man and a great practising instrument with Tyrone, will greatly quiet these parts, and your Lordships can hardly think what a great change we find already by their so happy and timely cutting-off. As for Sir Finnin O'Driscall, O'Donnevan, and the two sons of Sir Owen MacCarty, they and their followers, since their coming in, are grown very odious to the rebels of those parts, and are so well divided in factions amongst themselves that they are fallen to preying and killing one another, which we conceive will much avail to the quieting of these parts. I, the Deputy, am this day going towards Dublin, whence your Lordships shall hear from me, according to the directions given me by your Lordships. And I, the President, am returning into Munster, to attend my charge there. We have been much importuned by the army in general touching an abatement of half-a-pound of beef upon every flesh-day, from every particular soldier, and of two herrings every fish-day, and the horse-troops likewise find themselves aggrieved that the victuallers charge them with two shillings and sixpence increase in the issuing of every barrel of oats, without any other warrant than a private letter from Master Wade, Clerk of the Council; which although we conceive Master Wade hath signified over upon such purpose of your Lordships, or other good ground, yet in regard of importunities of the captains, and to prevent a general mutiny of the army, in regard the soldiers are weak and much enfeebled by the last siege of Kinsale, and that the prices of all things are increased above all measure, by reason of the new standard coin, and that the country is generally much harried and wasted, and thereby great scarcity and wants grow here; we hold it meet, and accordingly gave direction to the commissary of the victuals to issue oats, as formerly, at six shillings the barrel, and allow the soldier two pounds of beef and eight herrings a day, according as it was formerly accustomed, till your Lordships' resolution were returned in that behalf, which we humbly pray and expect. And so, having no other matter at this time worthy the presenting to your Lordships, we most humbly take leave.

. . . . . .

The same day, after this letter was signed, the Lord Deputy took his journey towards Dublin, but was surprised with an ill disposition of health, which so increased upon him that the next day he was forced to be carried in his horse-litter, and so continued until he arrived there. And the President, the aforesaid day returned towards Cork, was surprised with the like accident, inasmuch as he was not able that night to journey any farther than to Master Geralt Comerford's [1] house, not distant from Kilkenny above three miles, and there it appeared that he was in a burning fever. Nevertheless, being transported with a desire to be in his province, the next day he removed, and so, by easy journeys, resting some days upon the way, at last, upon the third of April, he

---

[1] This gentleman was one of the judges. He had been Attorney-General of Connaught under Sir R. Bingham's regime. The Low Burkes, who were seldom out of rebellion, charged him with being "a great stirrer-up of wars," a curious charge to come from a nation so awfully given to fighting as were the Low Burkes.

came to Cork, but was exceedingly weak, and in many men's opinion in danger of death.

The actions, accidents, and services of mark related in this second book, for the reader's better memory, I will briefly recount, which were as followeth: viz. the sending of forces out to Munster into Connaught to withstand the entrance of Connaught and Ulster men into Munster; the taking of James FitzThomas, the reputed Earl of Desmond; the apprehension of Florence MacCarty; the sending of a regiment into Connaught for the service of that province; the sending of James FitzThomas and Florence prisoners into England; the restraint of certain principal gentlemen of Munster that were apt to rebel; the arrival of the Spaniards at Kinsale; the Lord Deputy's coming into Munster; the siege of Kinsale; the landing of seconds from Spain at Castlehaven; the remarkable sea-fight in that harbour; the revolt of divers of the provincials; the coming of Tyrone and O'Donnell to raise the siege at Kinsale; the famous victory obtained against them and the Spaniards; the flight of O'Donnell, Redmond Burke, etc., into Spain; the honourable and advantageous composition; the rendering of Castlehaven and the castles at Baltimore to Her Majesty; the surprising of the castle of Donboy by O'Sulevan Beare; the transporting of the Spaniards into Spain; and the departure of the Lord Deputy out of Munster.

THE END OF THE SECOND BOOK.

MAP OF THE ARMY ON THE BEARE COUNTRY.

PACATA HIBERNIA.

THE THIRD BOOK OF THE WARS IN IRELAND,

Whereby that Country was reduced to Subjection and Obedience.

———◆———

CHAPTER I.

The estate of the province of Munster after the siege of Kinsale—The war of Ireland censured to be lawfully maintained by the rebels in the opinion of the learned men of Spain—The names of the doctors of Salamanca who censured the lawfulness of the rebellion in Ireland.

ALTHOUGH the Spaniards, as is related, were sent away out of Ireland, and the province of Munster cleared of strangers, yet to regulate and draw into order the Provincials who were revolted was a task of no small labour for the President to undertake, being not unlike the state of men's bodies, wherein relapses are far more dangerous than the first sickness. Before the coming of these Castilians the province, as you have heard, was in so good conformity that the civil justice, without all contradiction, had as current passage as in any of the former years of peace, and every man's cattle, without loss or danger, lay day and night in the fields.¹ But now the rebels and their hired bonoghs swarmed everywhere, and especially in Carberry, Beare, Desmond, and Kerry, insomuch that there was no place in them, or adjoining them, free from these caterpillars, who, beholding the grievousness of their offences, grew to be desperate, concluding themselves to be the children of perdition, and not capable of Her Majesty's gracious mercy, whereby their obstinacy was increased. In the tract of land aforementioned there were no castles which were held for the Queen but those which the Spaniards rendered and which were guarded by the two Captain Harvys, and Castle Mange, in Kerry, wherein a guard of Sir Charles Wilmot's had continued all the time of the siege at Kinsale; all the rest were in the possession of the rebels. In this distemper the province remained when the Lord Deputy left the same.

But before I enter further into the progression of the affairs of Munster I beseech the reader to pardon me for this ensuing digression, in which he may perceive how the learned men of Spain, at Salamanca, maintained and approved the rebellion in Ireland, which was handled upon the seventh day of March, 1602, *stilo novo*.

In the name of God, Amen: The most renowned Prince Hugh O'Neale doth make war for the defence of the Catholic faith with the Queen of England and

---

¹ This, which would seem to us to be a modest achievement in the way of administration, was in the sixteenth century regarded as a wonderful success. Perrott relates that all over Ireland in his time the cattle "would lye abroad at nights." Plainly the age was far removed from the time when a lovely young maiden could travel Ireland from end to end, singing and bearing gold and exhibiting her beauty in a conspicuous manner.

the English people; that is to say, that it may be lawful for him and the Irish freely to profess the Catholic religion, which liberty the Queen of England doth endeavour to take from them by force and arms. There are two matters now in question about this war. The one is, whether it be lawful for the Irish Catholics to favour the aforesaid Prince Hugh with arms and all other means in this war. The other is, whether it be lawful for the same Catholics to fight against the aforesaid prince without deadly sin and to favour the English in this war, either with arms, or by any other means, especially when, if they deny this kind of help to the English, they expose themselves to a manifest danger of their life or of losing all their temporal goods. And, furthermore, since it is permitted by the Pope that the Irish Catholics may obey the aforesaid Queen of England, and acknowledge her as their lawful Queen by paying tribute to her; for it seemeth that what belongeth to subjects to do may be performed, that is to say, to fight against the Queen's rebels, who deny their due obedience to her and seem to usurp the land which is subject to her dominion.

That both these questions may be decided we must hold it for certain that the Romish Bishop hath power to bridle and suppress such as forsake the faith, and those who oppose themselves with arms against the Catholic faith, when other means are not ministered to overthrow so great an evil. And, further, it must be concluded for infallible that the Queen of England doth oppugn the Catholic religion, neither doth permit the Irish publicly to embrace the Catholic faith, and that for the same cause the aforesaid prince and others before him, of whom the letters apostolical of Clement the Eighth make mention, made war against her. These being thus set down, the first question is easily resolved, for it is questionless, that any Catholics whatsoever may favour the said prince, Hugh O'Neale, in the aforesaid war, and the same with great merit, and hope of most great and eternal reward; for seeing that the aforesaid prince doth make war by the authority of the High Bishop for the defence of the Catholic religion, and that the Pope doth exhort all the faithful by his letters thereto (as by his letters is manifest), and that he will extend his graces upon the favourers of the prince in that war in as ample a manner as if they made war against the Turks, no man will in equity doubt that both the present war is just, and that to fight for defence of the Catholic religion, which is the greatest thing of all, is a matter of great merit. And concerning the second question, it is most certain that all those Catholics sin mortally who follow the English standard against the aforesaid prince; neither can they obtain eternal salvation nor be absolved of their sins by any priest, except they first repent and forsake the English army, and the same is to be censured of those who in this war favour the English, either with arms or victuals, or give them anything of like condition besides those accustomed tributes which it is lawful for them, by virtue of the Pope's indulgence and permission, to pay to the kings of England or their officers, so long as the Catholic religion shall flourish in the same. This assertion is confirmed by this most manifest reason, because it is sufficiently proved by the letters of the High Bishop that the English make unjust war against the said O'Neale and those that favour him. For seeing that the Pope doth declare that the English fight against the Catholic religion, and that they should be resisted as much as if they were Turks, and that he bestows the same graces upon those who resist them; who doubteth the war which the English make against the Catholic army to be altogether unjust? But it is not lawful for any to favour an unjust war, or to be present thereat, under the pain of eternal damnation. The Catholics therefore most grievously offend who bear arms in the camps of heretics against the aforesaid prince in a war so apparently impious and unjust, and all those who assist the said war with arms, victuals, or by any other means which of themselves further the proceedings of the war, and cannot give account of their indifferent obedience, neither doth it anything avail them to scandal the apostolical letters of *surreption,* for *surreption* cannot happen where no petition of them is declared, in whose favour they were dispatched. But the High Bishop doth openly teach in those letters that he and his predecessors had exhorted the Irish princes and all faithful men to make that war, and to provoke them the more thereto he doth enrich them with great favours and indulgences. How may it then be that those letters were surreptive which only contain in them an exhortation, strengthened with many great favours, for such as did fulfil them? Neither therefore can the Catholics who assist the English defend themselves by the reasons alleged in the second question, for no mortal sin is to be committed, although either life or goods stand thereupon; but those things which further and help to execute an unjust war are manifestly deadly sins. It is permitted likewise to the Catholics to perform such kind of obedience to the Queen as doth not oppugn the Catholic religion; neither ever was, nor could it be the meaning of the Pope to allow them to use that obedience towards the Queen which doth manifestly disagree with the end and scope which he had to spread the Catholic faith and religion in Ireland; but that it was his meaning and scope his letters manifestly declare. By all which it remaineth sufficiently apparent that the most famous Prince Hugh O'Neale and other Catholics of Ireland making war against a heretical Queen who opposeth herself against the true faith, and no rebels at all, neither do deny due obedience nor usurp unjustly the Queen's dominions, but rather that they revenge themselves and their country from impious and wicked tyranny by a most just war, and defend and maintain the holy and right faith with all their power, as becometh Catholics and Christians. All and every of which we, underwritten, do judge and approve as most certain and true. Salamanca, the seventh of March, 1602.[1]

John of Segvensa, Professor of Divinity in the College of the Society of Jesus, of this famous city of Salamanca, do so censure.

I, Emanuel of Royas, Professor of Divinity in the said College of Jesus, do agree in the same.

And I, Gaspa of Mena, Professor of Divinity and Holy Scripture in the said College, do hold with the opinion of these fathers, as being altogether true.

I, Peter Osorius, expounder for the sacred Canons in the same College of the Society of Jesus, am

---

[1] It would appear from this that the Pope only favoured the Irish rebellion so far as it had or purposed to have a religious object, and that in his view any insubordinate movement not having such a purpose would be wicked rebellion. The Royalist Irish were all Catholics, but held that the Pope had no power to absolve them from their duty to their sovereign. Generally speaking, the Catholic Irish have always shown, and still show, a disinclination to take their politics from Rome. Even O'Connell tore up a Papal rescript.

altogether of the same opinion with the aforesaid fathers.

. . . .

The President, as is said, being returned to Cork, after a few days began to recover, and finding his strength increased, and consequently his health, began to apply himself to his business. But before I speak further of his progressions I must look a little back to say something of things past.

CHAPTER II.

The Earl of Thomond directed to march with an army into Carberry, and his instructions—The Castle of Donboy fortified by the rebels—The Earl of Thomond having placed convenient garrisons in the west, returned to Cork—The Lord President resolved to besiege the Castle of Donboy—The list of the army in Munster—The Lord President advised not to enterprise the winning of the Castle of Donboy, and the reasons why—The Lord President perseveres in his resolution, and causeth the army to march towards Donboy.

To make trial whether the rebels in the country of Carberry would submit themselves upon the sight of an army, having been lately wasted and spoiled by the garrisons at Baltimore, Castlehaven and Bantry, upon the ninth of March (which was the day the Lord Deputy departed from Cork) the President directed the Earl of Thomond, with two thousand five hundred foot in list (which were by the pole but twelve hundred foot and fifty horse) to march into Carberry, and thence into Beare, there to view in what manner the castle of Donboy was fortified, of the incredible strength whereof much was noised. Many other directions he had, and, for the better satisfaction of the reader, I here insert the instructions themselves:—

INSTRUCTIONS GIVEN TO THE EARL OF THOMOND, THE NINTH OF MARCH, 1601.

First, as soon as possible you may, your Lordship is

to assemble your forces together, consisting of two thousand five hundred foot in list and fifty horse, and because they lie dispersed, for the more expedition's sake to take them in your way westward, as they are garrisoned.

The service you are to perform is to do all your endeavour to burn the rebels' corn in Carberry, Beare, and Bantry, take their cows, and to use all hostile prosecution upon the persons of the people, as in such cases of rebellion is accustomed.

Those that are in subjection, or lately protected (as O'Driscall, O'Donevan, and Sir Owen MacCarty's sons), to afford them all kind and mild usage.

When you are in Beare (if you may without any apparent peril) your Lordship shall do well to take a view of the castle of Donboy, whereby we may be the better instructed how to proceed for the taking of it when time convenient shall be afforded.

Captain Flower I think is now in Bantry, very weakly accompanied; for his relief you are to hasten towards him and for your better understanding to know in what state he is, to send presently to him, and accordingly to proceed.

There is direction to the victualler to send three months' victuals for five hundred foot to Baltimore, and the like proportion for Beare; and to the master of the ordnance to send to each of those places one last of powder, with lead and match proportionably; your Lordship is to call upon the ministers of those offices to see the same presently sent away. The powder and victual sent for Beare are directed to Baltimore, there to stay until the place be known where Captain Flower resteth, and thence to be thither directed by your Lordship.

When your Lordship hath met with Captain Flower, and depart from him, you are to leave with him five hundred foot, or more, if in your judgment you shall think it requisite, and likewise the like proportion of strength to Captain Harvy, more or less, as in your opinion shall be thought meet.

If the Abbey of Bantry be the place found fittest for Captain Flower to remain in, and the same be so ruined that of necessity, for the safe and well keeping of the victuals and munitions, cost must be bestowed, whatsoever your Lordship shall lay out for the repairing of it, upon your bill of disbursements it shall be forthwith repaid to you, always praying you to use as little charge as possible you may. Money to intelligencers and messengers is likewise allowed.

For the garrison at Kinsale victuals are likewise ordered to be sent, whereof the victualler must be reminded.

The capital rebels that are to resist you are O'Sulevan and Tirrell. Your Lordship must leave no means unessayed to get them alive or dead. The way, in my judgment, in which that service may be effected I have already made known to your Lordship, wherein I pray you to use your best endeavours.

Give all the comfort you may to Owen O'Sulevan,[1]

---

[1] Now putting himself forward as the Queen's O'Sullivan. He was eldest son of Sir Owen O'Sullivan, now dead, the chieftain whom Donal, the present O'Sullivan Bere, had displaced by appeal to the Queen invoking English law against Irish. Here in this little principality we perceive the presence and operation of one of the causes which all but foredoomed to failure the great rebellion headed by Tyrone. There was a Queen's Mac or a Queen's O ready to start up in every region invaded by the State. Tyrone took care to keep the Queen's O'Neill under lock and key, viz., Henry O'Neill, son of Shane.

by whose means you know the affairs of those parts will be best composed.

Dermond Moyle MacCarty is most assisted by the O'Crowleys.[1] Have a special care to prosecute and plague him and his assistants, and, if you can find any good means to work upon him, spare not your endeavour. Sir Owen MacCarty's sons, if they be well handled, will prove the best means, knowing, as you do, that he stands between them and the Lord of the country.

If Teg O'Norsy's[2] castle and Rannell Duff's shall in your opinion be meet for the service, do you take

---

Owen O'Sullivan's castle of Carriganass i.e. the Rock of the Waterfall, is beautifully situated over foaming rapids where a little river, the Ouvane, runs down from the mouth of the defile of Cæmaneea to the sea. Probably many of my readers have seen it, for it lies close to the highway which connects Macroom, Inchigeela, and Glengariffe.

About this time, O'Sullivan reduced the castle into his possession, battering it, according to Philip, with brazen cannon and bringing mantelets and other contrivances against it. For a while the Queen's O'Sullivan had to undergo a good deal of suffering.

I may mention that all the later Irish O'Sullivans, including the famous Murty Ogue, one of the heroes in Froude's "Two Chiefs of Dunboy," as distinguished from those of Spain, are descended from Owen of Carriganass, the Queen's O'Sullivan.

So when Froude makes Murty talk of his ancestor's heroic defence of Dunboy against Carew and the English, his historical romance becomes quite unspeakably unhistorical, for Murty's ancestors were aiding and abetting Carew and what Froude calls the English on that occasion.

[1] The Castle of the O'Crowlies, a small sept subject like the O'Sullivans and all the other western septs to M'Carty More, may be seen from the train by those who travel between Dunmanway and Bandon.

[2] This means Teigue of the Dorses. He was probably educated by Philip O'Sullivan's father Dermod, a very fine old Irish gentleman and soldier, lord of the Dorses or Dursey Island. It was he who conducted Vasco Sahavedro from Baltimore to Dunboy, after that fight in which O'Sullivan came to the relief of the Spaniards. Philip's father was a seaman as well as a soldier, and in the Desmond wars won a considerable naval battle, celebrated in Latin verse by his son.

them into your hands and leave wards in them; but let not your intent be discovered until you be possessed of them.

The like you are to do with Donneshed, Sir Finnin O'Driscall's house, in which of necessity I think the store of victuals and munitions for the garrison of Baltimore must be laid, for the castle of Donnelong, where Roger Harvey is, is too small for that purpose.

Lastly, I pray your Lordship of all your proceedings to give me as often advertisement as you may, and have correspondence with Sir Charles Wilmot,[1] for between your two forces all the Munster rebels remain.

The Earl, being gone with his army, marched as far as the Abbey of Bantry,[2] about threescore miles from Cork, and there had notice that Donnell O'Sulevan Beare and his people, by the advice of two Spaniards, an Italian, and a Friar called Dominick Collins, still continued their works about the castle of Donboy; the barbican whereof, being a stone wall of sixteen feet in height, they faced with sods intermingled with wood and faggots (above four and twenty feet thick) for a defence against the cannon. They had also sunk a low platform to plant their ordnance for a counter-battery, and left nothing undone, either within or without the castle, that in their opinions was meet for defence. But

---

[1] Wilmot was now governor of Kerry. Thomond was to try and get into touch with him. I may here remark, that in contemporary parlance South Kerry was known as Desmond. The larger designation of Desmond had fallen into disuse.

[2] There are hardly any remains of this once fine Abbey, founded by the O'Sullivan chieftains. Its site was a little to the west of Bantry, just below the house called Beechmount.

when it came to trial it appeared that their judgments failed, as afterwards you shall hear, for the barbican was not above six or eight feet distant from the castle, the height whereof was exceedingly high, not remembering that the ruins thereof would quickly fill the void space between them and make a fair assault when a breach was made, whereby all their earth and sod works proved vain and fruitless, not so much as one cannon-shot being bestowed upon them, but as near as the cannoneers could take their aims above it, as the President had directed Tirrell,[1] in the meantime, with the other Bownoghs, had so well placed himself in the mountains of Beare that he could not with his army pass any further without apparent danger. Hereupon the Earl left with Captain George Flower, besides his own company, the companies of Sir John Dowdall, the Lord Barry, Captain Francis Kingsmill, Captain Bostock, and Captain Bradbury, which were seven hundred men in list, in the Whiddy, an island [2] lying within the Bay of Bantry, very convenient for the service, and himself with the rest of his forces returned to Cork, where, having made relation of the particulars of his journey, it was found necessary that the President, without any protractions or delay, should draw all the forces in the province to a head against them. And although the time of the year was not so convenient (the spring being newly begun), yet present order was taken for all the army to repair to Cork, except those which Sir Charles Wilmot

[1] Tyrrell, a most experienced soldier, planted himself in the defiles of Glengarriffe and repelled Thomond.
[2] This island was used as a prison by the O'Sullivan chieftains. Consequently if there was no castle here, there must have been a strong moated house.

employed for the reduction of Kerry. Upon a longer delay a double inconvenience depended. First, Her Majesty should be burthened with a greater charge; and, secondly, though the Spaniards had an intention of sending another army, yet if they might be certified that the castle of Dunboy was taken, which was the only possession which they had in Ireland, and the country reduced to Her Majesty's obedience before they were put to sea, it might peradventure persuade them to new counsels, and alter the former determinations.

But before I proceed any farther it is pertinent to set down the forces which the Lord Deputy left for the prosecution of the war in Munster, which as they stood in the list (but very weak by the pole) were as followeth :—

Of Horse.

The Lord President . . .	100
The Earl of Thomond . . .	100
Sir Charles Wilmot . . .	25
Sir Anthony Cooke . . .	50
Captain William Taffe . .	50

Of Foot.

The Lord President . . .	200
The Earl of Thomond . . .	200
The Lord Barry	100
The Lord Audley . . .	150
Sir Richard Percy . . .	150
Sir Charles Wilmot . . .	100
Sir George Thornton . . .	100

Sir Gerard Harvy	150
Sir Francis Barkley	150
Sir John Dowdall	150
Sir Samuel Bagnall [1]	150
Sir Anthony Cooke	150
Sir Alexander Clifford	150
Sir Arthur Savage	150
The White Knight [2]	100
Captain Roger Harvey	150
Captain George Flower	150
Captain William Saxey [3]	100
Captain Francis Slingsby	100
Captain Henry Skipwith	100
Captain Francis Hobby	100
Captain Francis Kingsmill	100
Captain William Power	100
Captain George Kingsmill	100
Captain Robert Collome	100
Captain John Bostock	100
Captain Gawen Harvey	100
Captain Charles Cooke	100
Captain William Stafford	100
Captain John Owsley	100
Captain George Blundell	100
Captain Edward Dodington	100
Captain Ralfe Sidley	100
Captain Thomas Bois	100

[1] A base son of Sir Nicholas Bagenal, Marshal of Ireland, and brother of the famous Sir Henry, slain at the battle of the Blackwater. "Bagenal, Mr. Sam," figures a good deal in the State Papers prior to this time.

[2] Now out of rebellion, and "a great favourite boy" with the Government.

[3] We saw him marching out of Kinsale when Don Juan was entering.

Captain —— Holcroft . . . 100

In all . . $\begin{cases} \text{Horse} & . \ 325 \\ \text{Foot} & . \ 4400\ ^1 \end{cases}$

The enterprise of the siege of Donboy[2] was by the best subjects of the land and by the President's particular friends dissuaded: the one in regard of the public, and the other in the love they bore him; and also out of England had he advice that he should be very wary how he proceeded lest he should fail in the enterprise, whereby the Queen and State should undergo a fruitless charge and scorn; for by all men it was thought that the place was impregnable by reason of its situation, whereunto no approach by land-forces could be made nearer than the Bay of Bantry, being short of Donboy four and twenty miles, the ways being in many places im-

---

[1] Nearly all these captains were English, but for reasons already detailed, perhaps *ad nauseam*, we must conclude that nearly all their men were Irish.

[2] The perspective of history is, I think, lost sight of in Stafford's long account of the operations against O'Sullivan and Dunboy. The story is right well told, and is essentially so interesting, dramatic, and even tragic, that it is not at all surprising that the fate of the O'Sullivans should have caught the world's ear. The last chief of Dunboy has certainly found his poet, and curiously enough in one of his conquerors. How many scores of Irish castles, quite as strong as Dunboy, were stormed, and yet no one has heard about them. The O'Sullivans were in fact a small and weak sept, ground down to the earth by the tyranny and exactions of MacCartie More, their overlord, who seems to have been an awful rackrenter. And as regards MacCarty More himself, I cannot forget Shane the Proud's speech to the Queen's ambassadors: "I will not be an Earl, but something higher and better than an Earl. You have made a wise " (foolish) " Earl of MacCarty More " (Earl of Clan-Cartie); " I keep better *men* than him."

Yet Stafford, by the magic of his most graphic pen, has given a degree of renown to the last O'Sullivan Bere, hardly less than that of Shane, who regarded O'Sullivan's overlord and rackrenter as a mere nobody.

passable for horses and carriages, and there being in some places such straits and craggy rocks that it was impossible for men to march but in file, whereby one hundred that were to make defence might forbid an army to pass; if he purposed to transport his army by sea that he should find no landing place for his ordnance near to it, and, being landed, the wit of man was not able, without an infinite number of pioneers, to draw them to the castle; for all the grounds near it were either bog or rocks; and also that there was no conveniency of ground to encamp in, no good water near, nor wood for necessary use, nor gabion stuff, within three miles of it. The Earl of Ormond, in his love both to the service and to the President, wrote to him a dissuading letter, for the causes before recited, and therefore advised him to forbear the enterprise. But the President, foreseeing the importance of the service, and prophesying (as it fell out) that the winning of that place would discourage the Spaniards from any new invasion, gave a deaf ear to all persuasions, hoping that he should find the difficulties less than they were believed or related to him. The well-affected Irish, fearing the event, solicited him vehemently not to attempt it. His answers were that bogs nor rocks should forbid the draught of the cannon; the one he would make passable by faggots and timber, the other he would break and smooth with pioneers' tools; and with this constant resolution he caused the army to be assembled, which at Cork was in list near three thousand, but by pole not exceeding fifteen hundred, by reason that the companies had been extremely weakened by the long cold and hungry winter siege. The President, though feeble and weak in his own state of health, drew forth from Cork the three-and-twentieth of April, 1602, and encamped that night at Owneboy, being the very place where Tyrone lodged at the time that he received the great overthrow near Kinsale.

The four-and-twentieth we rose and marched to Tymolegge, where the army lodged; and three rebels who were taken and brought before the Lord President were executed.

The five-and-twentieth we drew to Roscarberry, where our army lodged.

The six-and-twentieth we departed Rosse over the Leap to Glanbarahan, near Castlehaven, where the army encamped, and the Lord President went to Castlehaven to view the castle and harbour, not removing Captain Gawen Harvy's company (who had the guard thereof) thence.

The seven-and-twentieth the army dislodged, and the Lord President with his regiment drew to Baltimore, and the Earl of Thomond and Sir Richard Percy with their regiments drew to a castle called the Ouldcourt, three miles from Baltimore, where, by reason of revictualling the army, we lodged two two nights, in which time the Lord President took view of the harbour thereof, and was ferried over into the Island of Innishshirkin, where he likewise took view thereof, and sent to the Island of Clare and the Sound between them, not removing Captain Roger Harvy's company thence, they being divided to guard the castles of Donneshed, Donnelong, and Cape Clear,

The nine-and-twentieth we encamped on the mountain at a place called Recareneltagh, near Kilcoa, being a castle [1] wherein the rebel Conoghor, oldest son of Sir Finnin O'Driscall, knight, held a ward.

[1] Still standing.

The thirtieth the army dislodged and drew to Carew Castle, built in ancient times by the Lord President's ancestors, and by the Irish called Downmark, or the Marquis's house,[1] being two miles distant from the Abbey of Bantry, where we encamped, as well to give annoyance to the rebels as to tarry the coming of the shipping with victuals, munition, and ordnance; at which place Captain George Flower with his garrison (left there by the Earl of Thomond) fell in unto us.

[1] This is absurd. Dun-a-m-barc means the Castle of the Ships, and has nothing to do with Marquis. Carew's ancestors had been Marquises of Cork, and a wily old Shenachie or territorial historian whom he discovered here, descendant of those who had been family historians to the ancient Irish de Carews, and who doubtless knew better, told him this bit of nonsense.

CHAPTER III.

Divers spoils done to the enemy—A letter from the Lord President to the Spanish cannoneers in Donboy—Captain Bostock and Captain Barry sent to Sir Charles Wilmot. A digression of Sir Charles Wilmot's proceedings in Kerry—Divers rebels slain—A traitorly soldier hanged—A ward put into Carrickfoyle—The Castle of Lixnaw taken by composition—The Castle of Ballihow taken and the Knight of Kerry defeated—Castle Gregory and Rahun taken.

THE first of May, Captain Taffe's troop of horse, with certain light foot, were sent from the camp, who returned with three hundred cows, many sheep, and a great number of garrans they got from the rebels.

The second, Captain John Barry brought into the camp five hundred cows, three hundred sheep, three hundred garrans, and had the killing of five rebels; and the same day we procured skirmish on the edge of their fastness with the rebels, but no hurt of our part.

The third, Owen O'Sulevan and his brothers, sons of Sir Owen O'Sulevan (who stand firm, and deserved well of Her Majesty, being competitors with O'Sulevan Beare¹) brought some fifty cows and some sheep from the enemy into the camp.

The fourth, O'Daly was convented before the Lord

---

¹ The Queen's O, stepping out as usual.

President and Council, and in regard it was proved that he came from the rebels with messages and offers to Owen O'Sulevan to adhere and combine with the enemy, which the said Owen first revealed to Captain Flower, sergeant-major of the army, and afterwards publicly justified it to O'Daly's face, the said O'Daly was committed to attend his trial at the next Sessions.

This O'Daly's ancestor had the country of Moynterbary given to him by the Lord President's ancestor many hundred years past, at which time Carew had for his inheritance the moiety of the whole kingdom of Cork, which was first given by King Henry the Second to Robert FitzStephen; the service which O'Daly and his progeny were to do for so large a proportion of lands to Carew and his successors was, according to the custom of that time, to be their rhymers, or chroniclers of their actions.[1]

The fifth and sixth, the weather was so tempestuous that we could not stir out of the quarter.

The seventh, the Lord President, understanding that the Spanish cannoneers were still in Donboy, as well in regard they were strangers but especially to deprive the enemy of their services, wrote a letter in Spanish to them to persuade them to relinquish the rebels, assuring them that they should not only come safe and remain safely with him, but that he would embark them for Spain. This letter, by the means of Owen O'Sulevan, was delivered to them; but, as it

[1] O'Daly, while flattering Carew's notions, took care to specify a very considerable district as his share of Carew's expected grant. Moynterbarry, strange as it may seem, means the People of Mary, i.e. the land appertaining to a religious community devoted to the service of Mary. The local pronunciation of this name to-day is Mounther-a-wauria. The Irish Carews were descended from William de Carew, brother of Maurice Fitzgerald, ancestor of the Geraldines.

appeared, they little deserved the favour proffered; for if they had pleased they might have made an escape; but at last, when the castle was taken, they paid the price of their inconsiderate obstinacy. The letter (Englished) was thus:—

A Letter from the Lord President to the Spanish Cannoneers in Donboy.

When Don Juan de Aguila, General of the Spanish Army for His Majesty in Ireland, departed from the city of Cork, having a care of your safeties he requested me to favour you, saying that contrary to your will the traitor Donnell O'Sulevan by force held you in his castle of Donboy, there to serve him as cannoneers. I, now calling to mind his desire (in the love I bear him, being so great a captain and so honourable a person as he is) and in consideration of the promise I made him, write this letter to you, promising, for the reasons before mentioned, that, when I shall encamp with my forces before the castle where you are, if then you will quit the same and come to me I will, by the faith of a gentleman and a Christian, make good my promise to Don Juan de Aguila not only to secure you in coming to me, and in the like safety to be with me, but also to relieve and supply your wants, and likewise, at your pleasure, to accommodate you with a ship and my passport safely to pass into Spain, in such manner as hath been already accomplished to the rest of the Spaniards that are returned to their country. This above written I am obliged by my promise to Don Juan to fulfil. But if you have a desire to find or receive further favours at my hands, you may with facility deserve them, that is, when you leave the castle to cloy the ordnance or maim their carriages, that when they shall have need of them they may prove useless, for which I will forthwith liberally recompense you answerable to the quality of your merit. Lastly, if there be in your companies any strangers (English and Irish excepted) who are likewise by force held as you are, these my letters shall be sufficient to secure their repair to me, and also to depart, as hath been before mentioned, conditionally, that you and they present yourselves to me before our ordnance shall begin to batter the castle of Donboy aforesaid. But if on your part default be made, I hold myself clearly acquitted of my promise made to Don Juan, and to be free from breach of faith on my part, and you ever after incapable of this favour of my promised offer. Return me your answer by this bearer in writing, or by some other in whom you have more confidence. From the camp near Bantry, the seventh of May, 1602.

To the Spaniards held by force in the
    Castle of Donboy.

. . . . . .

The eighth, the Lord President sent forth three hundred light footmen secretly by night through the enemy's fastness, under the command of Captains John Bostock and John Barry, with command that they should make their repair to Ardentully, Mac-Finnen's[1] house, and there join those forces with Sir Charles Wilmot's regiment, who, being united,

---

[1] MacFineen was chief of a minor sept of the O'Sullivans. His chief house was Ardea, a place, to me at least, memorable as that from which P. O'Sullivan the historian sailed for Spain. After the battle of Kinsale, O'Sullivan shipped off for Spain a good many of his women and children, the future historian amongst them.

Tirrell and the rest of the Irish rebels, who before had vaunted that they would keep our army from joining together, and lay in a place of advantage fit for that purpose, were so discomforted that they quitted the strength they possessed and sought only to avoid our forces, but in no way to resist or interrupt them.

But now leaving the progression towards Donboy for a while, expecting fair weather and prosperous winds to bring our provisions from Cork by sea, we will by way of digression say something of Sir Charles Wilmot's proceedings in Kerry before his coming into our camp. It may therefore please the reader to understand that the army, being risen from before Kinsale, the Irish defeated, the composition made with the Spanish general, and the forces returned to Cork, the Lord President about the beginning of February dispatched Sir Charles Wilmot with a regiment of one thousand seven hundred foot in list, but by pole very weak, and a troop of horse, into his former government of Kerry, not doubting but he, who had the skill to cure the former rebellious diseases of that country, could also recure the residuation thereof. In his passage between Askeiton and the Glen, Hugh MacSwine[1] (with the O'Connors and O'Neals) possessed a place through which he must necessarily pass, whereof being advertised, he lodged short of the wood an English mile, and rising before daylight assailed them in their quarter, where he slew twelve of their men, took all their baggage and horses, with fifty of their arms, and chased them three miles, but they were too swift of foot. Had it not been for

---

[1] A northern captain of Condottieri in the pay of the Baron of Lixnaw.

a Connaught man of the White Knight's company, who purposely discharged his piece to give them warning, whereat they took an alarm, they had been, as it was afterwards confessed, all, to the number of two hundred, surprised sleeping. The traitor, as he well deserved, was hanged for his labour.[1] The castle of Carrickfoyle he found empty and ruined; nevertheless he left a ward in it and gave the charge thereof to Captain Collum. When he came to the river of Cassan, which he passed the same day with some difficulty, being forced to swim his horses, John FitzThomas, young Captain Tirrell, Hugh MacSwyne, Owen O'Mayly, Rory O'Connor, Phelim O'Connor, and Gerald FitzMaurice, brother to FitzMaurice, the Baron of Lixnaw, with five hundred foot and a few horse assembled at Lixnaw near it to have stopped his passage over the Cassan, FitzMaurice himself being then gone into Desmond to persuade Donnell MacCarty, Donnell O'Sulevan, and William Burke to draw to the rest, to hinder his passage as aforesaid; but before they had knowledge of his being near them he made such expedition that he had got over the river.

And within a few days after, hearing that the Lord of Lixnaw was in Lixnaw Castle, he marched thither, and ere he was set down before it, FitzMaurice, fearing to be shut up in his castle, although he had a strong guard of five and forty good men well victualled in it, leaving his brother for his constable, posted into Desmond to procure aid from O'Sulevan Beare for the relief of the same. The castle stands

[1] Compare the opening story in the Bog of Stars. This poor fellow gave up his life for his friends, and yet he might have been a reliable soldier in other parts of Ireland.

close to the river-side, there being but a pike's length of ground between them, which made the ward negligent to have any store of water beforehand, thinking they might fetch it at their pleasure. Sir Charles, having knowledge thereof by a woman who came from them, found the means to place a choice part of his men upon that little plot of ground, whereby the ward could get no water; in which attempt Lieutenant Russell, who served under Captain William Saxey, and one soldier were slain. The ward, by this means debarred of water, rendered the place upon composition, which Sir Charles yielded to that he might prosecute services of more importance.

And being now come to Castle Mange,[1] wherein he had left a ward before the siege of Kinsale, he sent the one half of his companies of horse and foot into the Knight of Kerry's country (who, as the rest in those parts, had relapsed into rebellion) to prey the same, and to drive the cattle they should take to the Dingle; and for their succour, if need required, himself with the remainder of his forces marched after them as far as Ballyhow, ten miles from Castle Mange, where he found the Knight of Kerry with one hundred of his own followers and two hundred bonoghs, upon a bog not half a mile from the castle, where the Knight had a ward. To draw him to hard ground, in his sight a few men were appointed to assault the castle, himself with his foot and horse standing in a body without moving. The soldiers fired the castle door, and within three hours possessed themselves of it. The Knight all this while stood at gaze. The castle being won, Sir Charles drew

[1] Castle-Maine, Co. Kerry. See the Plate.

towards him to procure him to fight; he, finding the advantage of the ground he was in, where the horse could not harm him, charged our troops. Sir Charles, seeing himself engaged, and in danger if he should retreat, drew up his colours to the head of his pikes and joined with the enemy. It was long disputed which should have the better, and with pike and sword between them twenty were hurt and slain. The horsemen, seeing how doubtful the success was, valiantly and resolutely alighted from their horses, upon whose coming the enemy fled, and were chased more than a mile; but their footmanship was too good for us, and in the chase very few of them were slain. In this encounter Phelim O'Connor was killed, and all the chiefs amongst them (the Knight excepted) were hurt. The next day Sir Charles, leaving his foot at Ballyhow, rode to the Dingle,[1] at whose coming thither numbers of people repaired to him humbly imploring Her Majesty's gracious protection. The fifth of March he also took, from the Knight of Kerry, Castle Gregory and the Rahane, his chief manor house. And lastly, hunting him as a fox whose earth is stopped, pursued the scent so freshly that he constrained him to a new covert, following the Lord of Lixnaw into the mountains of Desmond.

---

[1] It is curious how many Irish towns at this date wore the definite article as a prefix, "the Newry," "the Naas," "the Neal," "the Dingle," etc.

CHAPTER IV.

The forces which the rebels had in Kerry in bonaght—The voluntary submission of Donnell MacCarty—Sir Charles Wilmot required by the Lord President to come to the camp at Carew Castle—A great prey taken from O'Sulevan More's sons—The Knight of Kerry upon humble suit protected—Sir Charles Wilmot with the forces of Kerry and the munitions and victuals from Cork arrived at the camp then at Carew Castle—Munition and victuals sent by the Lord President to the Lord Deputy—Dermond Moyle MacCarty, brother to Florence MacCarty, slain.

AFTER these good successes many of the country (as their manner is to take part with the strongest) submitted themselves to the governor, the principal amongst whom was Dermond O'Sulevan, brother to O'Sulevan More,[1] by whom he understood the force of the rebels there, namely, the Baron of Lixnaw, in his country of Clanmorris, had entertained William Burke with three hundred bonoghs, the Knight of Kerry as many under MacCab's sons and the MacSwynes, and Donnell MacCarty (usurping again the title and possessions of MacCarty More, with the help of the O'Sulevans) gave bonaght to Captain Tirrell with four hundred men, so that their forces were one thousand strangers.

At this time Sir Charles Wilmot had certain traffic

[1] O'Sullivan More was chief of another O'Sullivan sept whose country lay on the north side of the Kenmare river.

with William Burke, who seemed very desirous to become a subject. The Governor required him to do such service as might merit both his pardon and reward, which he yielded to, yet with limitations, namely that he would never betray the lives of any, but he would undertake to get into his hands all the prey of Kerry and Desmond and deliver the one half to the garrison, so that he might have licence to depart into Connaught with the rest.[1]

The Governor in the interim of this intercourse ceased not to follow the prosecution of FitzMorris, and prevailed so well therein that, having slain many of his kerns and got all his tenants into subjection, he banished him the country of Clanmorris and caused him to fly for his safety into Desmond. Hereupon Donnell MacCarty, who bore a good affection to the Lord President, since his former submission, and relying much also upon the Governor's kindness, whereof beforetimes he had good experience, without any capitulation or protection came in his own person to Sir Charles and brought with him five thousand cows, besides sheep and garrans in great numbers. The Governor, hereby perceiving his loyal simplicity, would take no advantages against him, but gave him all countenance and contentment that his place could afford.[2]

The Governor, having cleared all Kerry, so that no enemy was left upon his back, drew the forces towards Desmond about the middle of April, to pursue such services as that mountainous and desolate country

---

[1] *Noblesse oblige* did not affect this pretty gentleman, son of a Baron, grandson of an Earl.

[2] This gentleman was also son of an Earl, the Earl of Clan-Carty.

would permit him to effect. But by reason of the
dangerous passages, the whole country being nothing
else but mountains, woods, and bogs, he thought it
not safe to venture any further than Listree, a castle
seated twelve miles within Desmond. Whilst he
remained there in camp he received letters from the
President giving him to understand of his journey
to Donboy and how far he was proceeded therein,
willing him to take the best order that he could for
the speedy settling of those parts that he might
repair to him, upon a day assigned, to Carew Castle.[1]
The rebels, also receiving notice that the President
had marched so near to the country of Beare, withdrew
out of Desmond, as before, into Glangarve, whereby
opportunity was offered to the Governor of performing
some good service. For Donnell O'Sulevan, son of
O'Sulevan More, a malicious rebel, remained with
great store of cattle and certain kerns in Juragh, which
being made known to Sir Charles, upon the fifth of
May he secretly dispatched a party of men, who
burned and spoiled all the country and returned with
four thousand cows, besides sheep and garrans.
The Knight of Kerry, finding that the Queen's forces
prospered so well, and that the rebels were daily
impoverished and distressed, sought in all humble and
submissive manner for protection, promising the best
security that could be devised for his future loyalty,
which the Governor was the more willing to accept
because those parts should enjoy thereby a more
quiet establishment during his absence with the
President. These things thus ordered, he intended
meeting the President's army. Many difficulties
appeared to give impediment thereto; for the rebels,

[1] So Carew was resolved to call Dunamare.

knowing that these forces should join, and that there was no way for Sir Charles to march but by the Abbey of Erillah, and so over the Mangart,[1] a most hideous and uncouth mountain, they plashed and manned all the places, straits and advantages thereof, giving forth that they would set up their rest and either kill or be killed before they would permit him to pass. But to proceed.

The ninth, the Lord President went over into the Whiddy Island to take view thereof, and returned to the camp that night; and the tenth he rode towards the mouth of the harbour to see the entrance thereof.

The eleventh, the President drew forth all the regiments, leaving only a competent number to guard the quarter in his absence, and marched two miles from the camp, beyond Carrigness,[2] to the edge of the strait, where Tirrell, with the rebels, was lodged to give disturbance to Sir Charles Wilmot's coming to the camp, to the intent if the enemy had given upon Sir Charles he might give him seconds. But the passage was quitted, and the forces came through the same without a blow; and the very same day the ships arrived in the harbour, which brought the victuals and munitions from Cork, it bringing great gladness to the army, then being in so great want that we must have been forced within two days to have returned towards Baltimore.

The twelfth, the Lord President received letters from the Lord Deputy by John Pavy, his servant, whereby he was required to send a great proportion

[1] The mountain denounced in this manner is our admired Mangarton.
[2] This was the castle of the Queen's O'Sullivan. The "strait" was the picturesque gorge of Cæmancca, *Gælicé, Cucm-an-fiudh,* "the deer's leap."

of munition and victuals out of his province to his Lordship, which he performed accordingly, and returned his man. The same day, also, the hoy which brought the ordnance, and the *Trinity* (belonging to James Goagh of Waterford) with the remainder of the munitions and victuals, which was left for her guard, both safely arrived at Carew Castle, where we still encamped.

The thirteenth, whilst we were thus detained by unseasonable weather, there was a notorious rebel accidentally slain upon this occasion. The President, at his coming from Cork, had commanded all the subjects in Kinalmecha, Kirrywherry, and Kinalcy to draw the cattle northwards into the plain towards Youghal and Castle Lyons, so that if the rebels should draw thitherwards while he was at the siege of Donboy they might not receive any relief from those parts, amongst whom MacCarty Reugh would not drive away his cattle, pretending to keep them secure from the rebels, under the garrison of Kinsale; and indeed the reason was because the principal rebels in Carberry, being his dear friends and near kinsmen, he did not stand in fear to receive damage from them. But it fell out that Dermond Moyle MacCarty, Florence's brother, being distressed for want of victuals for himself and his followers, having no other means to supply his wants, thought to make bold with his cousin MacCarty for a few cows, and therefore came amongst his tenants with thirty men in his company, and, seizing upon some part of their prey, offered to retire towards his fastness. The churls who attended the cattle raised the cry, whereupon some forty of the country, with such furniture as came next to hand, speedily followed in rescue of their goods. The rebels, not fearing any enemy, made no great haste away, and thereby were soon overtaken; these sought to rescue their prey and they to defend them, in such sort that in process they fell to a light skirmish, and not many shots were made before one lighted on the chief rebel, Dermond, and killed him on the spot; which being known it bred no less astonishment in the one party than in the other, all the country being equally grieved for the loss of such a principal pillar of the Catholic cause, and therefore conveying his corpse to the Abbey of Timoleg,[1] he was there interred by a Friar in great solemnity. MacCarty Reugh sent present letters hereof to the President, signifying the vigilant care and impartial regard that he carried against the rebels, which his Lordship might well perceive by his service against his nearest kinsman, and the President was content to give him thanks, although he knew how little he had deserved the same.

[1] P. O'Sullivan says that MacCarty Reagh, Lord of Carberry, headed this rescue party.

CHAPTER V.

A resolution in Council that the army should be transported by sea to the great island and thence to the main—The rebel Tirrell desirous to parley with the Lord President—All our horse sent from the camp to guard Kinsale, and likewise certain foot—Tirrell failed twice to parley with the Earl of Thomond, and the reason why.

THE fourteenth, the Lord President, the Council, and the better sort of the captains assembled together and consulted touching the way for the conduct of the army to Bearehaven, where in regard the way by land was found impassable as aforesaid, for that the passage must be made through such huge rocks, mountains, bogs, and straits, that it was not possible for a man to march, carry arms, and use his weapons if he should have occasion to fight, much less to carry any victuals, munition, or baggage; and for that also Owen O'Sulevan and all the other gentlemen who best knew the country described the same to be so full of dangerous and unavoidable straits that the enemy, being first possessed thereof, might, with the twentieth part of the force they had there, give annoyance and impediment to the greatest army; for which and other reasons it was resolved, by general consent, that the army should be transported over the arm of the sea to the great island, and thence pass to the main.

The fifteenth, the traitor Tirrell sent two of his most trusty friends into the camp as messengers to the Lord President to invite and pray a parley the day following with his Lordship, which he refused. Then he desired that he might speak with the Earl of Thomond, which was granted at a place upon the edge of a river, about a mile distant from our camp. And the same day Captain Taffe and his troop of horse, all our carriage, garrans, and drivers, and one hundred choice foot, selected out of all our regiments, were sent back to the Castle ny Park to guard the town of Kinsale and the ordnance there; Captain Hobby and Captain Skipwith, being there before with their two weak companies, not being thought sufficient in this uncertain time to secure those places.

The sixteenth, the Earl of Thomond, well attended, drew forth his regiment, and went to the assigned place; but Tirrell, failing to be there, excused by his former messengers his not coming by the approach of the evening, praying his Lordship's patience, promising there to attend his Lordship the next morning.

The seventeenth, the Earl the second time (according to promise) drew down to the appointed place, where Tirrell only made a show of his whole force on the other side of the river, in the view of our army, but never came to the place where the Earl was, whose treacherous intent the Earl perceiving, and scorning to expect any other issue, returned to the camp. Tirrell, as we afterwards understood, would fain have gone to the Earl, but the Jesuit Archer, FitzMorris, and Donald O'Sulevan would not permit him.

From the seventeenth to the six-and-twentieth nothing happened worthy of note, only we were detained in our camp with contrary winds and with strange, unseasonable, and tempestuous weather.

The six-and-twentieth the wind turned fair, and the shipping drew forth, but immediately the weather proved so tempestuous that they were constrained to return to their former road; and the same day a sergeant of the Earl of Thomond's, with a party of his company, drew to Down Manus,[1] whence he brought a prey of three-score and six cows, with a great many garrans.

The seven-and-twentieth, the eight-and-twentieth, the nine-and-twentieth, and the thirtieth, we were detained with like contrary winds and unseasonably foul and stormy weather.

---

[1] Still standing. It is singular that this wild western country, where there was so little to defend, quite teemed with castles.

CHAPTER VI.

The Army dislodged from Carew Castle—The regiments transported to the Great Island—Teg Rough MacMaghon slain—The Castle of Donmanus surprised—A Spanish ship arrived—The conference between the Earl of Thomond and Richard Mac-Goghagan—The Lord President rides to the place where the forces were to land—The vigilant care of the Lord President—Two regiments directed to land in the Little Island, the other two to make to the main—The rebels deceived—The rebels defeated, and Captain Tirrell wounded.

THE one-and-thirtieth the weather grew fair, and we took advantage thereof and drew forth, on which day our army dislodged from Carew Castle, leaving our sick men (who were many) with a strong guard in the Island of Whiddy, and marched to Kilnamenogh, on the seaside, in Mountervarry, where we encamped that night.

The first of June, the Earl of Thomond and his regiment were embarked for the Great Island, as also Sir Charles Wilmot and his regiment, after whose departure the Lord President removed his camp to a headland, three parts whereof were environed by the sea, while the rest was intrenched.

The second, Sir Richard Percy and his regiment followed the other two; and lastly the Lord President with his landed in the Great Island, where the other regiments had formerly arrived.

The Lord President, being wearied with his long

stay there, spending the time without advancing the service, for that the hoy, with the pieces of battery, could not so well turn to windward as the rest, without which he could effect nothing of his intended service, sent Captain Slingsby aboard (who had before been conversant in sea affairs) to use his best diligence in getting those vessels to the Great Island, near the castle of Donboy, which service, by towing the hoy at the stern of the *Trinity*, of Waterford, and other diligence used, he effected and arrived at the Great Island.

The third, Teg Reugh MacMaghon, a principal rebel in an island adjoining the Dorseys, was casually shot through the body by his own son, whereof he died the third day following.[1]

The fourth, Owen O'Sulevan and two of his brothers, with a party of men, went to the castle of Donmanus, which was held and guarded by the rebels, which they surprised, and kept the same, killed four of the guard, and took the prey and spoil of the town.

The fifth, a Spanish ship arrived at the Bay of Kenmare, near Ardea, in Desmond.

And the same day Richard MacGoghagan, the Constable of Donboy, came to the Great Island and spoke with the Earl of Thomond; but whether he was sent by the President's entreaty to see whether he could persuade MacGoghagan upon promise of reward to render the castle to the Queen, or whether Richard MacGoghagan entreated the Earl that he might have a

[1] An outlawed and landless chieftain of Clare. He stole a ship and took to piracy. Coming to Berehaven, he was made prisoner by O'Sullivan, who rowed with him to the ship, intending to seize the ship too. Teigue stood up in the boat and called to his men to fire on O'Sullivan's party. They did so, and he himself fell, shot by the fire of his own people, possibly, by his son.

safe-conduct to speak with him, I am uncertain, but of this I am sure, that the Earl's meeting with him was not without the President's knowledge and allowance. All the eloquence and artifice which the Earl could use availed nothing; for MacGoghagan was resolved to persevere in his ways, and, in the great love which he pretended to bear the Earl, he advised him not to hazard his life in landing upon the main; "for I know," said he, "you must land at yonder sandy bay, where, before your coming, the place will be so intrenched and gabioned that you must run upon assured death." The Earl, disdaining both his obstinacy and his vain-glorious advice, broke off his speech, telling MacGoghagan[1] that ere many days passed he would repent that he had not followed his counsel.

The sixth, being Sunday, a foul and stormy morning, the Lord President very early, taking but one footman with him, rode two or three miles from the camp, to the place where the boats were assembled to pass the army (which that day was to rise) over into the main. The cause which moved him to be stirring so timely was to view the landing-place, which was less than half a mile from the place of embarking, whence he might easily discern a low, sandy bay,[2] between

[1] A soldier of fortune of a sept once powerful in Westmeath. It will be seen that all through he acted like a soldier and a gentleman. See the two figures in the Plate, of Thomond and M'Geoghagan, an absurd representation of the parley. Compare the attitude of the figures with the words of the text.
[2] Sandy Bay was the harbour of the little town called Castletown. The green island is called Deenish and is as green as ever. The place where Carew was expected to land for the island was on the strand on the west, now called Caomtreenan. Here Tyrell had thrown up his fortifications. Castletown was once called Castle Dermot, such being the name of the castle round which it is built, and which will be found marked in the Plate.

high ground, of very little capacity, where the descent was to be made, which was intrenched and barricaded with gabions of earth; in which trench, and behind the gabions, the enemy had placed three musketeers, and their gross at hand to give them seconds. But, not contented with a view so far off, the Queen's pinnace, the *Merlin*, riding not far from him, he commanded Captain Fleming to pass him over into a little island, called Donghe Irish, which lay between the Great Island and the main, and some part of it not twelve score from the sandy bay aforesaid. When he came to the said island, and taking an exact view of the landing-place, and how the rebel army lodged to forbid our descent, and the apparent danger he saw would ensue in the attempt, he rounded all the small island, and at last found a convenient place to land in the main; and the same, by reason of a rising ground in the midst thereof, was out of sight of the sandy bay. Presently he commanded Captain Fleming to land out of his pinnace in the island two falcons of brass, and haled them upon their trunks to a place naturally formed like a platform, and parapetted with an old ditch, as if it had been fashioned to that purpose. In this place the pieces were planted. From it to the mainland was not above one hundred paces; and although the distance from the sandy bay to this place was not four and twenty score, yet to come to it was more than half a mile, by reason of a gurt, or cleft rock, made by the sea; which ran up far into the land, which the enemy must compass before he could come to it. By the time that the President had performed as much as he intended in the small island the President's and the Earl of Thomond's regiments were embarked and under sail, whom the President, when they came near him, caused to land where he stood in the small island, and, drawing them to that end of the same which faced the sandy bay to amuse the rebels, being not distant from them, as is said, a musket shot, he formed them into a battalion and so stood firm confronting the enemy, as if thence he would pass them into the main. Sir Richard Percy and Sir Charles Wilmot with the rear regiments by this time were likewise embarked.

For you must understand that we had not boats sufficient to transport all our regiments at once, and they likewise made to the small island, but instead of landing in the same the President directed them to pass by the end of it, where he had placed the falcons, and to land directly in the main. Before the rebels found themselves deceived the two rear regiments were landed and formed into order ready to fight. Then the President drew his own and the Earl of Thomond's regiment to the boats, not twelve score from them, which the rebels perceiving, and too late finding their error, in a disordered manner made towards our landing-place, but before they could compass the fret, or cleft rocky ground aforesaid, all our army were landed. Nevertheless they came on bravely, but our falcons made them halt; our vanguard made towards them and a good skirmish ensued which continued until the other regiments came up, but then they broke and ran faster than we could follow. Upon the place eight and twenty of them were slain, whereof two were officers, and thirty wounded, whereof Captain Tirrell was one, shot in the body, but not deep enough. There were only two prisoners taken, and presently hanged, whereof a servant of James Archer, the infamous

Jesuit, was one, and with him his master's sword and portace. And if the Jesuit himself had not been a light-footed priest he had fallen into our hands, and yet, nimble as he was, he escaped with much difficulty, and besides him, great numbers of them would have passed the edge of the sword had not they had a boggy wood at hand wherein they were sheltered. The loss on our side was only the hurting of seven men, none of mark. The skirmish being ended, we lodged that night upon the same ground, near Castle Dermond.

CHAPTER VII.

The Spanish ship which arrived near Ardea brought passengers, munition and money to the rebels—The distributors and distribution of some of the money—A letter from Owen MacEggan to Richard MacGoghagan at Donboy—A letter from James Archer, Jesuit, to Dominic Collins, Jesuit, at Donboy—A letter from John Anias to Dominic at Donboy—A letter from John Anias to the Baron of Lixnaw a little before his execution.

WITHIN two hours after the skirmish aforesaid the rebels had intelligence that there was a Spanish *patache* landed the night before at the haven of Kilmokilloc, not far from Ardea, in |the Bay of Kenmare. She was purposely sent from Spain to know the state of the castle of Donboy, whether it held still for the King of Spain. Some Irish passengers were in her, namely a Friar, James Nelane, a Thomond man, belonging to Sir Tirlogh O'Brian, who had the charge of the treasure; Owen MacEggan, the Pope's Bishop of Ross, and Vicarius Apostolicus, with letters to sundry rebels and twelve thousand pounds, as the President was credibly informed by one called Moylemurry MacEdmond Boy MacSwyny, then a rebel, who saw it, besides munition, which put such fresh spirit into the rebels, who formerly were advising rather to break and disperse than to endure a siege, that they solemnly vowed to persevere in the defence of the castle, assuring the messenger (which they confirmed by their letters) that they would hold the same until Michaelmas, within which time they prayed aid, which the messenger confidently promised; "for," said he, "two thousand men were drawn to the Groyne before I departed thence. And the next morning, being the fifteenth, he set sail for Spain, carrying with him Brian O'Kelly and Donnagh MacMahon O'Brian. The distribution of the money by appointment in Spain (as Moylemurry aforesaid affirmed) was left principally to the disposition of Donnell O'Sulevan Beare, Owen MacEggan, James Archer, and some others; and Ellen Carty, wife to Owen O'Sulevan, then a prisoner with Donnell O'Sulevan Beare, saw some part of that treasure disbursed in manner following.

To Donnell O'Sulevan Beare . . .	1500 li.
To James Archer, Jesuit	150
To Donogh Moyle MacCarty : . . } To Finnin MacCarty . . . . }	160
To Dermond Moyle, Florence's brother . .	300 li.
To O'Donevan	200
To Sir Finnin O'Driscall and Connor, his son	500
To Connor MacNemarra . . . } To Richard Blake . . . . }	100
To the Lord of Lixnaw	100
To John FitzThomas	200
To O'Connor Kerry . . . . } To the Knight of the Valley . . . }	100
To Donnell MacCarty, the Bast . . .	400
Sum.	3710 li.

And likewise the said Moylemurry saw four great boat-loads of wine, munition, and money taken out of the *patache* and carried on shore by O'Sulevan Beare into the Castle of Ardea;[1] but how much munition was brought he did not know; part thereof was presently sent to Donboy, to encourage the rebels in the castle. Owen MacEggan wrote a letter to Richard MacGoghagan, which is here ensuing truly related, and another written by Archer, the Jesuit, to Dominic Collins, the Friar, and a third from John Anias, who conceived himself to be a good engineer: all which letters here ensue:—

A LETTER FROM OWEN MACEGGAN TO RICHARD MAC-GOGHAGAN AT DONBOY.

MASTER RICHARD,—I commend me to you, being very glad of the good report I hear of you, whereby I cannot but expect much (with God's assistance) in that lawful and godly cause of you. I am sorry but it was my luck to confer with you and with the rest of your company and inform you of all the state of the matters of Spain; but upon my credit and conscience there is no piece of service now in hand in all Christendom for the King of Spain than the same that ye have. How great it is to God and necessary for our country affairs you know. Moreover within a few days you shall have relief of men come to help you thither out of Spain. The great army of fourteen thousand men is forthcoming. You shall all be as well recompensed, both by God and by the King's Majesty, as any ward that is in all the world again. Have me, I pray, commended to all, and especially to Father

---

[1] Another O'Sullivan castle on the shore of Kenmare river.

Dominic, and bid him be of good courage. There comes with the army a Father of the company, an Italian, for the Pope's Nuncius, in whose company I came from Rome to the Court of Spain, and there he expects the armies coming hither. He shall give all a benediction, yea I hope within your castle there, spite of all the devils in hell. From the Catholic camp this present Wednesday, 1602.

Your assured friend,
Owen Hegaine.

In my sacrifice and other poor prayers I will not fail to commend you and your good cause to God. Our ship arrived three days ago, and our letters are come to the King by this time, Nisi Dominus custodierit civitatem, etc.

A Letter from James Archer, Jesuit, to Dominic Collins, Jesuit at Donboy.

Your letters of Thursday last came to our hands, but our disagreeing in some matters makes to be slack in performing your desire; yet you must take better order for the premises. Meanwhile, however becomes of our delays or insufficiencies, be ye of heroical minds, for of such consequence is the keeping of that castle that every one there shall surpass in deserts any of us here, and for noble, valiant soldiers shall pass immortal throughout all ages to come. For the better encouraging, let these words be read in their hearing. Out of Spain we are in a vehement expectation, and for powder, lead, and money furnished. Now, to come to more particular matters, understand that there are but two ways to attempt you, that is, scaling with ladders or battery. For scaling, I doubt not but your own wits need no direction ; and for battery, you may make up the breach by night. The higher you raise your works every way the better, but let them be thick and substantial. Raise to a greater height that work Captain Tirrell made betwixt the house and the cornel. Make plain the broken house on the south side. For fire-work direction do this : prime the holes and stop in the balls with powder mixed through the material well, and some powder uppermost that shall take fire. The rest you know, as you have heard me declare there. By all means possible send me one ball and the rest of the saltpetre. This in haste till better leisure : camp this Thursday.[1]

Your loving Cousin,

JAMES ARCHER.

To father Dominic Collins, these in haste.

A LETTER FROM JOHN ANIAS TO DOMINIC COLLINS, JESUIT AT DONBOY.

Be careful of your fortifying continually; with a most special care raise in height the west side of your port; fill your chambers on the south and north side with hides and earth; what battery is made suddenly repair it like valiant soldiers ; make plain in the south side the remnant of the broken houses; make ways out of the hall to scour and cast stones upon the port, and, if the enemy would attempt the like, dip deep that place we first began and a trench above to defend the same, as I have said to you. Although we expect speedy relief out of Spain, yet be you wise to preserve

---

[1] We have already read of Archer's sword which was captured in the battle of Sandy Bay.

the store of victuals discreetly. Devise yourselves all the invention possible to hold out this siege, which is the greatest honour in this kingdom; with the next I shall prepare shoes for you; send me the cord or long line and the rest of the saltpetre, withal the iron barriers, seven pieces in all. Salute in my name Richard MacGoghagan, praying God to have of His special grace that care of your success. From the camp, the —— of June, 1602.

Your loving Cousin,
JOHN ANIAS.

To Father Dominic, Bearehaven, these.

In November following, this John Anias, who in October was taken prisoner by John Berry, the constable of Castle Mange, was executed by martial law. Whether he was a priest or no, it was held doubtful. The day before his execution he wrote this ensuing letter to the Lord of Lixnaw.

A LETTER FROM JOHN ANIAS TO THE BARON OF LIXNAW A LITTLE BEFORE HIS EXECUTION.

In trust is treason : so Wingfield betrayed me; my death satisfies former suspicions, and gives occasion hereafter to remember me; and as ever I aspire to immortalize my name upon the earth, so I would request you, by virtue of that ardent affection I had towards you in my life, you would honour my death in making mention of my name in the register of your country : let not my servant Cormock want, as a faithful servant unto me; let my funeral and service of the Catholic Church be observed for the soul. Here I send you the pass and letter of that faithless

Wingfield, having charged the bearer upon his duty to God to deliver this into your hands. O'Sulevan was strange to me, but inures himself to want me. Commend me to Captain Tirrell, O'Connor, your sister Gerode Oge. This the night before my execution, the eighth day of November, 1602; and upon this sudden I cannot write largely.

Your loving bedfellow [1] sometimes,
ISMARITO.

---

[1] When men made a solemn contract they often slept together afterwards. It was probably the custom in mediæval Europe, for some of the greatest Norman lords observed it in Ireland. In this letter, one of the countless tragedies of this terrible time reveals itself as in a flash. Wingfield was one of Carew's captains. Wingfield apparently sent the writer a "pass" or protection, and then broke his word. A forged protection was one of the many ugly tricks resorted to by the State at this time. A brother of the Earl of Clanricarde was so caught and executed. Yet the House of Clanricarde was now on the side of the State.

The "Ismarito" which finishes the letter I cannot explain, unless it be a mis-spelling of *Dhe-is-Maire-with*, i.e. "God and Mary be with you."

CHAPTER VIII

The Lord President vieweth the castle of Donboy—The Lord President finds good ground to encamp in and to plant the battery, contrary to all men's opinions—Two spies of the rebels hanged—The artillery landed—The camp intrenched and the artillery drawn into the market place—Our approaches begun—The Island of the Dorseys taken, and in it divers rebels slain and taken prisoners, besides artillery, munition, and much other spoil—The rebels taken in Dorseys executed and the fort razed—Captain Kingsmill maimed with a shot—An attempt of the rebels given on our camp—Sir Samuel Bagnall brings letters to the Lord President from the Lord Deputy and from Don Juan de Aguila—A fair escape—The artillery planted before Donboy—Donboy battered and a breach made—The breach assaulted—Divers of the rebels slain in seeking to escape by a sally—Others slain in the water—The Lord President's colours placed on the top of the castle, but the vault still maintained by the rebels—Sundry rebels voluntarily yielded themselves—The remainder made election of a new captain, whose resolution was extraordinary—A battery made upon the vault—The rest surrendered themselves—A desperate resolution of Richard MacGoghagan—Eight and fifty rebels executed ; the rest reserved for a time—The whole number of the ward in Donboy—The loss we received in the siege—Captains, men of quality, and others wounded—Artillery, munition, and spoils got in the castle.

THE seventh, the President drew his forces to a neck of land within a mile of Donboy, opposite it, an arm of the sea passing between the castle and the camp, whence the President, taking Sir Charles Wilmot and one hundred foot for a guard with him, stole out of the camp and marched directly to the castle to view it and the grounds adjoining, in doing whereof some small shot was bestowed upon them, but no other

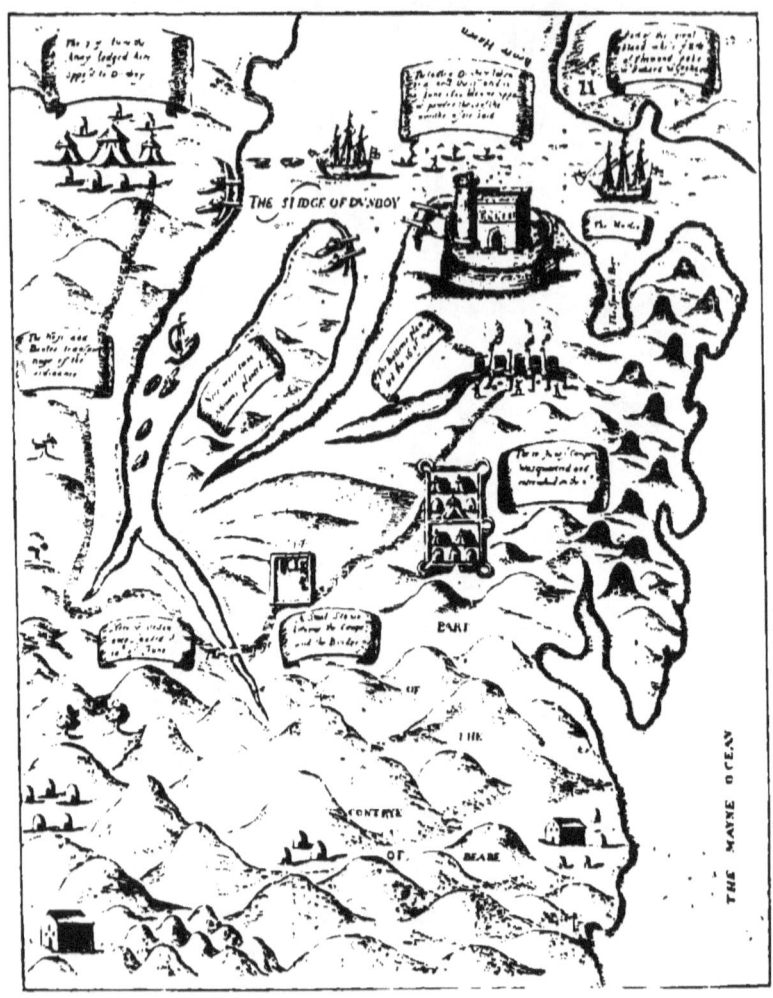

MAP OF THE SIEGE OF DUNBOY.

hurt done than Sir Charles Wilmot's horse shot in the foot. There they found, contrary to the reports of all men who had seen the same, a fair place of good ground, and of capacity sufficient to encamp in, within twelve score of the castle, and yet out of sight of it by reason of a rising ground interjacent; and also, upon the top of a small ascent in the midst of the rocks, a fair green plot of ground, not a hundred and forty yards distant from the castle, like a natural platform, of just sufficient largeness to plant the artillery upon. At their return, the report being made, it was hardly believed. For the Lord Barry, the White Knight, Cormack MacDermond, Captain John Barry, and Owen O'Sulevan,[1] who was born and bred in the castle—all of them, being in the camp, constantly averred that there was no other than rocky ground near it, and surely I conceive they did think it to be so, supposing that the plots of ground aforementioned were too little to lodge in and to plant the artillery. Further, the President assured them that, with God's favour, he would plant the ordnance without the loss of a man, and, within seven days after the battery had begun, to be master of all that place. Hereat the whole army much rejoiced, for the general opinion was that it would be a long siege; but afterwards, as you shall hear, the President kept his promise aforesaid. The same day, seven great shot were made from the castle to the camp, but no harm was done.

The eighth, we planted two falcons, taken out of the Queen's pinnace, upon a point of land on the

[1] Remember this gentleman was the son of the preceding chieftain and dwelt here until his father was driven out by Donal and the Government.

north side of the castle, hard by our camp, which beat upon the enemy, who were then carrying turf and earth to advance their works. And the same day the hoy was brought aground, and two culverins were unshipped and put into boats, and two spies sent by the enemy into our camp were taken and hanged. And we also sent soldiers to the wood to cut gabion stuff and to bring the rafters of an old church to make joists for the platform to plant the ordnance on.

The ninth, the Sergeant-Major, Captain George Flower, was sent by sea to take view of the Spanish bay near Donboy, to see whether there was any good landing for the ordnance there, and found the ground rocky[1] and unfit for draught.

The tenth, Captain Francis Slingsby, whom I cannot too much commend, in the hoy with the demi-cannon, and the three boats laden with two culverins and one demi-culverin, passed the point underneath the castle, within one hundred feet of the same, whence their great shot were made at the hoy, but all without harm, for his muskets so plied the artillery that the gunners durst scarcely stand by the same. And the same day we landed the two culverins and the demi-cannon, and encamped within musket-shot, but not within sight of the castle, by reason of a rising ground aforesaid which shadowed us, although oftentimes their great and small shot came over the camp and amongst us into the same.

The ordnance could not be drawn from the place where we landed to the place where we made our quarters, but there was a small creek very near the castle of Donboy, which being once

---

[1] So called still, a shallow rocky little harbour, but very picturesque.

entered into, they might ride in safety, being then covered with a hill between them and the castle, but all the way of their coming thither was open to the play of the ordnance of the castle, until they were within that creek,[1] whose mouth was not above forty yards distant from the castle. The President commanded the ordnance to be shipped into boats, and to carry them into that creek, which, by the help of dark nights and still rowing, was effected undiscovered. But the cannon and culverins were of such weight that no boat there could carry them, and none durst venture in the hoy to carry them by night. In this difficulty Captain Slingsby desired the President that he would commit that to his charge and give him but thirty shot, and he would (by God's grace) carry that ordnance by daylight into the creek or sink by the way, if his Lordship would please to venture the ordnance; which was accepted and performed the same day without the loss of a man, though many shot were made from the castle; for he had placed all his shot in the hold upon the ballast, so that the deck was breast-high above them, so that they had only their pieces and head and shoulders above the deck to play with their small shot; and that he that steered the hoy might be in safety (which much concerned the effecting of that service by his safe conducting) he placed him in the hold, and ordered it so that with two cackles he might steer the hoy either to starboard or to port as he was willed above by the captain, who stood aloft by the mizen-mast to order her course as he saw cause; but it was so fine and fresh a gale of wind that though they sailed above half a league in play of the

[1] This creek is the estuary of the only river in this neighbourhood.

ordnance and small shot of the castle, yet she made that way that they could not above twice discharge and lead their ordnance before she attained the creek, where she was then in security from any further annoyance of the castle.

The eleventh, we entrenched our camp, mounted our ordnance, and drew them all into the Marketplace; and the same day, about eight o'clock in the evening, the Lord President gave direction to have a demi-culverin drawn within shot of the castle, which made but two shot that night and was withdrawn. The Spanish cannoneers, finding the shot, willed the Irish to be of good courage, for that piece would do them no harm. He also caused two minions to be landed out of the Queen's ship, and placed them upon a point of ground on the north-west side of the castle, which overlooked it, to annoy the rebels whilst we were about our work. The same night we began our approaches, the care whereof the President imposed upon Captain Francis Slingsby, a discreet and dexterous gentleman, making him trench-master, who performed with commendations the charge which was laid upon him, having all the day before employed a great party of men in the wood,[1] which was a long mile and a half distant from the camp, to fetch more wattle to make gabions, and was constrained to send a strong guard with them for their defence. This day the enemy made a sally out of the wood upon some of our guards, but were immediately repulsed.

The twelfth of the same, understanding that the enemy had fortified the Island of the Dorseys, and

[1] The wood near Castle Dermot to which Tyrrell's men ran after their defeat.

carried thither three pieces of Spanish ordnance, and placed a strong ward of forty choice men in the same, reserving that as their last and surest refuge, the Lord President made special choice of Captain John Bostock, and sent him with Owen O'Sulevan and Lieutenant Downings[1] (officer to Sir Francis Barkley), and gave them (as also to Captain Thomas Fleming, who had command of Her Majesty's pinnace) secretly in charge that, now, whilst their army was occupied in besieging Donboy and making their trenches and approaches, and the enemy secure from any suspicion that we would give any attempt elsewhere, they should presently take Her Majesty's pinnace and four boats, and put into them one hundred and sixty foot men and set sail for the Island of the Dorseys, which charge they effected accordingly, and arrived there with the forces early the next morning, and being on land drew to the north point of the island, where they found the walls of a ruined chapel.[2] Captain Bostock, under the safety thereof, lodged Lieutenant Downings and a party of men, and then returned on board the Queen's pinnace to give direction what he would have done, and thence took the boat of the pinnace and rowed about the island to discover a fit landing place for himself and the rest of his soldiers; then, coming back to the pinnace, so soon as the tide served he caused the pinnace to warp up nearer the place, and appointed thirty soldiers and a serjeant to attend her, and sent to Lieutenant Downings, on shore, advising him that, at the very instant that he should land in the eastern part of the fort, he should give an attempt on the north

[1] The name of Downing is still common in Berehaven.
[2] *A Bonaventura Hispano Episcopo extructum.* P. O'Sullivan.

side. Then he divided his men into three boats, and the pinnace beating upon the fort with her ordnance, he and Lieutenant Downings (at the other two places first agreed upon) assailed the outermost fort, which, after a good defence made, their resolution and valour carried, and there they possessed themselves of three iron pieces of the Spanish ordnance, and forced the rebels into their second fort, where they entertained a good fight for the space of two hours. But our men, being encouraged with their first good fortune, gave on them so eagerly that the enemy, amazed, rendered themselves, and presently all the weaponed men came forth and delivered him possession of the fort, which was a place of exceeding great strength; and in the same, at the yielding up thereof, was the wife of Owen O'Sulevan, who since February last had been held prisoner by O'Sulevan Beare. There were found within the fort seven barrels of powder, with a small proportion of lead, and above threescore shot for their great ordnance, as also a quantity of wheat, oil and vinegar. In the island there were taken five hundred milch cows. Of the rebels, four were killed and two hurt, who with all the rest were brought into the camp and afterwards executed.[1] The fort, for that it was conceived to be an unnecessary charge, and unmeet to be held, the Lord President caused Lieutenant Downings to ruin and lay it even with the ground.

The same night the Lord President, the Earl of Thomond, Sir Richard Percy, Sir Charles Wilmot, Captain Francis Slingsby, and Captain George

---

[1] Philip O'Sullivan relates that they here slew old men, women, and children. Drove them first together into a crowd and then shot and stabbed them all to the number of three hundred, "most of them tenants of my father," writes Philip.

Kingsmill, with others standing round together in conference, a musket shot came amongst them from the castle and shot Captain George Kingsmill through the left hand and broke many of his bones.

The thirteenth, about midnight, Tirrell, with the rebel forces, came as near our camp as he durst, and gave us a hot alarm, pouring shot into our camp, shot through many of our tents and cabins, which did us little or no hurt, who being resisted from the north side of our camp, where a little sconce was the same day raised to hold a guard in, the charge whereof was imposed on Lieutenant Jeffrey, and good seconds sent from us, they ran away. This day Sir Samuel Bagnall arrived at the camp by sea, and brought letters to the President from the Deputy, commanding him to send all the forces to his Lordship, except those of the old list of Munster. He also brought with him a letter from Don Juan de Aguila, which had come by a merchant of Dublin to the Lord Deputy's hands.

The fourteenth and fifteenth our men were busy making gabions and drawing the trenches nearer the castle, Captain Francis Slingsby being, as aforesaid, trench-master.

The same day the President, the Earl of Thomond, and Sir Charles Wilmot, taking a guard of foot with them, rode, for recreation, out of the camp towards our last camping-place, and riding softly by the seaside, all three in rank, having left their foot behind them, they espied a gunner in the castle traversing a piece of ordnance. "This fellow," said the President, "will make a shot at us." The word was no sooner spoken than fire was given. The President, knowing that gunners always lay before a moving mark, reined his horse and stood firm. The Earl and Sir Charles started forward, and the ball grazed their horses' heels, beating some of the earth upon them. The President, glad to see them past danger, laughing, said that if they had been as good mechanical cannoneers as they were commanders they would have stood firm as he did. Also this day a whole culverin was drawn out of the camp and certain shot were made. The balls being found, the gunners liked it not, and began to fear their success. The day following, the whole culverin having been formerly withdrawn, certain shot were made out of the demi-culverin aforesaid. Upon sight of the shot they much rejoiced, supposing that our culverin had received some mischance, and scorned at any offence we could do them.

The sixteenth, the gabions, trenches, and platforms were finished, and in the night the demi-cannon and the two culverins were drawn down and planted against the castle, within 140 yards.

The seventeenth, about five o'clock in the morning, our battery, consisting of one demi-cannon, two whole culverins, and one demi-culverin, began to play, which continued without intermission till towards nine in the forenoon, at which time a turret annexed to the castle, on the south-west part thereof, was beaten down, in which there was a falcon of iron placed, upon the top of the vault, that continually played at our artillery, which also tumbled down. With the fall of the tower many of the rebels were buried therein. That being ruined, the ordnance played on the west front of the castle, which, by one o'clock in the afternoon, was also forced down. Upon the fall thereof the enemy sent out a messenger offering to surrender the place if they might have their lives and depart with their arms, and a pledge given for the assurance thereof; nevertheless they continued shooting all the while the messenger was coming between them and us, whose message being delivered, the Lord President turned him over to the Marshal, by whose direction he was executed. And then, the breach being in our opinion assaultable, the Lord President gave command to have it entered; whereupon the captains of the Lord President's regiments, which were commanded by Captain Henry Skipwith, lieutenant-colonel thereof, who were to give the assault, cast the dice for the point, and who should give seconds; and it fell to Captain Doddington's chance, and to be seconded by Sir Anth. Cooke, their lieutenants, Francis Kirton and Thomas Mewtas, to give on first, and the rest of the regiment to second them. The Earl of Thomond's regiment was to second the Lord President's, and during the assault the two regiments of Sir Richard Percy and Sir Charles Wilmot were commanded to stand in arms in the Market-place, as well to assure the camp as also to answer all other occasions. All things being thus disposed of, Lieutenant Kirton, according to the direction, giving on first, in entering the breach was, at the push of the pike, on the top of the same, who, although he received three shot and hurt in the right arm, yet with valour and resolution kept the place and made it good till Lieutenant Mewtas came up to his second, and both they until the Lord President's colours and the rest climbed up and placed their ensigns upon a turret of the barbican, reinforced with earth and faggots of great thickness, to which was added a large spur on the south-west part of the castle, of the height of sixteen feet, as in like manner all the turrets and curtains of the barbican were reinforced, at the top whereof they barricaded themselves with barrels of earth, and at the first approach there were within it some of the enemy with a falcon of iron, whom our men forced to quit the place and to retreat into a turret adjoining upon the south side, which was ramparted with earth some sixteen feet high, flanking the first, it being well manned, and therein a demi-culverin and a saker of brass loaded with hail-shot; the one whereof they presently discharged upon our men that were possessed of the south-west turret and spur, and going to load her again, their gunner was slain at his piece; whereupon, being for the present deprived of the use of those ordnance, and the place we possessed playing directly into it, they were forced to retreat under the safety of the east part of the castle, which was standing, where the enemy had placed pikes at the corners of the walls to receive them; the way between it and the curtain of the barbican being but six or eight feet broad, which passage they so well defended that we could neither annoy them nor go betwixt the two turrets aforesaid without disadvantage and apparent danger of great loss, where the shelter of the wall and the narrowness of the passage deprived both us and them of all use of shot, and there for the space of an hour and a half it was disputed with great obstinacy on either side; the enemy still making good defence, and beating with shot and stones upon us from the stairs and likewise from that part of the castle which stood from the top of the vault, and from under the vault, both with pieces and by their throwing down stones, iron balls, and other annoyances, wherewith many of our men were slain and wounded, and we oppressing them in all those places by all means we might, and still attempting to get up to the top of the vault by the ruins of the breach, which was maintained by the enemy so that we were divers times forced down again. And whilst in each of these places our men were thus employed, Captain Slingsby's sergeant, who had got to the top of the vault of the south-west tower by clearing the rubbish thence, found that the ruins thereof had made a way that led to a spike or window that looked into it and commanded that part of the barbican of the castle which the enemy possessed and defended, he having been there two hours before he discovered the same, by which passage our men, making their descent to the enemy, and gaining ground upon them, they being then in desperate case, some forty of them made a sally out of the castle to the seaside, whither our men pursuing them on the one side, and they being crossed by Captain Blundell with a small party of men (on the outside of the barbican) on the other side, we had the execution of them all there, saving eight who leapt into the sea to save themselves by swimming. But the Lord President, supposing before that they would in their extremity make such a venture to escape, had appointed Captain Gawen Harvy and his lieutenant Thomas Stafford,[1] with three boats to keep the sea, who had the killing of them all; other three leapt from the top of the vault, where our soldiers killed them, amongst whom a notable rebel called Mellaghlen Moore, being the man who first laid hands upon the Earl of Ormond, and plucked him from his horse

---

[1] No doubt the gentleman to whom we owe Pacata Hibernia.

when he was taken prisoner by Owhny MacRory, was slain.

After this, the courage of the enemy decreasing with their numbers, and not able nor daring to make such defence as they did before, we gave a new assault to the top of the vault, where having a difficult ascent, the shot from the foot of the breach giving good assistance, after some hours' assault and defence, with some loss on both sides, we gained the top of the vault and all the castle upwards, and placed our colours upon the height thereof, the whole remainder of the ward, being threescore and seventeen men, being constrained to retire into the cellars, into which we having no descent but by a straight winding stony stair, they defended the same against us, and thereupon, upon promise of their lives, they offered to come forth, but not to stand to mercy. Notwithstanding, immediately after a Friar born in Youghal, called Dominick Collins, who had been brought up in the wars of France, and there under the league had been a commander of horse in Brittany (by them called captain Le Branch), came forth and rendered himself. The sun being by this time set, and strong guards being left upon the rebels remaining in the cellars, the regiments withdrew to the camp.

The eighteenth, in the morning, three and twenty more likewise rendered themselves simply to Captain Blundell, who the night before had the guard, and afterward their cannoneers, being two Spaniards and an Italian (for the rest were slain), likewise yielded themselves. Then MacGoghagan, chief commander of the place, being mortally wounded with divers shot in his body, the rest made choice of one Thomas Taylor, an Englishman's son, the dearest and most intimate man with Tirrell, and married to his niece, to be their chief, who having nine barrels of powder, drew himself and it into the vault, and there sat down by it with a lighted match in his hand, vowing and protesting to set it on fire and blow up the castle, himself and all the rest except they might have promise of life, which being by the Lord President refused, for the safety of our men his Lordship gave directions for a new battery upon the vault, intending to bury them in the ruins thereof, and after a few times discharged, and the bullets entering amongst them into the cellar, the rest that were with Taylor, partly by intercession, but chiefly by compulsion (threatening to deliver him up if he were obstinate), about ten o'clock in the morning of the same day constrained him to render simply, who, with eight and forty more, being ready to come forth, and Sir George Thornton, the sergeant-major, Captain Roger Harvy, Captain Power, and others entering the vault to receive them, Captain Power found the said Richard MacGoghagan lying there mortally wounded (as before), and, perceiving Taylor and the rest ready to render themselves, raised himself from the ground, snatching a lighted candle, and staggered[1] therewith to a barrel of powder (which for that purpose was unheaded) offering to cast it into the same. Captain Power took him and held him in his arms, with intent to make him prisoner, until he was by our men, who perceived his intent, instantly killed, and then Taylor and the rest were brought prisoners to the camp.

The same day fifty-eight were executed in the

[1] Observe that this man, being mortally wounded with divers shot in his body, had been lying stiff and bleeding for a day and a night. What a heart this man must have had!

Market-place, but the Friar Taylor, and one Tirlagh Roe MacSwiny, a follower of Sir Tirlagh O'Brian, and twelve more of Tirrell's chief men, the Lord President reserved alive, to try whether he could draw them to do some more acceptable service than their lives were worth. The whole number of the ward consisted of one hundred and forty-three selected fighting-men, being the best choice of all their forces, of which not one man escaped, but were either slain, or executed, or buried in the ruins, and so obstinate and resolved a defence had not been seen within this kingdom. On our part we lost in the place Thomas Smith, Captain Francis Slingsby's lieutenant, and some others; and many of our men were burnt with powder and fireworks, which the enemy cast amongst them as they were in fight. Men of note hurt: Captain Dodington, shot with two bullets in the body, but not mortally; his lieutenant, Francis Kirton, shot in the arm and thigh; divers sergeants and sixty-two soldiers maimed and wounded, of which some are dead since, and others like to follow. And amongst the rest Sir Anthony Cooke, Sir Garret Harvy, Captain Skipwith, and Captain Roger Harvy received several bruises with stones and iron bullets flung upon them, but, being well armed, they received no great hurt. In the castle we gained ten pieces of ordnance, whereof four were brass, two of them being broken by our battery; and another piece of brass was likewise broken by our ordnance before any part of the castle fell, which the prisoners say is so deeply buried in the ruins that the search of the metal is not worth the labour. All the carriages were by the fall of the castle and by our artillery so broken that not one of them was left serviceable. Moreover, there were of powder nine barrels, and some great shot, but their whole store, by reason of the ruins, we could not well find out. There were also in the castle some quantities of wine, vinegar, oil, corn, beef, and hides, which the soldiers made pillage of.

    Philip O'Sullivan's description of this storm agrees substantially with our author's, though he naturally praises with greater warmth the valour of the defenders. He adds that Carew hanged women as well as men.

    This heroic defence must be attributed, not to the O'Sullivans, but to Tyrrell's Condottieri, drawn chiefly from Westmeath and Connaught. Tyrrell, a first-rate commander, evidently chose his men well and trained them well to bring them up to this pitch of perfection. The bonoghs seem to be the most respectable portion of the Irish nation at this time. When they undertook to fight, whether for the Queen or for an insurgent lord, they did fight.

CHAPTER IX.

Tirrell's proffers for the redeeming of his men—Our ordnance (with those which were gained there) shipped—The services propounded to Tirrell he refuseth, and the reasons of his refusal—The castle of Donboy blown up with powder—Tirrell's men who were respited executed—The army shipped and transported into the Great Island—The Downings taken—Leamcon Castle taken—The castle of Lettertinless taken and burnt—The Lord President returned to Cork—The companies sent for by the Lord Deputy delivered over to Sir Samuel Bagnall—The confidence the Irish had of supplies from Spain made them obstinate.

THE nineteenth, proffer was made by the traitor Tirrell to do some acceptable service that might redeem the lives of his men, so that their execution might be respited, which was for that time forborne. And the same day all our ordnance, and the Spanish pieces that we gained at Donboy, were put aboard and shipped, as also our boats sent to the Island of the Dorseys to fetch Lieutenant Downings, our men, and the ordnance thence, which were in number twelve, viz. demi-culverin one, sakers four, minions five, falcons two.

The twentieth, Tirrell, understanding, as is said, that his men's lives were respited, sent his trusty servant Laghlin Odallye to the Lord President to signify to him that he would perform any service that should be within his power to purchase the lives and liberties of his followers. Answer was returned him, and a stratagem propounded in the effecting thereof, that he should obtain pardon and liberty for himself and his dependents, but the reply which he made thereto was that he would ransom the prisoners with money, if that might be accepted, but to be false to the King of Spain, whom he termed his master, or to betray the Catholic cause, he would never; upon which answer his twelve men, before respited, two days afterwards were executed. The reason why he so suddenly swerved from his first promise of service was the hopes which he received by Owen MacEggan, the Pope's Bishop of Ross, lately arrived at Ardea, in the Bay as aforesaid of Kenmare. The President, therefore, perceiving that they conceived great hope of Spaniards, advised the day following with the chiefs of the army as to what course was best to be taken with the castle of Donboy, half ruined, who were all of opinion that a garrison which should be left there could not defend themselves or give any great annoyance to the Spaniards, if they should fortune to land there; for being so remote from all seconds and succours, were unavoidably left to ruin. And besides, though the Spaniards came not, the service that they could do in that country would not countervail Her Majesty's charge in maintaining them. Therefore they resolved to bestow the powder which was recovered in the castle to blow up the same; committed to the charge of Captain Slingsby.

The two-and-twentieth, the castle of Donboy was accordingly blown up with powder, the outworks and fortifications being utterly destroyed;[1] and the

---

[1] Dunboy was afterwards occupied and to some extent re-erected by a party of Cromwell's soldiers. The ruins are interesting in themselves and trebly so owing to historical associations. The blowing

same day Lieutenant Downings, with our men and boats, returned from the Dorseys to the camp, and also twelve of Tirrell's chief men, formerly spoken of, were executed.

But Taylor, and Dominick Collins the Friar, were carried prisoners to Cork, where being found, by due proof, that Taylor was one of the principal murderers of his captain, George Bingham,[1] at Sligo, besides being guilty of an infinite number of other foul and traitorly acts, he was shortly afterwards, without the city of Cork, not far from the north gate, hanged in chains; and the Friar, in whom no penitence appeared for his detestable treasons, not yet would endeavour to merit his life either by discovering the rebels' intentions (which was in his power) or by doing some service that might deserve favour, was hanged at Youghal, the town wherein he was born.

The same day, also, all our carriage and baggage being laid aboard, at the entrance into our boats, because we were not able to carry the cows, horses, and mares which we had taken, being at least six or seven hundred heads, the President commanded they should be killed, which was performed.

The three-and-twentieth we shipped our whole army back from Donboy, who all arrived that day in the Great Island, and thence the Earl of Thomond and Sir Charles Wilmot and both their

up of the castle reminds me that the chieftain's grandfather was killed in the castle by an accidental explosion of gunpowder.

[1] George Bingham, brother of Sir Richard, lay in garrison in Sligo Castle. His lieutenant was Ulick Burke, surnamed "of the Broom," nephew of the Earl of Clanricarde. Between the captain and lieutenant a quarrel so deadly broke out, that Burke, forming a party amongst the men, murdered Bingham, gave up the castle to Hugh Roe, and joined the confederates. Taylor has been already mentioned as an Englishman and son-in-law to Tyrrell.

regiments, were transported by shipping to Killaminog, being the place we encamped in, as we went, in Mounterbarry.

The same day the Lord President was advertised by Lieutenant Saunders that he had taken a great boat belonging to Teg MacConnor O'Driscall, brother to Connor Oge O'Driscall, of the Downings, wherein were slain Dary MacConnor, his brother, and three more of his best men, and that two days afterwards he took the strong place of the Downings, which is seated upon a high rock in the sea, disjoined from the land, so that there is no coming to it but over a little drawbridge of wood, resembling the seat of Dunluce in Ulster.

The four-and-twentieth, the Lord President and Sir Richard Percy, with their regiments, were embarked, and they arrived in the evening at the Island of Whiddy, where we had no means, for want of boats, to unship our men, and the night approaching were forced to leave our two regiments aboard, and the Lord President lay that night in the island.

The five-and-twentieth, the Earl and Sir Charles, with their regiments, marched by land from Killaminog to the old camping-place at Carew Castle, where, when the boats came to us, we unshipped the remainder of the army, and there we encamped all that night.

The six-and-twentieth, the companies required by the Lord Deputy were assigned and commanded to prepare themselves and attend Sir Samuel Bagnall till he brought them to his Lordship; and the same day the castle of Leamcon,[1] near Crookhaven,

---

[1] A very fine castle and in perfect preservation, strongly situated on the point of a promontory. The name means the Hound's Leap. A rock in the sea hard by is called Inis Bran, Bran's Island. Bran was a famous hound of the heroic ages.

which the rebels warded, was recovered from them by an officer and party of men of Captain Roger Harvy's company.

The seven-and-twentieth, the Earl of Thomond and Sir George Thornton embarked in the Queen's pinnace for England, and the army dislodged from Carew Castle and marched to a place in the mountains called Becarien Eltagh, where we encamped that night.

The eight-and-twentieth, the Lord President departed thence, taking the captains and officers of those companies that were to go to Ulster along with him, that they might perclose their accounts and dispatch all things at Cork against their companies should come thither; and by the way they came to the Castle of Lettertinless, belonging to Conogher, Sir Finnin O'Driscall's son, where the enemy had a ward of seventeen men. After some defence made and shot discharged, when they saw the army draw before the castle they sued for their lives, which granted them they yielded it up; and after the soldiers had made pillage of the goods, we burned and destroyed the castle and stone hall, and rode thence to Tymolagg, leaving the army behind us that night in Ross.

The nine-and-twentieth, the Lord President went to Kinsale and took view of the fortifications at Castle Park, and gave order and direction for the better forwarding and ending of the works there, and thence rode that night to Cork, appointing the companies that were to depart the province to march the shortest way, and to lodge at Downdanyer, Donnell MacCarty Rough's castle, and the rest to come to Kinsale.

The thirtieth the companies which were to go with Sir Samuel Bagnall came to Cork and had their supplies delivered them with order for their present departure.

The first of July, the captains that were to go along with Sir Samuel Bagnall spent the day in staying for their sick men, who were coming after, and preparing themselves for the journey; and the day following they all arose from Cork and marched thitherwards.

The President, in his return from Donboy, as is said, passed through Carberry, where many were still in action, not doubting but now they would have submitted themselves, seeing their supposed impregnable citadel was destroyed and Dermond Moyle MacCarty, their Ante-fignane, slain. He found it, however, much otherwise, for those who before offered to do service for their pardons stood aloof, and those who before were distracted, and prepared to fly either to Spain or Ulster, had received new life, and made fast combinations to hold out till their expected aids from Spain should arrive; yea and some also who before were subjects, and forward to give the best intelligence, did now palpably betray both by their countenance, their words, and their actions that their hearts were otherwise affected, all which alteration arose from the arrival of Owen MacEggan, so often mentioned, who not only bestowed the Spanish treasure which he brought with him bountifully amongst them, but put them in hope of more, with full assurance of a fresh army to come to their succour. His credit, the feeling of a few ducats, and his persuasions so prevailed that they verily believed that they should within a few months be so reinforced with Spanish aids as to be enabled to drive the English out of Ireland.

CHAPTER X.

Supplies of a thousand foot sent out of England for Munster—Sir Charles Wilmot with his regiment sent into Kerry—James Archer and Conner O'Driscall fled into Spain—Sir Owen MacCarty's sons revolt—Divers castles taken in Carberry by the garrisons there—The description of Bearchaven—The description of Baltimore Haven—The description of Castlehaven—The Spanish hostages licensed to depart—A letter from the Lord President to Don Juan de Aguila.

THE President, being come to Cork, found Sir Edward Wingfield with a thousand supplies lately come from England, all which were disposed in the weak companies that came from Donboy; in the taking whereof, and the marching thither, with the return, ten weeks were consumed, many men lost by the way, and by sickness very much weakened. Notwithstanding, so many of the army as were above the old list of Munster were presently sent to the Lord Deputy by Sir Samuel Bagnall, who came for them (as aforesaid) whilst the President was at the siege of Donboy. Sir Charles Wilmot, with his regiment, was sent again into Kerry (which country, having therein great store of corn and cattle, would otherwise have been left open to the rebels' relief) with direction to remove all the inhabitants, with their goods and cattle, over the mountains into the small county of Limerick, and such corn as could not be presently reaped and conveyed, as aforesaid, he was commanded to burn and spoil; the reason whereof was, that the President, having occasion of service near the heart of the country, as you shall hereafter hear, and also receiving daily intelligence of a great army provided in Spain, did not think it safe nor convenient to employ so great a part of his forces in places so remote, considering that good and strong garrisons were needful in the chief cities of the province, which otherwise would be open to the enemy that should attempt them. But in effecting hereof the Governor found great difficulty; for the harvest, by reason of that winter-like summer, was very backward, and (besides the Irish) the Bishop of Kerry, and certain English families who had of late planted themselves there (whose whole estate consisted in that summer's profit), importunately solicited some longer stay. The President, being acquainted herewith, unwilling to give any just occasion of grievance to the Irish and loss to the English, consented to tolerate their stay for the present, requiring the Governor in the meanwhile to put in execution such services upon the rebels as occasion might minister. The fifth of July, James Archer the Jesuit, and Connor O'Driscall, eldest son of Sir Finnin O'Driscall, having got a small bark, fled into Spain.

The two Captain Harvys were left at their old garrisons in Carberry, Captain Roger at Baltimore, the Lord President's horse there; Captain Gawin at Castlehaven, the Lord Barry's company at Littertonless, the treasurer's company at the Abbey of Strory, Captain Stafford at Old Court, and Captain Slingsby at the church of Shadone, where they wasted and foraged the country, so that in a short time it was not able to give the rebels any relief, having spoiled and brought into their garrisons the most part of their corn being newly reaped; from whom the President was certified that the Cartys of that country daily relapsed, insomuch as Donnah Moyle MacCarty and Finnin, his brother, with their followers, who attended the President at the siege of Donboy, had received three hundred pounds impress from Owen MacEggan, commonly called the Apostolical Vicar, in the name of the King of Spain. They, I say, upon the tenth of July, 1602, joined with the rebels; but in the end they could not greatly vaunt of their winnings, for Captain Roger Harvy got several draughts upon them, whereby he took their preys and had the killing of many of their men; besides he took from them divers castles strongly seated near the sea, where ships might safely ride, and fit places for an enemy to hold, as namely, the Castles of Dunmanus, Leamcon, Donegal, the Downings, Rancolisky, and Cape Clear, and, in a word, all that stood upon the sea coast between Donboy and Castlehaven, except only the Castles of Kilkoe and Cloghan.

But because we have had often occasion in this relation to speak of the three famous harbours of Bearehaven, Baltimore, and Castlehaven, it seems to me necessary in this place to speak something more particularly thereof, according to an exact view taken by the Lord President, and by him remitted to the Lords of Her Majesty's Privy Council. First, therefore, the haven of Beare is situated twelve miles to the northward of that promontory or foreland so well known by the name of Mizen Head, or Caron Head. That which we properly call Bearehaven is the sea which enters between the Great Island (before mentioned) and the main, or country called Beare, or

O'Sulevan's country. At the entrance of the harbour it is not above a musket-shot over, I mean from the Castle of Donboy to the Great Island. Being entered, the tides are slack, there are a good anchorage and convenient places to bring ships on ground, and smooth water, five fathoms deep at low-water mark. Towards the north end it grows much larger, is at the least a league over, and of capacity sufficient to contain all the ships of Europe.

The Great Island and the main as aforesaid makes the haven, which island is seven miles in length, at the south end whereof it joineth with the Bay of Bantry. When Donboy was unruined it commanded this spacious and goodly haven, which affords no small profit to O'Sulevan Beare whilst his castle was standing; for the coast yields such abundance of sea-fish as few places in Christendom do, and many ships, whereunto at the season of the year (I mean at the fishing-time) there was such a resort of fishermen of all nations that *communibus annis*, although the duties which they paid to O'Sulevan were very little, yet at least they were worth to him five hundred pounds yearly.[1]

The second of these harbours named is Baltimore, called by the Spaniards Valentimore, which is likewise caused by an island called Innisherkin, two leagues to the east of Cape Clear. The haven's mouth, at the south end of the island aforesaid, is ten fathoms at low water, but exceedingly narrow, by reason of a great rock lying in the same (always above the water),

---

[1] Here we see a very strong reason why O'Sullivan should object to the extension of the power of the State in this direction. He was Admiral on this coast, and his Admiralty in Berehaven meant £500 a year.

which, being within half a caliver's shot of the better shore, gives good opportunity to secure the port. After you are entered there is a pool about half a league over, where infinite numbers of ships may ride, having small tides, deep water, and a good place to careen ships. At the other end of this island, with good pilotage a ship of two hundred tons may safely come in by day, but by reason of many sunken rocks that lie in the entrance it is not possible for the best pilot in the world to assure his entrance by night. The President, for the safety thereof, thought it meet to erect blockhouses there, which undoubtedly he would have done if he had continued for any considerable time in Munster, being so exceeding dangerous to fall into the hands of a powerful enemy, as it would be a work of much difficulty after it were once fortified to displant him; besides an enemy there seated would command the best part of Carberry, the soil whereof is good, whereby he might furnish himself with victuals at easy rates.

The last, and indeed the least of these three havens, is Castlehaven, by the Irish called Glanbarraghan, renowned for that memorable sea fight lately acted there by Sir Richard Levison against Pedro de Zubiaur, commonly called Suryago, the Spanish Admiral. The passage into the harbour is so narrow that a ship of great burden, especially in a storm, cannot safely enter, and, being entered, there is no great space for any number of ships to ride in; but for all other commodities it is like the havens before mentioned, for there are eight fathoms at low-water mark. The castle aptly commands every part of the harbour, but the grounds round about it so command the castle that it can by no reasonable charge be made tenable against the cannon; but to proceed.

When the composition was made with Don John de Aguila for the rendering of Kinsale, among other articles it was agreed that the Spaniards should be shipped away in English or Irish bottoms, and for the safe return of the ships to Ireland there were three Spanish captains (as is formerly declared) left in Cork as hostages. The Spaniards being all safely arrived at the Groyne, and the ships returned, the Lord President, according to the composition, set the pledges at liberty, and, having provided a bark for their transportation, he wrote to Don John de Aguila, which letter (Englished) was as follows:—

A LETTER FROM THE LORD PRESIDENT TO DON JUAN DE AGUILA.

According to the agreements made at Kinsale between the Lord Deputy and your Lordship, these two captains, Pedro Suaco and Diego Gonzales Sigler, who remained in Cork pledges for the security of the ships and the subjects of the Queen my mistress who transported the Spaniards to the Groyne, are now in this passage, in a ship called the *Marie* of Cork, returned to Spain. The third pledge, Don Pedro Morijon, went with the Lord Deputy to the city of Dublin, whence, as I understand, he is departed into his own country. Now the agreements which were made between the Lord Deputy and your Lordship are on either part fully accomplished. Your Lordship's letter of the second of April I have received, but the wine and fruits came not to my hands. Nevertheless I acknowledge myself much obliged, and render your Lordship humble thanks for your favours, and especially in that I am retained in your memory. The occasion I did not receive them was my being at that time at the siege of the Castle of Bearehaven, which I thank God is taken, as also are many others possessed and held by the rebels, and the defenders of them chastised, as appertaineth to traitors. Your Lordship's present unto me was delivered by the messenger to the Lord Deputy, he conceiving that it had been directed to his Lordship, whereof I am extremely glad, and am as well satisfied with it as if it had come to my own hands; for the love I bear to his Lordship is no less than to myself. I am much grieved, and at nothing more than to see that this country produces nothing worthy to be presented to your Lordship, that I might in some proportion manifest in what esteem I hold the favour of a man of your quality, honour, and merit. If Ireland may yield anything which may be to your Lordship's liking, you may be assured that your Lordship hath power, at your pleasure, to command both it and me. So, being ready to do your Lordship all the possible service I may, the differences between our sovereigns reserved, in which both your Lordship and all the world shall evermore find me to be a true Englishman and a faithful servant to my Queen and mistress, I recommend your Lordship to God, beseeching Him to preserve you. Cork, the thirteenth of July, 1602.

    Beso las Manos de V. S. Su Servidor,
           GEORGE CAREW.

Muy Ilustre Señor.

CHAPTER XI.

The taking of the Castle of Donboy was the cause that the army prepared in Spain for Ireland was stayed—Two thousand supplies of foot were sent out of England for Munster—John FitzThomas's practice to deceive the Lord President, but failed—A false rumour of a Spanish fleet on the coast of Munster—Sir Samuel Bagnall with his regiment commanded to stay in Munster.

THE President daily received advertisement, as well by some of the country that had conference with Owen MacEggan, as also by merchants and their agents out of Spain, which all agreed in that succours were being prepared and ready to embark for Ireland; but hearing the loss which the rebels had received in Beare, and that the Castle of Donboy was razed, where they purposed to secure their landing, new directions were brought from the Court of Spain to the Earl of Caracena, Governor of the Groyne, to stay their proceedings in the voyage till the King's pleasure were farther known; but still the army was not dissolved. The examinations sent by the Lord President into England to the Lords were found to agree with the intelligence which was sent to Her Majesty out of Spain; wherefore, to prevent what danger hereby might ensue, it pleased Her Majesty to take present order that the fleet of ships, some her own, and some merchants', that had been upon the coast of Spain the greater part of the summer, should be revictualled and lie off and on, in the height of Cape Finisterre, till towards Michaelmas, so that if they proceeded in the intended invasion either they might fight with them at sea, or at least follow them to such harbours of Ireland where they should arrive, and there distress them; but the happy success in the siege of Donboy altered the Spanish councils, for now they had no place in Ireland that held for them. Nevertheless the coming of new forces from Spain for Ireland being still doubted there were sent from England two thousand foot for the supplying of the list. By this time Sir Charles Wilmot, as he was directed, had come out of Kerry, and all the subjects, with their goods and cattle, were drawn on this side the mountain of Slewlogher, whereby the bonoghs who had lived these five months principally upon O'Sulevan Beare, and by that means eaten him up, began to consult about leaving the province, there being no man now in action who was able; for the Cartys in Carberry had been so much wasted and impoverished by the two Harvys that though their hearts were good, yet their means failed them to uphold a war, or for long to hold them together. Therefore John of Desmond, brother to the Sugan Earl (prisoner in the Tower of London), laboured Tirrell instantly to take bonaght of them in Connilogh, and for that purpose had inveigled Morris FitzThomas, called the Lord of the Clenlis, to deliver to him the strong castle of Glancoyne, the custody whereof, to save Her Majesty's charge, had been committed to him the year before, and because no suspicion might be conceived of the said John FitzThomas's practice, he now became a suitor by James Walsh, who had been his brother's secretary, for a protection, desiring, as he pretended, to become a subject upon these conditions. First, if his brother James,[1] the titulary Earl, might be set at liberty, he would be content to become a pledge for him, either in the Castle of Dublin or elsewhere the State should appoint; which being refused and rejected, he offered to do service so that he might have his pardon and some means to relieve him in the future. But as the President would not be drawn to accept any of these conditions, so it was thought that he would have drawn back if they had been accepted; but all this negotiation was but to colour his practice laid for Glancoyne, which castle, and the fastness near adjoining, would have commanded a great part of that country. But all these jugglings were discovered by one V. B. whom the President without suspicion maintained amongst them. Wherefore he sent Philip Northcot, the sheriff of the county of Limerick, with private instructions to surprise both Maurice FitzThomas and the said castle, but either to take both at one instant or to meddle with neither. The sheriff, watching many opportunities, and not speeding of his purpose, the President, to prevent future danger, committed the custody of the said castle to Sir Francis Barkley, and so disappointed the rebels of that hope.

[1] It is pleasant to find that this shifty gentleman, who stepped in and out of rebellion as if it were his doublet, was loyal to his brother, and indeed the fact is, that if we cease to regard these sixteenth century Irish gentlemen from a religious or patriotic point of view, we shall find in them many virtues. Treated simply as men and dynasts, they might be exhibited with a certain Homeric grandeur. Achilles, too, was a poor patriot, and yet what has Homer made of him as a man?

About the latter end of this month of August a rumour was generally divulged through the province that the Spaniards were upon the coast, and that certain ships were discovered from the Old Head of Kinsale, and presently after that four and twenty sail were arrived at Bearehaven, and hereupon you might see horsemen galloping this way and that way, to and fro, with such signs of gladness and apparent joy, as though the day of their deliverance were near at hand; but, as it fell out, this was but a false alarm, the ships that were descried being a fleet of Easterlings bound to the southward. The President hereby discerning with what assured hopes they apprehended their coming, and with what glad hearts they should be welcome, being come, became an earnest and humble suitor to the Lord Deputy that Sir Samuel Bagnall's regiment lately called out of Munster by his Lordship's command might with his favour be returned again. The Lord Deputy, taking an honourable care of that province, finding by his own intelligence that the Spaniards purposed to make their descent either in Munster or in parts of Connaught not far disjoined, condescended to the President's request, whereupon the said colonel with his regiment was directed to Limerick, there to remain in garrison.

During the siege of Kinsale there was a young gentleman of the Cartys called Teg MacCormock, son of that well deserving gentleman, Sir Cormock MacTeg, who, being of the President's troop of horse, through the enticements of the rebels and promises of the Spaniards, was induced to combine with the enemy, and, stealing away his horse and hackney, entered into action; but the success of his confederates not proving so fortunate as they hoped, he grew weary of the rebellion and made himself a suitor to the President to be received to mercy, as may appear by his letter here ensuing :—

CHAPTER XII.

A letter from Teg MacCormock Carty to the Lord President, entreating the remission of his offences—Cormock MacDermond Carty accused of sundry treasons—Cormock MacDermond committed—The Castle of Blarney in the custody of Captain Taffe—The Castle and Abbey of Killcrey rendered to the Lord President—Mocrumpe besieged—Cormock's wife and children imprisoned—Cormock MacDermond plotted his escape.

A LETTER FROM TEG MACCORMOCK CARTY TO THE LORD PRESIDENT, ENTREATING THE REMISSION OF HIS OFFENCES.

RIGHT HONOURABLE,—My duty most humbly remembered; having long forborne, though thereby disquieted in mind, and ashamed of myself to send unto your Honour; yet, presuming upon Her Majesty's mercy and your favour, I have made bold to become a petitioner to your Honour, that it may please you to admit me thereto, and to forgive and forget my faults, considering they were not malicious, but youthful, and not of pretence to hurt Her Majesty or her subjects, but in hope to recover against my cousin, Cormock MacDermond,[1] some means to maintain

[1] This was that Lord of Muskerry of whom we have read several times already. His seignorie ran along the banks of the Lee. The writer very frankly says that he only went into rebellion in order to recover a piece of land. Indeed, all these magnates were more eager about land than anything else, and the land question was the root of all the wars.

my decayed estate, and still likely to be suppressed by his greatness, who will by no means give me a portion of land to live upon, as was promised upon the delivery of Kilcrey [1] by your Honour, wherein, as of the rest, I do again humbly beseech your favour, and so, as with a repentant and penitent transgressor of the laws, I do humbly submit myself to Her Majesty's grace, and will endeavour myself hereafter by my good deeds and services [2] to wipe out the memory of my former follies. Expecting your favourable answer, I most humbly take my leave. From Carrigifuky, this ninth of June, 1602.

Your Honour's most humble
to command,
TEG MacCORMOCK CARTY.

But the President had conceived such a deep displeasure (and not undeserved) against him that he protested against all favour to be extended towards him except he merited and deserved the same by some signal service. This young man, finding himself exposed to a desperate fortune, and abandoned to ruin, unless he could work his reconciliation, and besides bearing no goodwill to his cousin Cormock MacDermond, the Lord of Muskerry, for some controversy about title of lands between them, desired a safe-conduct to come to the President, promising to reveal to him such matters of importance as might happily make satisfaction for his former offences. His motion was hearkened unto, and a protection granted

---

[1] Kilcrea Abbey, an interesting relic in fine preservation.
[2] Teg fulfilled this promise at all events. When O'Sullivan was retreating, Teg fusilladed him vigorously as he marched northwards through West Muskerry.

for three days, within which time he presented himself before his Lordship, and delivered to him in private that he was able to vouch and prove divers capital matters of notorious treasons in his kinsman Cormock MacDermond. First, that he had underhand traffic with Don John de Aguila, letters ordinarily passing between him and the said Cormock, and in particular he averred that he saw Don John himself deliver to James Galde Butler (Cormock's wife's brother) two letters, the one from the King and the other from the Church, but from what particular churchman he could not certainly affirm, but by all probability it should seem to be from the Pope. These two letters were by him sent to be delivered to Cormock aforesaid, together with his own commendations in these words: "Commend me to your brother-in-law Cormock, and deliver him these two letters, the one from the King and the other from the Church," which were the same night delivered. Moreover he was deposed, by virtue of which oath he affirmed, that, upon his knowledge, Cormock had secret conference with Owen MacEggan since his last arrival out of Spain, and that from him he had received eight hundred ducats impress, and thereupon had accorded to yield into the Spaniards' hands, immediately upon their landing, his strong castle of the Blarney, situate within two miles of Cork, which deposition was afterwards confirmed by the testimony and evidence of sundry other credible personages. These informations concurring with the examinations of Dermond Mac-Carty, by the Spaniards called Don Dermutio (executed at Cork, of whom you have before heard), and also manifold proofs existing of his frequent combination with Tyrone, O'Donnell, Florence Mac-

Carty, and James FitzThomas, with other trivial treasons ordinary amongst these provincials, the President, with the advice of the Provincial Council, thought it a matter of very dangerous consequence to permit such gross and palpable treasons to escape unpunished, the toleration whereof might breed such intolerable boldness in these people that Her Majesty's politic government and authority temporal would grow no less contemptible than the ecclesiastic, against which the best seeming subjects were refractory. To prevent therefore such future mischief as might ensue by longer protraction it was thought fit that during the time of these sessions (then in hand) the said Cormock should be apprehended and committed to safe custody until such time as the original and depth of his offences, being found out, he might be brought to his trial according to due course in law. The day and time therefore being appointed for his commitment, which was about the eighteenth of August, the President, the same morning, to avoid all suspicion, took a journey to Kinsale to view the fortifications in Castle ny Park, leaving behind him double directions concerning Cormock: first, for his Castle of Blarney, which is one of the largest and strongest castles within the province of Munster, for it is four piles joined in one, seated upon a main rock,[1] so that it is free from mining, the wall being eighteen feet thick and well flanked at each corner to the best advantage. Considering therefore the diffi-

[1] The castle now shown as Blarney is apparently a poor *remanet*. The point of the allusion to its being upon a rock is this, that it could not be undermined and blown up.

The MacCarties of Muskerry, it must be remembered, were one of the Irish clans by which the Queen dragged down the Earl of Desmond.

culty that might grow in taking this castle by force, the President gave direction to Sir Charles Wilmot and Captain Roger Harvy (taking for their guard a sergeant with four and twenty foot) to make show of going only to hunt the buck in the parts near adjoining, and being hot and weary between the hours of ten and eleven o'clock in the forenoon, to take the said castle on their way homeward, and calling for wine and usquebagh, whereof Irish gentlemen are seldom unfurnished, should, if it were possible, themselves first and their soldiers afterwards, draw into the castle and gain possession thereof; and the Chief Justice Saxey likewise had direction to call Cormock before him in the public sessions, and, taking occasion of defect and delay about certain prisoners whom he should have forthcoming at these assizes, should at the same hour before appointed commit him to the Gentleman Porter till the President's pleasure should be farther known at his return from Kinsale. This latter order concerning his person was accordingly effected, but the former stratagem about the castle was frustrated; for the warders, whether out of the jealous custom of the nation in general (which is not to admit into their castles any strangers in their master's absence), or whether Cormock in his guiltiness had given them such directions, I know not, but sure I am that neither Sir Charles, though he much importuned to see the rooms within, nor any of his company were permitted to go into the gate of the castle nor hardly to look within the gate of the bawn. The President was no sooner returned to Cork than one of Cormock's followers saluted him with a petition relating at large the hard measure that his master had received from the Chief Justice, to whom answer was made that he would call for the Chief Justice before him, and, being satisfied from him of all particulars, order should be taken that no unjust or sinister proceedings should be taken against him; in the meantime he must be content to submit himself and be amenable unto law. Now did the time better permit the offences formerly committed to be pursued by course of justice, for could he but have gathered by probable conjecture of the discovery of any part of these treacheries before his apprehension he had in readiness one thousand men of his own followers, well armed, to have stepped with him into action upon the first alarm.[1]

The combination lately contracted by Cormock with the priest, Owen MacEggan, being manifestly proved by several witnesses, subject to no exceptions, the Gentleman Porter, called Master Ralph Hammon, was commanded to bring the prisoner before the President and Council, who were assembled at Shandon Castle, who, making his appearance, was charged with the several treasons before recited, who insisted very much upon his justification, pretending that these accusations were injuriously devised and slanderously suggested by his enemies, especially for the last article concerning the conspiracy with the priest MacEggan, which indeed was so cunningly and secretly carried, as he supposed, that it was rather presumed than proved against him. He renounced all favour and pardon if it would be justified by lawful testimony. The President replied that this was the only matter of substance that he was charged withal, the former being

[1] And the Queen had had the benefit of this military strength so far.

pardoned since the perpetrating thereof, being only inducements and presumptions whereby they were the rather moved to give ear and credit to the latter accusation; but he, still persisting in his innocence, was at last urged with this dilemma, namely, that either he should confess his fault, and so entreat Her Majesty's mercy, or else, in token of his loyal and guiltless heart, he should deliver unto the State his Castle of Blarney, upon condition that if the fact whereof he was charged were not evidently proved against him the said castle should be redelivered to him or his assignees by a day appointed. At first he seemed very inclinable to the motion, but in process it was perceived that he intended nothing but juggling and devices; wherefore a warrant from the whole body of the Council was directed to the said Gentleman Porter, straightly charging and commanding that he should be kept in irons closer than before until he should demean himself in more dutiful conformity; and, besides, they appointed Captain Taffe, in whom Cormock reposed much trust, to persuade him to surrender the said castle into the President's hands, undertaking upon his credit to retain the same and all the goods in it, or near thereunto, belonging either to himself or his followers, from loss and danger, either by subject or rebel. Cormock, at last, finding that the President was resolved either to make him bend or break, caused his constable, though much against his will, to yield the said castle to Captain Taffe, so that no other whosoever might have the charge or custody thereof. The prisoner, besides the Castle of Blarney, had two places, kept by his dependents, of good importance to command the country; the one, an abbey called Kilcrey, distant from Cork six miles, and the other a castle called Mocrumpe, sixteen miles distant from Cork; the former situated upon the south and the latter upon the north side of the River Lee. The Castle and Abbey of Kilcrey was rendered to Captain Francis Slingsby, sent thither by the President; but Mocrumpe, seated in the heart of Muskerry, and environed by woods and bogs, could not be got without the countenance of an army; therefore the President sent first Captain Flower, and afterwards Sir Charles Wilmot, with a competent number of foot and horse, to lie before it until such time as they might gain it by sap or mine, or by some other stratagem, as time and occasion should minister opportunity. During this siege the President cast about for his wife and children, and, having got them likewise into his hands, confined them within the walls of Cork. These things thus accomplished the President dispatched letters both to the Lords of Her Majesty's Privy Council of England, and to the Lord Deputy and Council of Ireland, relating to them the apprehension of Cormock and the reasons inducing him thereunto, desiring also to receive their Lordships' pleasures for his further proceedings in this business; but before answer could be returned, an unfortunate accident unexpectedly altered the whole platform of this intended service; for Cormock's followers had plotted his escape, and likewise to procure Cormock Oge, his eldest son, who was then a student in Oxford,[1] to be conveyed secretly out of the University and brought to Ireland, or, as some

[1] Divers sons of chieftains were already finding their way to Oxford. The most conspicuous of these so far were Brian of the Battle-axes, O'Rourke, Prince of Leitrim, Richard Burke, Earl of Clanricarde, and the son of O'Kelly, captain of Hy-Many.

thought, to be sent into Spain; for effecting whereof, John O'Healy, one of Cormock's old thieves, was (the next passage) to be sent into England. Advertisement hereof was brought to the President, who, to prevent both of these designs, first sent for the Gentleman Porter and delivered unto him at large the great prejudice that should arise to Her Majesty's service if the prisoner should escape, that the Queen's charge and his own pains and laborious travail were all frustrated; yea, if the Spaniards should arrive (as they were expected) the whole kingdom of Ireland should receive hazard and prejudice by it; wherefore he charged him upon his duty to the State, his allegiance to Her Majesty, and in the love he bore unto himself that he would be no less careful of his safe-keeping than of his own life, which in some sort depended thereon. Answer was made by Hammon that his Lordship should not need to trouble his mind with any such imaginary doubts; for if shackles of iron, walls of stone, and force of men (for he had certain soldiers allowed him for a guard) could make him sure, then should the prisoner be forthcoming whensoever the State should be pleased to call for him; and for John O'Healy, the President held a watchful eye over him, but it was not thought good to make stay of him until he should be aboard the ship, that such intructions and letters as should be sent by him might with himself be apprehended, whereby the whole circumstance of these plots, and the chief agents therein, might be discovered. To be brief, the wind was fair, the master hasteth aboard, the mariners and passengers purposing to set sail the next tide; amongst the rest John O'Healy, unregarded as he thought, is also on board; but he was much deceived in his opinion, for presently a messenger, sent from the State, found him in the hold; when he began to search him for his letters, he making show to deliver them willingly, suddenly threw both his letters and money into the sea; which although it plainly demonstrated apparent guiltiness, yet could he never afterwards be brought to confess either the contents of the one or the sum of the other, pretending ignorance in both, whereupon he was committed to the common gaol.

But let us leave Cormock for a while with the Gentleman Porter, and his man in the gaol, and speak of other accidents and matters of State which at this time were handled.

Upon the second of September, the Lord President received letters from the Lords of the Council, wherein they signified to him how well Her Majesty and themselves liked his services performed in Munster, with many other things worthy to be remembered, which importeth me in this place to relate the true copy of the original letter :—

CHAPTER XIII.

A letter from the Lords of the Council to the Lord President—Instructions for Captain Harvy to write to Spain—A letter written by Her Majesty's own hand to the Lord President—A letter from the Lord President to Her Majesty—A letter from Captain Harvy to Pedro Lopez de Soto, the Spanish Veador—A letter from O'Donnell to O'Conner Kerry—A letter from Don Juan de Aguila to the Lord President—A letter from the Lord President to Don Juan de Aguila—Captain Harvy's passport sent to the Veador—The Lord President's passport for Captain Edny into Spain—Spanish intelligence sent from Master Secretary Cecil to the Lord President—The Lord President's opinion sent to Master Secretary of a defensive war in Ireland.

A Letter from the Lords of the Council to the Lord President.

AFTER our heavy commendations: We have, according to our duties, imparted to Her Majesty your dispatch of the seven-and-twentieth of July, who hath conceived so great liking of your proceedings, as she hath commanded us to take notice of the same in the most gracious terms that our own heart could wish, being likewise most desirous that the army under you, as well in general as those gentlemen and officers in particular who have so valiantly exposed themselves to danger, as appeareth by your particular relation, may know that they have ventured their lives for a Prince who holdeth them so dear, as if she could preserve her estate and them without the loss and hazard of them there is nothing which she possesseth (of her own) which she would spare to redeem their trouble and danger. It remaineth now that we acquaint what is done by Her Majesty to prevent the purposes of the King of Spain, wherein we cannot but much commend the apprehension you take of those advertisements you have, and the judgment you use in applying the same, for the safety of that province, the defection whereof, as we are sorry to find by so understanding a person as you are. So do we hope when it shall appear (as it doth daily in all parts of Ireland) that God doth bless Her Majesty's army against the rebels, and that the King of Spain shall find himself not so at ease as to employ any army there in haste, that lack of duty and ingratitude which doth now live in them will either die in itself and turn to the contrary, or else that God will, as He hath begun, confound them in their own malicious inventions. It is very true that Her Majesty's own advertisements do confirm that a pinnace of fifty tons was sent with some of O'Donnell's followers, and some treasure, to assure the rebels of an army to come into Ireland, which pinnace, being once put to sea, was forced back again to Vinera; but they parted thence again within three or four days after, which is the same that landed at Ardea, whereof your letters make mention. We have also assured advertisements that Her Majesty's fleet, being kept on the coast, hath much hindered the Spanish designs, not that they were fully ready to come forth, but because the fleet kept their preparations from drawing to a head, for this next month is the time which is the fittest for them to put to sea if Her Majesty's fleet do not hinder them; for which purpose, though now most of her ships, being long at sea, and come in with the carrick, yet they are going out again with all possible speed. You shall further understand that Her Majesty hath been acquainted of the letters of compliments between Don John and you, the copies being sent over by the Deputy, by Sir Oliver Saint-John, whereof you now send the original, at which time he sent Her Majesty his own and kept no counsel that he had intercepted your great bribe. We have also seen the letter of Soto to Captain Harvy, and the passport of whose conference (from which passport also proceeded) Her Majesty conceiveth that you may make some good use for her service, in this form following: Where it doth appear by O'Donnell's letter to O'Connor Kerry out of Spain that he is desirous to understand the state of Ireland, but so as if there be any bad it may be concealed from the Spaniards, Captain Harvy may in requital of the Veador's courtesy towards him use this freedom of a gentleman though an enemy to let him see how much the King of Spain is abused by the rebels, who seek to engage him upon false hopes, and conceal just causes of doubts, for which purpose he shall send him O'Donnell's own letter, which he cannot deny, and withal in any case (it being well overseen by you) make him a relation of the successes of Her Majesty's army. Now if it may be said that they will think this letter is posted, and take this to be a finesse in Harvy, the worst that can come is that this good may ensue: that under colour of sending that to him there may some person go in the ship who may discover what preparations there are in that place; for the better colouring whereof he may reply that where he hath sent him a passport for the safe-conduct of any person whatsoever he should send to negotiate in the matter (which passed between them in conference) that he looked rather to have received from him, who was the propounder of the same (with so great affection), some such overture from that side as might have given him foundation to break with the Deputy, or yourself, to send over to Her Majesty about it, for which purpose he may offer him as good a passport for any of his messengers as he hath sent to himself, it being very great reason that such a motion should proceed from that side rather, which hath opened itself with greatest violence, than from any of Her Majesty's Ministers, who have instead of their malicious attempt performed all offices of honour and humanity. And so much for answer of that point.

For your opinion concerning such places as are fit to be fortified, Her Majesty doth very well approve the reasons whereupon the same is grounded, being such indeed as ought to sway Her Majesty's judgment either one way or other; for as it is true that charge is well forborne which draweth with it peril, so it is a double danger to spend in any place where safety followeth not such a charge. And therefore if you do continue in the mind that Baltimore is like to be of greatest use to the enemy both in regard of the haven itself and of the country adjoining, and that some such fortification may be raised as may command the haven, without any great charge, Her Majesty is content that you do proceed; otherwise if you do think that whensoever any forces shall descend, that the place so fortified cannot hold out for any time, then Her Majesty doth like it better, both there and elsewhere, that those castles which you do win from the Irish, seated upon the sea, be utterly demolished rather than be left for the rebels to nestle in at their first arrival, and easier to be furnished by them for their great advantage. In which point of fortifications, because you may see the temper of Her Majesty's mind, that useth mean in all things, and knoweth when to spend and when to spare, in both which never prince was so little subject to private humour, either one way or other, further than stood with the safety of her State and people, over which her care is rather to be admired than matched, we do send you an extract of her own letter to the Lord Deputy, how he should govern himself in that point, whereof we fear you have not yet had notice, in respect that the distance between you and him is well near the longitude of Ireland. For the artillery which you have taken, if you find them necessary for that kingdom, she is well pleased that they be detained, as well to serve for a scourge to them that brought them (if again they renew their attempt) as to prevent the inconvenience and charge of their transportation hither. But if you find them not necessary for that place, but that iron may do as good service, you may transport them in some of the victuallers, when they do return from that province. And so we do commit you to God's protection. From the court at Greenwich, this eighteenth of July, 1602.

Your very loving friends,

THOMAS EGERTON, C.S.   THOMAS BUCHURST.
NOTINGHAM.   JOHN STANHOPE.
ROBERT CECIL.   JOHN FORTESCUE.

At the same time also he received a gracious letter

written by Her Majesty with her own hands, which multiplied his comforts, thinking all his laborious endeavours to be fully recompensed in that they were so graciously accepted.

A Letter Written by Her Majesty's Own Hand to the Lord President.

Your Sovereign, E. R.,—My faithful George, how joyed we are that so good event hath followed so toilsome endeavours, laborious cares, and heedful travels, you may guess, but we can best witness; and do protest that your safety hath equalled the most thereof: and so God ever bless you in all your actions.

Not many days after the receipt of this gracious letter the President in his next dispatch into England wrote to Her Majesty this letter following :—

A Letter from the Lord President to Her Majesty.

Sacred Majesty,—If I could sufficiently express the joy which my heart conceived when I beheld a letter written by your royal hand, and directed unto me (who in your service have merited little, though in zeal, faith and loyalty equal to any), your Majesty would not in your more than abounding charity mislike your pains, having thereby raised the dejected spirit of a poor creature, exiled from that blessing which others enjoy in beholding your royal person, whose beauty adorns the world, and whose wisdom is the miracle of our age.[1] Gracious Sovereign, three years are now almost fully expired, since my employment into this kingdom took its beginning; during which time, rest in body and mind hath been a stranger unto me; and, overwearied in both, I do most humbly beseech your Majesty (if this realm be not invaded from Spain, whereof in a few days true judgment may be made) to grant me leave, but only for two months this winter to attend you in your court; which small time of respiring, and at that time of the year, can be no hindrance to the service, and yet sufficient to relieve my mind, and enable my body, which now is not so strong as I could wish to do your Majesty that service I ought. Ireland is destitute of learned men of English birth, and with Irish physicians, knowing the good will they bear me, if they were learned I dare not adventure; the longer I am without remedy, the less and the less time I shall be able to serve you. But as I am your Majesty's creature, so I do submit the consideration of my humble and just suit to your princely consideration, at whose royal feet, and in whose service, I am hourly ready to sacrifice my life. From your Majesty's city of Cork, the nine-and-twentieth of September, 1602.

<blockquote>Your sacred Majesty's most
humble vassal and servant,
GEORGE CAREW.</blockquote>

[1] All the Queen's chief servants were in the habit of addressing her in language of this description. They all affected to be in love with her, and she rather affected a tender feeling for them. It was an affectation, no doubt, but not quite such an affectation as we might imagine. There was a sort of cult of Elizabeth going on at this time, something like that which led to the deification of the Roman Emperors.

After the President had received their Lordships' instructions (in their letters afore-mentioned) he framed an answer for Captain Harvy, written in French to the Veador; and also a French passport, the copies whereof, Englished, I think it meet to relate, and with them the letter from O'Donnell, formerly touched upon by their Lordships.

A LETTER FROM CAPTAIN HARVY TO PEDRO LOPEZ DE SOTO, THE SPANISH VEADOR.

SIR,—After your departure it pleased God to visit me with such extreme sickness that all my thoughts were fixed upon another life, supposing that my days had been determined; by reason whereof, together with my feebleness and absence, I had not the means to acquaint the Lord President with the passages betwixt us until now that the time prefixed in your passport is almost expired, which I could not by any means remedy. Sir, I have of late received a letter from you, dated the ninth of April, 1602, by which I perceive that you are desirous that I should send a messenger to give you a taste (as I conceive) concerning the discourse which passed between us, which truly I would willingly have done if I had not been visited with sickness. But now, finding by the opinion of all men that His Majesty is resolved to continue the war against the sacred person of my Sovereign; although in my heart, as a Christian, I wish a firm unity between their Majesties, which by their ancestors hath been so long, to the comfort of their subjects, religiously continued; yet now, understanding the great preparations which the King is making for the invasion of Her Majesty's dominions, I confess I am not so passionate for the peace as I was, and I have no reason to make any overture of your discourse to the Lord President, there being so little probability of a peace to ensue. Wherefore if you think it good that the matter we speak of should be set on foot, because you were the first mover of it (wherein you manifest your zeal), I pray you to write to me that I may understand whether His Majesty will give ear to a peace or not, whereof you need not be scrupulous to speak freely, since you see by experience that when your design gave us cause of revenge we entreated you with honour and humanity. When I shall know your answer I will deal effectually with the Lord President, with whom, as well in kindred as in affection, I have such interest as you have heard, and of whose worth and sufficiency you have been well informed, assuring you that if he will put his hand to it, it will much advance the business. I am not in despair of his inclination to a peace if by your answer he may perceive that you proceed roundly. I marvel much that His Majesty and the Lords of his Council lend their ears so much to this traitorly, barbarous nation, who from their cradles have been nourished in falsehood and treasons, masking, of late, their actions under the veil of religion, whereof the truth is that in their hearts they have neither fear of God nor faith to men. And that henceforth you may not be blinded, and see their fraud, wherewith they beguile His Majesty, to whom they protest sincerity, I send you here enclosed a letter signed by the hand of the traitor O'Donnell, written to a friend of his in this province of Munster, called O'Connor Kerry, which was found in the Castle of Bearehaven, which by Her Majesty's forces, under the conduct of

the President in person, was within the space of seven
days taken and razed, and the rebels put to the sword,
and their companions, with all their forces, lodging
near them; but, according to their custom, they durst
not second or aid them, but left them to destruction;
by which letter you shall see, as clear as the day, how
this traitor O'Donnell only tempers a bait to deceive
the King your master, like all the rest of this nation,
who do but temporize to work their advantage by it.
To relate unto you truly in what estate these rebels
live at this present, howsoever they may protest and
dissemble their affairs, or write from hence, I protest
upon my soul that Tyrone works all he may to be
received into the favour and mercy of our Sovereign,
and that all the lords and chiefs of the North who
followed him on the day of the rout at Kinsale, and
others of those parts, have submitted themselves to
the Lord Deputy, and for security have put in their
pledges for their future loyalties. And Tyrone, with
his weak troops, has been so sharply prosecuted that,
as a fugitive being forced to quit his own country, he
seeks out coverts, bogs, and woods. The Lord Deputy
without impeachment passes from place to place, and
holds all Ulster in subjection. The other provinces of
Leinster and Connaught are reduced to obedience, and
the province of Munster (where I remain) is so much
at the command of the Lord President that if he
would receive to mercy all the traitors who seek to be
received and promise to live as good subjects there
would be no rebels left; and amongst others,
O'Sulevan, who hath given you the best assurance,
and of whom, as I think, you have most confidence,
doth daily make suit[1] to be restored to the Queen's

[1] The State Papers for this year are not published, so we cannot

favour, and this I assure you from the mouth of the Lord President. Moreover (as the vulgar can inform you) the President absolutely commands in this province, and the traitors, whose requests he rejects, are so few and so weak that they live like wolves and foxes, flying from one place to another, only to assure their lives, which kind of life cannot long endure. But if the King your master will persevere to aid these poor traitors, you shall see us, when you shall enterprise it, in better point than we were, it not being in your power to surprise any port or place of importance; and, if it be your chance to come hither in person, you shall find it to be true, whereof in my particular, in regard of the honour I bear you, I should be exceedingly sorry. The bearer hereof, Walter Edney, my lieutenant, whom you know by sight, in his fatherly love to his dearest son, whom he placed in the service of Captain Pedro Enriques de Tejada, lately deceased, hath entreated the Lord President to license him to see his son, to the end that he might supply his necessary wants, for default whereof he may otherwise perish; which occasion I willingly embraced whereby I might write to you, and by that means receive your answer, beseeching you to extend your favour to him during his abode in Spain. I will do the like for all such as depend upon you, if they shall happen to arrive in this kingdom. And to the end that I might the more fully know your answer, and have the better means to treat the more effectually in these affairs, which are of such consequence, I pray

check Captain Harvey's statements, but this statement is in itself extremely probable, and certainly O'Sullivan did make suit to James I. out of Spain, for restoration of his lands, promising to be a faithful subject. There is a break towards the end of the century in the published volumes of State Papers.

you to send one from you well instructed, that I may bring him to the Lord President, which will much advance the business you desire. And as you have given me a passport for such as I should send to you (whereof by reason of my sickness I could make no use), I send you the like here enclosed, which shall be of force until the end of February, 1602. Even so, sir, being ever ready (my allegiance to my Sovereign excepted) to do you all friendship and service, I pray God to preserve you in health according to your own desire. From Cork, the 17th of September, 1602.

Yours affectionately to do you service,

ROGER HARVY.

A Monsieur Pedro Lopez de Soto,
Veador-General for His Majesty of
Spain, deliver these at the Groyne.

Sir, I had forgotten one thing, which is to pray you to afford your favour to my lieutenant, that he may vend his merchandise transported thither, and return others, which he carries only by the means of traffic, for defraying his charges. I will do the like for any of yours that you shall send hither.

ROGER HARVY.

A PASSPORT OF CAPTAIN HARVY'S, SENT TO THE VEADOR.

I, Roger Harvy, captain of a foot company, and governor for Her Majesty of Castlehaven, Baltimore, etc. For certain causes concerning Her Majesty's service, I give this free passport to such ship and messenger as Don Pedro Lopez de Soto, Veador-General for the King of Spain, shall send into this province of Munster in Ireland between the date of this present and the last of February, 1602. And if it shall happen that any of Her Majesty's ships, or any other of her subjects, shall meet with the said ship, or that by force of wind they shall be forced upon the coast of England, or into any port within the realm of Ireland, in Her Majesty's name I pray and require all of them that they may be friendly treated, and that the messenger without any impediment may be permitted to have free recourse unto me and to vend their merchandise, being requisite for the Queen's service. Dated at Cork, the seventeenth of September, 1602.

ROGER HARVY.

To all admirals, vice-admirals, governors, magistrates, and officers, and to all other Her Majesty's loyal and obedient subjects unto whom this shall or may appertain.

A LETTER FROM O'DONNELL TO O'CONNOR KERRY.

What news is here, the doctor and Dermond O'Driscall may largely report to you; but of this one thing you may be fully assured, that the King will not omit the winning of Ireland if it cost him the most part of Spain. His Majesty doth send you money and munition. I pray let our information of you be found true, and your service encourage our King to further merit you. I pray you send me the relation of the news of our country, in such sort that if there be any bad it be concealed from the Spaniards and known to me; where the Deputy with the Queen's forces is

occupied, or where they are in garrison. At the Groyne, the four-and-twentieth of May, 1602.
Your loving friend,
Hugh O'Donnell.

To his loving friend O'Connor Kerry,
these give in Ireland.

At the same time that Pedro Lopez de Soto, the Veador, wrote to Captain Harvy, Don John de Aguila wrote to the Lord President, and sent him a present of wines, lemons, oranges, etc. And to do him a farther courtesy he gave him assurance that his passports should be sufficient for any man that he would employ into Spain if he had any cause to send thither. This letter the President sent to the Lords of the Council in England, who authorized him both to write to him and to return him a present, if he were so disposed. The copy of Don John's letter, and the President's to him, translated out of the Spanish, here ensue :—

A Letter from Don Juan de Aguila to the Lord President.

Muy illustre Señor,—To say the truth I am very glad that I am in Spain and that the passage was good which I was to make. I confess unto your Lordship that I am so much obliged for the honourable and good terms which the Lord Deputy and your Lordship used there in the service of your Prince in all things which concerned me that I desire some apt occasion to manifest myself to be a good paymaster (as I ought) for those courtesies, and for the assurance thereof your Lordship may send securely to me to command anything you please for your service. And your ship and passport shall be friendly received. And for that in this country there is no fruit of more estimation than wines of Ripadavia, lemons and oranges, these few are sent to make a proof thereof and the willingness I have to serve your Lordships, whom I commend to God. From the Groyne, the second of April, 1602.

Muy illustre Señor,
Besa las manos á
V.S. Su Servidor,
Don Juan de Aguila.

A Letter from the Lord President to Don Juan de Aguila.

Muy illustre Señor,—I doubt not but that your Lordship hath received my letters of the thirteenth of July, sent in answer to yours of the second of April by the Captains Suaco and Sigler, and I rest so well satisfied of the good terms wherein we stand that I am desirous to do your Lordship some agreeable service. At that time there was no occasion for me to make use of the passport and offer your Lordship made me for security of that man or ship which I should send into those parts. But now this bearer, Captain Walter Edney, whose son served Captain Pedro Enriques de Tejada (lately deceased), having prayed me to give him license and my passport to see his son, to supply him with his necessary wants, I beseech your Lordship that he may, according to your promise, safely and securely pass and return, which favour I shall thankfully acknowledge; and, whensoever your Lordship shall have occasion to send any of yours into these parts he shall be used with the like courtesy. I have received profit by the book of fortification which your Lordship left me at your departure, and hold it as a relic in memory of you, and as a good scholar I have put some things in practice, whereof your Lordship at your return hither again (which I hope in God will be never) may be a witness whether I have committed any error in the art or no. My greatest defect hath been the want of the help of so great a master as your Lordship is, of whom I am desirous to learn, not only that art but in all else concerning the military profession, in which I do give your Lordship the pre-eminence. To conclude, I rest in all I may (my duty reserved to the Queen my mistress) affectionately ready at your Lordship's service; and so, kissing your hands, I beseech God to preserve you with many happy years. From Cork, the seventeenth of September, 1602.

    Muy illustre Señor,
     Besa las manos á
      V.S. Su Servidor,
       GEORGE CAREW.

Although here is nothing to be had worthy the presenting to your Lordship, yet I make bold to present you with an ambling hackney.

The man whom the Lord President made choice of to carry these letters to Pedro Lopez de Soto and to Don John de Aguila was Walter Edney, lieutenant to Captain Harvy, who was an ingenious man of good discretion, and well experienced, as well in land as sea service; and the better to disguise his employment he had a son in Spain, a page to Captain Pedro Enriques, who, after the rendering of Kinsale, casting an affection to the boy, moved Don John to entreat the President that he might have the youth to serve him, which was granted, and within a few months after the Spaniards' return the captain died; and, to put farther mask upon his employment, the President freighted a small bark laden with Irish commodities, and in it a choice Irish horse, with a rich pad and furniture, and some other trifles which he sent to Don John de Aguila; and for his safety he had two passports with him, the one from Captain Harvy, the other from the President; the President's passport here ensueth.

BY THE LORD PRESIDENT OF MUNSTER, IN IRELAND.

I, Sir George Carew, Lieutenant-general of the artillery, for Her Sacred Majesty the Queen of England in that her kingdom, and her Highness's Lord President for the province of Munster, in Ireland, certify that I have licensed Captain Walter Edney to go into Spain to visit his son remaining there, and to return hither within two months after the date hereof, this being agreeable with the allowance and power which Don John de Aguila gave me at his being here, the copy whereof is hereunto annexed. Given at Cork, the seventeenth of September, 1602.

G. C.

Of these dispatches for Spain enough being said, it is time to return to the passages in Munster, but first I must relate to you the news from Spain sent in a letter from Sir Robert Cecil to the Lord Deputy, and the same transcripted, by Master Secretary's direction, to the President. The letter bore date the seventh of August, and arrived at Cork the second of September following, whereby the reader may see that the King of Spain's eyes were still, notwithstanding the rout at Kinsale, the dishonour he received in the return of his troops, and the loss of Donboy, whereby his footing in Ireland was lost, open upon that kingdom.

Although Queen Elizabeth, of happy memory, was dead before Lieutenant Edney returned, yet I hold it not impertinent in this place to recount his successes. When he was landed at the Groyne he understood that Don John de Aguila, by the accusation of the Irish fugitives, was in disgrace confined to his house, where shortly after he died of grief.[1] His letters and passports were taken from him by the Earl of Carazena and sent to the Court, and himself stayed until the King's pleasure was known. The Irish traitors inveighed much against him, saying that, under pretext of trade and

[1] I hope the reader is as sorry as I am for the fate which overtook Don Juan at the hands of my fellow countrymen. Don Juan, in a word, did his Irish work splendidly. I hardly know of a better soldier and more honourable or loyal gentleman operating in Ireland. And sure we may be that the country is the richer because Don Juan was here. The Irish refugees, many of whom had been in the Kinsale races, threw the blame off themselves and on to this excellent man. Under a tyranny it is almost more dangerous to succeed than to fail. We may be sure that if Don Juan had conquered Ireland and brought our woefully distracted nation under discipline, he would have been recalled in disgrace and possibly lost his head. At the same time, for such a nation as the Irish at this date a tyranny was the best. Had Tyrone conquered Ireland, he too would have established a tyranny. By sovereign irresponsible power alone could such men as we have been reading about been compelled to see that they were more than units.

bringing of presents, he came as a spy. Nevertheless he was well treated and had the liberty of the town and to wear his sword, with allowance from the King of a ducat *per diem* for his diet. His goods were sold for the best advantage, and his bark returned to Ireland; but the President's present to Don John, the Earl of Carazena detained to his own use; and after nine months' restraint Edney was enlarged and returned to England in July, 1603.

A little before this time Sir Robert Cecil, Her Majesty's principal secretary, wrote to the Lord Deputy the news of Spain, a branch of which that he also sent to the President, dated the seventh of August, and received the second of September, I hold meet to insert, whereby the reader may understand that the King of Spain had still his eyes open upon Ireland :—

. . . . .

One great cause of my writing this private letter is this, that where I see how much it doth distract your mind to think of Spain behind you and of the North before you, fearing to be diverted from the conclusion of your labours, you may perceive in what estate the preparations of Spain are now, as I am certainly advertised by one of mine own, who is newly from the port of Lisbon, where he took shipping the 21st of July.

There are two great ships, each of them of a thousand tons, one called the *Andrew* and the other (which shall be the vice-admiral) the name forgotten. Besides, there are twelve ships of two hundred tons and downward, in which it was resolved to send some fifteen hundred men, to have relieved the siege at Bearehaven, the news of the taking whereof was first known by a ship from Waterford to Lisbon, and not before. Of the fifteen hundred men, eight hundred came from the Groyne, being part of those who were transported out of Ireland. In the Groyne remaineth O'Donnell, and there is only the great *Saint Philip*, with ten small barks, with which he mightily importuned to be sent to the North. If these had been sent to Bearehaven, in Munster, hoping upon his arrival with some fifteen hundred men to have raised the siege, possessed some parts, and made a beginning of a plantation; hereof great benefit must needs have grown to the rebels; for those small numbers which should have been landed at Munster, with the bruit of the rest to follow (which is always multiplied), would have made a distraction of the Ulster prosecution, etc.

. . . . . .

Lastly in the said letter he prayed the President to set down his opinion what course were best to be taken in a defensive war if the King of Spain did invade Ireland with a royal army. The next passage, to give master secretary satisfaction, the Lord President wrote to him a long letter; but because many private things were handled in the same I will only relate so much of it as concerns his opinion touching a defensive war in Ireland.

THE LORD PRESIDENT'S OPINION OF A DEFENSIVE WAR IN IRELAND SENT TO MASTER SECRETARY.

Granting that the enemy will come no less powerful than is reported, and that the Irish will join with them (whereof there is no doubt), then consideration is to be had what in such a sea of troubles is meetest to be done that may best preserve the Queen's army with least charge, and the way to weary the enemy and the country. Because my opinion may perchance differ from other men, whose authority, greatness, and better judgment (in the world's opinion) bear more sway, I will forbear to deal in so weighty a business any farther than to yourself, using the liberty you have ever given me to say what I conceive to be the best counsel. If the army of Spain be so great as is both reported by those that come from thence and is expected here, let us make no doubt but he will be master of the field (for the present) and will so hold himself except the army of Ireland be reinforced to a far higher list, the charge whereof will make, if I be not deceived, both England and Ireland to groan; wherefore the best way, in my conceit, to moderate such huge expenses is for the present to be careless of the countries generally throughout the kingdom; for in seeking both to defend them and to make head against the enemy will be too heavy a burden. The principal regard which we ought to have is of the cities, in all of which I wish a strong garrison both of horse and foot, able to defend a siege. When the enemy shall see that we are dispersed into garrisons either he will presently, in his best strength, go to besiege one of those places, or else disperse, because he hath the country to friend, as we do. If he attempt the besieging of any of our places aforesaid there is no doubt but in such a business he will unite all his forces in one; then may we be bold to draw all our forces from their several garrisons to a head to relieve that place, and with God's favour make no doubt but to force the enemy to rise. If he disperse, then those garrisons will be able to master the countries about them, and leave no habitation to relieve either Spaniard or Irish; and upon occasion two or more of these garrisons may meet to effect greater services than otherwise can be done. This fashion of a war will in a short time destroy all the country, make the Irish curse the Spaniards and themselves for drawing them hither, drive the King to an inestimable charge and hazard by sea to victual and relieve his army which otherwise will perish, ease the Queen's charge, and secure the chief towns, which is chiefly (and above all other things) to be respected. Supposing the army would land in Munster, in it I would have principal regard of Cork, Limerick, and Waterford, in either of which cities I wish there might be a strong garrison of three thousand foot and three hundred horse, one thousand foot more to be dispersed for some poorer places must be kept, so that the Queen's forces should consist of ten thousand foot and one thousand horse. The rest of the kingdom (where the Spaniards are not) may be held in awe with some garrisons upon them as now they are. This manner of war, in my conceit, would little or nothing increase the charge the Queen is now at, and in a short time weary both the Spaniards and the Irish.

To make it appear more probable to you that these garrisons will be able to ruin all the country at their pleasures, although the enemy be ever so strong, it cannot be denied but six thousand foot and six hundred horse may be drawn from the garrisons, and yet those left against the Irish and townsmen sufficiently guarded. With such a light army the commander may go where he list, and lodge as near the Spaniard (without harm) as he thinks good; for we have the same advantage upon them that the Irish in lightness have of us, and with such an army (of the Irish) there is no doubt to be made; then it follows that we shall be able to go into every part of the province and retreat at our pleasures. On the contrary, if the Spaniard be strong, and we in his strength fight with him, the event of the battles (being dangerous and uncertain as they are), the loss of one field or one day's disaster would absolutely lose the kingdom; if he come with like numbers as he did last year (which I cannot believe, because the example hath taught him more wit) yet I do not wish that we should presently besiege them; for Kinsale was bought at so dear a rate that while I live I will protest against a winter siege, if it may be avoided. I speak within my compass, I do verily believe that at that siege and after the sickness were got we lost about six thousand men that died.[1] Thus may your Honour see what a fashioned war I conceive to be least in charge and most of use; but for a farther help it will be needful for some of the Queen's ships to be over upon the coast to keep the Spaniard from relief of victuals; and then there is an apparent hope that a Spanish army can not any long time subsist in Ireland, for between us and them, and the swarms of Irish that will draw into Munster, the province will be so harassed that neither the Spaniards nor rebels can avoid starving. I protest unto your Honour I do not project this

---

[1] So when Philip O'Sullivan says that the Queen's army lost 8000 men at Kinsale, he rather underrates than overrates the loss. Add to the 6000 who died, the great numbers who, according to Mountjoy, ran away, and Philip's estimate will seem small. Ten thousand would be nearer the mark. Now Don Juan during that period, as is evident from the foregoing documents, lost only about 2000 men.

manner of a war for any particular respect to myself, hoping thereby to have the managing of it, being unmeet for the lieutenant of the kingdom to be where there is not a royal army in the field to confront an enemy; and therefore, lest I may be mistaken, if the motion be liked let it not be mine. But the reason that leads me to that opinion is, because I am sure it is the easiest war for charge, the surest from hazard, and in the end must prevail. Dated 11 August, 1602.

G. C.

CHAPTER XIV.

Cormock MacDermond escapes—The Castle of Mocrumpe taken and most of the ward put to the sword—O'Sulevan and Tirrell repair with their forces into Muskerry—Cormock MacDermond makes means to be received to Her Majesty's mercy—The reasons that moved the Lord President to accept Cormock's submission.

CORMOCK MACDERMOND being all this time in the Gentleman Porter's custody, and his intended escape (as hath been said) made known to the Lord President, the same also came after to the ears of the Lord Bishop of Cork, who, according to his duty both of a subject and a councillor, acquainted the Lord President with it, who made answer that himself heretofore had intelligence thereof and had seriously admonished the Gentleman Porter to take an extraordinary care of his prisoner; yet, because that could not be too often repeated that can never be too sufficiently learned, he entreated the Bishop that he also, for *abundans cautela non nocet*,[1] would call for Hammon and give him warning to be vigilant and circumspect in his charge, knowing how much it concerned both himself and the State. The Bishop, having performed gravely and pathetically[2] the President's desire, left the execution thereof to his future care. Lastly Dominick Sarsfield,[3] the Queen's Attorney for that province, came to the President upon

---

[1] Too great caution does no harm.   [2] "Pathetically." Good.
[3] The Sarsfield sept were strong for the Crown in these wars.

the same errand, agreeing in all circumstances with former intelligence; whereupon the said officer was again called, the practice revealed to him, and for a perclose commanded to keep him close prisoner in a handlock, either with his own servant or some soldier of especial trust. Notwithstanding all these repetitions and reiterations of warnings, within two days of this last caution being given, namely, upon Michaelmas day, between seven and eight o'clock at night, Cormock, having no other attendant but his trusty servant Maghon Oge O'Lyne, who had broken a window that looked into the street, stripping[1] himself of his clothes, crept in his shirt out of the window, where were divers mantle-men waiting of purpose to receive him. An English woman, coming along the street at the very instant he was creeping forth, perceived his white shirt and thereupon raised the cry. They within the house, hearing the cry, looked for the prisoner, and finding the window open and chamber empty follow the pursuit, but all in vain,

[1] Why he should have stripped himself is not very apparent. Possibly to squeeze the better through the narrow window. The full story of Lord Muskerry's escape is as follows : Owen MacSweeney, one of that Lord's gentlemen, a mere lad, was the person who broke up the window. He also filed through one of the chains which connected the Lord's feet and hands. Meantime six of Lord Muskerry's people were below holding a blanket between them into which he was to fall. When his Lordship got on to the window-sill, nothing could persuade him to take that leap in the dark. Then Owen, for time pressed, took the matter into his own hands and precipitated his Lord by the strong hand. His men received him safely in the blanket and made off with him as fast as they and he could go. The rattling of his chains on the paved streets drew the watchman and a crowd after him. The hue and cry was raised, but the Lord's faithful followers got him safely over the city walls and to a spot where seven swift horses were ready to receive him and them. Swift flight then up the Lee Valley. Cormac being now in rebellion, made a treaty with O'Sullivan Bere. But no oath could bind Cormac, and he was soon back again with Carew.

for he, having the dark night, the town and country to friend, was conveyed over the city walls and so escaped. The President, although infinitely grieved with this unfortunate accident, yet thought it more necessary to prevent future dangers than to lament past disasters, and therefore wrote presently, first to Sir Charles Wilmot (being still before Mocrumpe) that if he could not gain the castle that night he should raise his siege and retreat with his forces the next morning, for nothing was more certain that now, Cormock having escaped, all his followers and dependents, who did infinitely love him, would presently turn rebels, which if they should, and join with Tirrell and Donnell O'Sulevan (as most likely), they would intercept the places and passages between him and Cork, so that he should not be able to retire without great danger and loss. These letters being sent away by a horseman, others were instantly written to the Lord Barry and the Lord Roche that they should make stay of all Cormock's followers and goods that were yet residing in their countries, not suffering either the one or the other to start aside till from himself they should receive farther directions.

Sir Charles was much distracted with this news, being exceedingly sorry to raise his siege before the work was finished, yet purposed to obey his directions, when behold a mere casualty gave him opportunity to effect his desires; for the warders, having killed a pig for their provision, and not having plenty of water to scald the same, were constrained to singe it (as the manner of some countries is) with straw, fern, and such like as they had within the walls. This fire, not carefully regarded, took hold upon a cabin within the bawn adjoining the castle wall, and the thatch thereof, fired and flaming aloft, happened, through a window, to catch hold of certain tallow and such combustible matter within the castle, raging so violently withal that the rebels were constrained to quit it and to make the bawn their last refuge, wherein they had little hope of safety; for they saw the two Captain Harvys, brothers, and Captain Thomas Boys ready to assault it, wherefore, mistrusting that weak defence, which could not be maintained, they resolved to sally and to venture the recovery of the woods adjoining; in which attempt about fifty of them were put to the sword; the rest were but few who, by favour of the dark night, escaped. At length, the violence of the fire being somewhat appeased, all industry was used to make the castle tenable, and a company being left within, well victualled and furnished with all necessaries, the army the next day returned towards Cork. The rumour of Cormock's escape having come to the ears of O'Sulevan Beare and Captain Tirrell, they incontinently drew their forces forth of Kerry and Desmond into the borders of Muskerry to confer and join with Cormock, making no question but their decayed party should receive great strength and encouragement by the Lord of Muskerry, his strong country, and multitude of dependents. The President, both to terrify Cormock and to secure the goods of the subjects in the Lord Roche's country, sent for Sir Samuel Bagnall with his regiment from Limerick to lie upon the confines of Muskerry, not making any other account but to begin a new war, chargeable to Her Majesty, painful to himself, and nothing profitable to the captains or soldiers, the country being already much impoverished with the former siege, the corn destroyed, and the cattle fled into places of greatest strength, when, as it pleased God, contrary to all expectation, to give this turbulent beginning a short and peaceful end, considering that the hopes of Spain began to be desperate and calm; for this Irish escaped Lord, having conferred with Tirrell and his associates, and discerning that they, being very needful and half starved, having been shut up so long within the mountains of Beare and Desmond, required bonaght upon his country, which was grievously wasted already by the English,[1] found the unavoidable ruin and destruction of himself and his followers if he entertained that course; and, secondly, finding the English possessed of all his strongholds, both on the sides and in the very heart of his country; and, lastly, his eldest son then, by the procurement of the President, prisoner in England, and his younger son, with his wife, daughter, and some of his most respected followers close prisoners in Cork, thought it his wisest course to adhere unto the State, if his humble submission might be accepted. Upon this resolution on the twelfth of October he wrote several letters to the Bishop of Cork, to the Chief Justice, and to Captain Taffe, earnestly soliciting each of these that they would become mediators and intercessors in his behalf to the Lord President that license might be granted to him to make his repair to his Lordship, protesting that he would do anything within his power to redeem his former offences. The whole body of the Council adjudging his suit reasonable, the President would not dissent from ther unanimous opinion, and therefore his request was granted. The one-and-twentieth

---

[1] It must be always remembered that English in contemporary parlance and when the civil wars of Ireland are spoken of, means the party of the State, the Royalists.

of October he came to the President and falling upon his knees, humbly, and indeed more passionately than I have seen any, besought Her Majesty's mercy, in no way standing upon his justification, but promising that his future services should deserve her gracious favours; only thus far in modest terms he alleged for his excuse, although he knew his offences great, and himself thereby subject to law, yet that in his heart he still retained the duty of a subject, and therein would remain so long as life and breath should remain within his body. The President and Council, beholding the man, and weighing his words, which proceeded from him not without evident testimony of inward grief and unfeigned sorrow (although peradventure arising like Esau's tears from the sense of his loss more than from conscience and feeling of his folly), thought good, upon advised deliberation, to receive him into Her Majesty's grace and favour; and as you have already heard the motives inducing him to demand it so shall you briefly understand the reasons by the weight and validity whereof the State was persuaded to grant it. First, considering the insupportable loss which he had sustained since his imprisonment in the taking of two castles and the burning of his third castle, wherein, as being the place of his most especial abode, his best movables, whereof he was very well furnished, were consumed and burnt; and also the harvest of his country, between Her Majesty's forces and the rebels (for in the same they had made their abode for a whole month), which was valued, as might be esteemed, at five thousand pounds, which as a just punishment was fallen upon him.

Secondly, it was well weighed, what a help and

courage his combination would have afforded to the rebels if he had obstinately run a rebellious course, for he was at that time the strongest man in followers of any one of the Irish in that province, and his country in strength and fastness equal with the worst part of the same, and that which required no less respect was the situation of his country, reaching even to the walls of Cork, whereby the greatest part of Her Majesty's forces must of necessity have been employed in Muskerry, which would have given great impediment to the prosecution of the service in other parts; whereas by receiving him the war would be removed farther off and the greatest tempest of disturbance avoided; that he was deeply infected and foully stained with manifold treasons was too manifest, yet this difference was made between him and others, that they were in public action professed traitors, and he a juggling traitor; and though he had joined with a foreign enemy, yet not in so heinous a manner as some others; for they solicited strangers to invade the kingdom, but strangers having invaded the kingdom solicited him to partake with them. The three castles before mentioned no doubt were great bridles upon him, and in time, no doubt, would have wrought the effect desired, which was to banish him out of his country. But considering the charge and encumbrance, subject to some loss, that would grow in victualling them, and many lewd and unsettled persons ready to join with him if they had perceived him inclinable to continue a rebel, which might have bred new broils and protracted the wars of Munster *in infinitum*. Again the benefit that by his prosecution and extirpation might have redounded to Her Majesty was that thereby his land should have escheated unto her, which in the opinion of all wise men would have proved too dear a purchase. Farther, besides his submission and his son, who was a prisoner in England, his second son also, and his Castle of Blarney were held as pledges upon him ; and, whereas the Lord Deputy had devised the form of an oath for the northern protectees, he was content to swear and subscribe to the same oath ; and lastly himself, with four of the best barons of Parliament in Munster, were bound in three thousand pounds for his future loyalty and subjection, so that he was bound in heaven and in earth, before God and before man, by law and by nature, and nothing but hell was remaining for his farther assurance.

CHAPTER XV.

The Lord President offers the Lord Deputy to send him of his list one or two regiments—O'Donnell's death—Tirrell's quarter assailed by Sir Samuel Bagnall—The loss on the rebels' part—Tirrell rageth in fury against the inhabitants of Muskerry and retireth into Beare and Desmond—The death of Captain Harvy—Captain Flower succeeded Captain Harvy in the government of Carberry—Cloghan summoned—The Constable's brother hanged, and the castle rendered.

CORMOCK being now reduced, the Lord President wrote to the Lord Deputy signifying him thereof; and withal that, if his Lordship had any use in Connaught for the forces of Munster, he might dispose of one or more of the regiments of the same as he pleased; and he also certified him that one called James Blake, of Galway, lately arrived from Spain, constantly affirmed that O'Donnell was dead, both which pieces of news you may believe were welcome to the Lord Deputy.

The morning immediately following the day of his submission, which was the two-and-twentieth of October, Sir Samuel Bagnall, placed, as you have heard, with a regiment of foot and one hundred horse on the borders of Muskery, had occasion of service by this means. Tirrell, with eight hundred foot and forty horse, was still remaining in the westernmost confines of Muskerry, environed with such fastness of woods and bogs that he thought himself secure. The cause of his stay was that he expected the return of

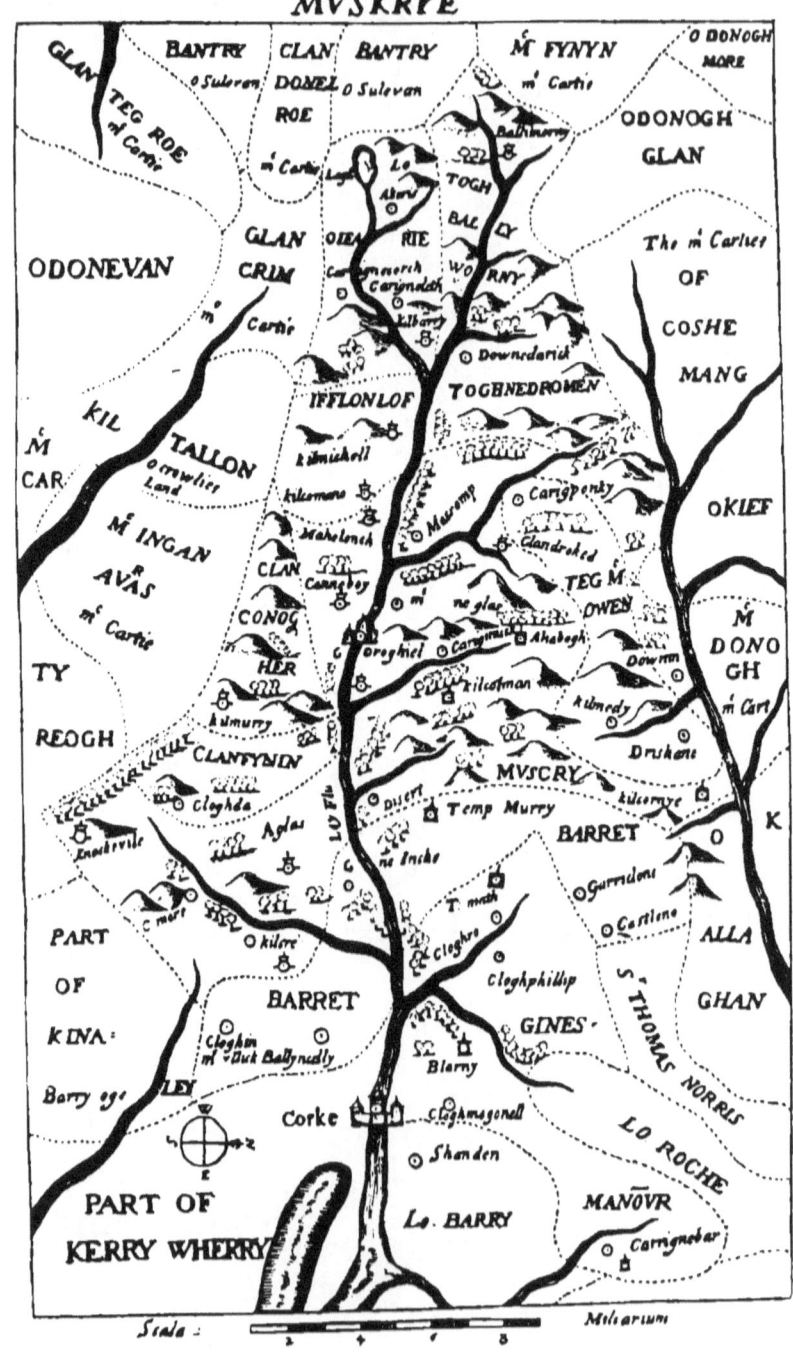

Cormock, by whom he made account to be waged, for Cormock indeed had not acquainted him with his intent of submission. Sir Samuel Bagnall, therefore, conjecturing that so soon as he should hear of this Lord of Muskerry becoming a subject he would retire to his old haunt in the mountains of Beare and Desmond, thought the time now or never to do service upon this light-footed enemy, and therefore he called upon Owen MacTeg of the Drisshan, one of the MacCartys of Muskerry (whom the President had appointed to attend his directions), and requested him, in the edge of the evening, to make trial if he could go unperceived to Tirrell's camp and bring him word in what place and in what manner the rebels were lodged. This Owen MacTeg very willingly and faithfully performed his employment, and about midnight returned and reported that he had found the rebels secure, as he imagined, from all fear or suspicion, and he would undertake to conduct and guide the forces directly to their camp. Upon this intelligence it was not long before Sir Samuel and his companies were all in arms. Disposing them into two bodies, Captain Sidley (who had the point) had five and twenty out of every company, with officers proportionable for his numbers, and Sir Samuel himself, with the rest, marched close up after them, and the horse came in the rear, for the night was dark and the way deep and woody. In this manner they held on till they came so near to the rebels' quarters that they might discern their fires. Then they made halt and sent Owen MacTeg, with his cousin Owen O'Lough, one of the MacSwynes, to discover whether they could perceive any stirring amongst them, and to descry more particularly the manner of their encamping.

They, gathering courage by the countenance of the army, which approached so near that precisely viewed every part thereof, and returning to the colonel certified him that they were lodged in three quarters, a little distant one from the other; at their back a strong wood, before their face a main bog half a mile broad, and on either side cragged and rocky mountains. The colonel therefore directed Captain Sidley with the vanguard to divide his troops and to give on upon all the three quarters at one instant, and commanded the sergeant-major, Captain William Power, and Captain Bostock with the battle to be his seconds; and to make good their undertakings himself marched in the rear, a very small distance from them. And because there was no ground for the horse to serve in near the camp they were commanded to attend Captain Minshaw, lieutenant of the President's horse troop, upon the farther side of the bog, to intercept them in their flight. These forces marshalled into this order, the foot were come up within less than a furlong of the rebels' quarter, and no doubt had surprised them unperceived if a piece by mischance had not fired by the stumbling of one of the new supplies, which giving the alarm, some of them drew speedily into arms; yet our men killed eight of them in the place; Tirrell ran away in his shirt, leaving both his garments and weapons behind him, and his wife followed no better clothed. Our men got fifty horses and hackneys, one thousand cows, sheep and garrans, a great store of arms and baggage, and that which seldom hath been seen in Irish spoils—some remnants of velvet, holland, gold and silver lace, English apparel of satin and velvet, and some quantity of Spanish coin. Amongst the rest there was a portmanteau found by the soldiers, wherein Tirrell's Spanish money was confessed to have been, but they that got it had more wit than to proclaim it in the market-place. But whosoever sweetened their mouths with these Spanish drugs, sure I am that the soldiers came all with good courage well pleased to Cork, except only seventeen who were hurt in the skirmish. All our captains and commanders deserved well, and particularly Captain Minshaw, who had his horse slain under him, and was wounded with a pike. Tirrell, finding himself to have sustained this irrecoverable loss of men, money, clothes, and arms, and hearing withal that Cormock was with the President at Cork imagining that this plot had been contrived by him in revenge of this defeat wreaked his anger upon divers churls and poor people in those fastnesses, first burning their corn and cabins, and afterwards putting them to the sword, wherein he little offended the State, these being only such as had fled from the garrisons into those fastnesses because they would not be subject to law; and this was towards the latter end of October. Tirrell, having found by this woeful experience that the fastness of Muskery could not secure him from the pursuit of the English, retired into his old lurking dens in Beare and Desmond, not fearing but that he might quietly spend the remainder of this winter in those desolate parts, and the rather because he committed no outrage upon the subjects adjoining.

The President, perceiving their resolution, being now freed from the cloud he formerly conceived of foreign invasion, and knowing them to be much discouraged and out of heart by reason of their late overthrow, which now was past hope to be recovered, either by Spain or Cormock, thought it a fit time in these respects to make a speedy prosecution, foreseeing that the former good fortune, effectually pursued, might strike a good stroke to break the heart of the rebellion in Munster; towards the effecting whereof he incontinently resolved to environ them with garrisons; but the difficulties that encountered him in this business were many and great: the long ways, being nearly fourscore English miles from Cork to Beare, the plains so deep and boggy, the mountains so rough and craggy, and the carriage-garrans, that are never strong, were not able to travel six miles a day; and, besides, easterly winds are so rare upon this coast that it would take a long time to transport their victuals and munitions by sea. Notwithstanding, wading through all those inconveniences with industrious travel and laborious diligence, he had planted Sir Charles Wilmot with one regiment at Donkerran, Sir Richard Percy at Kinsale, Captain George Flower, the sergeant-major, at Bantry, and Captain Roger Harvy at Baltimore. But the present service received no small prejudice by means of the untimely departure of Captain Roger Harvy, whose heart, being overwhelmed with an inundation of sorrows and discontentments taken, though on my conscience not willingly given, by one who had been his honourable friend, became blown like a bladder, as the surgeons reported, and was no longer able to minister heat to the vital parts, and therefore he yielded to that irresistible fate which at last overtaketh all mortal creatures. The untimely death of this young gentleman was no small occasion of grief to the Lord President, not only that nature had conjoined them in the nearest degrees of consanguinity, but because his timely beginnings gave apparent demonstration that his continual proceedings would have given comfort to his friends, profit to his country, and a deserved advancement of his own fortunes. Great were the services which these garrisons performed, for Sir Richard Percy and Captain George Flower, with their troops, left neither corn, nor horn, nor house unburnt between Kinsale and Ross. Captain Roger Harvy, who had with him his brother, Captain Gawen Harvy, Captain Francis Slingsby, Captain William Stafford with their companies, and also the companies of the Lord Barry and the Treasurer, with the President's horse, did the like between Ross and Bantry.

Not many days after the death of Captain Roger Harvy, Captain George Flower, having the charge of Baltimore and the commanding of the garrisons thereabouts, which formerly were under Harvy's direction, understanding that the Castle of Cloghan was guarded by the rebels, and that in the same there was a Romish priest lately come from Rome, taking with him Captain Francis Slingsby and Captain William Stafford with their companies of foot, besides his own, marched to it, in hope to gain it, the rather because he had in his hands one called Donnell Dorrogh, a traitor, brother to the constable that had the charge thereof. Upon his summons they refused to yield. Then he told the word that if the constable did not presently render the castle to him, he would hang his brother in their sight. They said the constable was gone abroad (but therein they said untruly, as afterwards was proved). In conclusion, to save the priest (whose life they tendered), they persevered obstinately not to yield; whereupon Captain Flower, in their sight, hanged the constable's brother. Nevertheless, within four days afterwards, the priest, being shifted away in safety, the constable sued for a protection and rendered the castle to Captain Flower. I relate this incident to the end the reader may the more clearly see in what reverence and estimation these ignorant, superstitious Irish hold a Popish priest, in regard of whose safety the constable was content to suffer his brother to perish.

CHAPTER XVI.

A branch of a letter from the Lords of the Council to the Lord President—The ensigns of magistracy re-delivered to the Corporation of Kinsale—Of Spaniards defeated at Kinsale in the time of King Richard the Second—The rising-out of the country committed to the charge of the Lord Barry—The Lord Deputy requires the Lord President to meet him at Galway—Sir George Thornton appointed to join the Lord Barry—A messenger from the rebel Tirrell to the Lord President, and his answer—The Knight of Kerry defeated—The Knight of Kerry, Thomas Oge, and O'Sulevan More's son make their submission—A foul murder committed by O'Sulevan More's son.

THE Lords of the Council, by the letters dated the sixteenth of December, signified their pleasures to the President: That in regard Florence MacCarty was a prisoner in the Tower, his children, to avoid Her Majesty's charges, should be set at liberty, and also the children-pledges of others, except the President saw cause to the contrary, to be enlarged; that Her Majesty was pleased that the President should deliver to the corporation of Kinsale their charter and other ensigns of magistracy, and to impose upon them, instead of a fine, the rebuilding of their walls, at their own charges, and certain workmen towards the finishing of the fort of Castle ny Park; that Her Majesty was pleased at the President's request that a fair and strong house should be built for the President, where he thought it convenient, to be defrayed upon the fines and casualties of the province;

that the fort of Haulbowlin should be presently finished; lastly, thanks in Her Majesty's name for his services, liking well his proceedings with Cormock MacDermond, the courses he had taken in his return from Donboy, the well disposing of the garrisons, his raising and making fortifications, etc.

By this letter it appears that the President was directed to re-deliver to the burgesses of Kinsale their charter and other ensigns of magistracy, among which was a fair large standard of damask with the arms of England on it. This standard was first delivered to them (by command of King Henry the Eighth) by Sir George Carew, the Lord President's cousin-german, when he arrived at Kinsale, who, not long before the siege of Boulogne, was admiral of some of the King's ships. In the hands of Sir George it was left in safe keeping when the Spaniards arrived there, and by the same Sir George Carew, by Queen Elizabeth's command, it was (as is said) re-delivered to them again. Although this petty note may seem to some scarce worth relating, yet for the rareness of the incident I thought it meet to be remembered; and that the reader may also understand what a fatal place Kinsale hath been to the Spaniards in former times, as well as now, I think it not impertinent to relate what happened to them in that port in anno 1380, and the fourth year of the reign of King Richard the Second. My author is Thomas of Walsingham, who lived in those days, and thus Englished in Hollinshed:—

"In this meanwhile that the Earl of Buckingham was passing through the realm of France, the French and Spanish galleys did much mischief on the coast

of England, but about the latter end of June, by a
fleet of Englishmen of the West countries, part of
them were forced to retire, and take harbour in a
haven in Ireland called Kinsale, where, being assailed
by the Englishmen and Irishmen, they were vanquished, so that to the number of four hundred were
slain, and their chief captains taken, as Gonzales de
Vorse and his brother, Martin de Motrigo, Turgo,
Lord of Morrans; also the Lord of Reath, Peers
Martin of Vermew, John Moditt of Vermew, the
Seneschall of Wargarie, the Seneschall of Saint
Andrews, Cornelis of Saint Sebastiano, Paschale de
Biskaya, John Martinez, Sopogorge of Saint Sebastiano, and divers others. There were taken four of
their barges, with a ballenger, and one and twenty
English vessels recovered, which they had robbed and
taken away from their owners. There escaped yet
four of their notable captains from the hands of our
men: Martin Grantz, John Perez Mantago, John
Husce Gitario, and one Garcia of Sebastiano."

Thus far Hollinshed, craving the reader's patience,
for to some this old story may seem to be a needless
curiosity. But to proceed.

The President, to make the speedier prosecution
and expedition in the affairs of the province, caused
the rising-out of the country to be assembled to the
number of sixteen hundred, at their own charges,
under the conduct of the Lord Barry. These provincial forces were not prepared for any great need
that was of their service; it was thought meet to
draw as many hands together as conveniently might
be, who, according to their manner, for spoil's sake
would not spare their dearest friends. And also it
was thought no ill policy to make the Irish draw

blood one upon another, whereby their private quarrels might advance the public service. The President had first determined himself in person with five hundred English, joined to the provincials, to have taken the field; but his intentions were casually diverted by letters from the Lord Deputy, who, signifying that his Lordship purposed to be at Galway about the two-and-twentieth of December, required him (all other business set apart) immediately to repair thither to consult about certain affairs much importing the service of the State, by reason whereof the President appointed Sir George Thornton with 500 English soldiers, inhabitants as Undertakers in Munster, to accompany the Lord Barry with the provincials, and all these to meet together, about the twentieth of this present, at Donkerran, which was the place of their rendezvous.

In the meantime the rebel Tirrell, not liking to stay any longer in the air of Munster, wherein he had run many dangers, bethought himself of a retreat out of the province, hoping that the President would condescend to any composition rather than be troubled with his company, whereupon he sent his intimate servant, Laghlin O'Dally (before mentioned in this discourse), to Cork, who, coming to the President, told him that his captain (meaning Tirrell) would be co tent to leave the province, and would after this, so as he might have a pardon, a pension, and a company of foot in Her Majesty's pay, serve the Queen and deserve the reward demanded by his future services. The President, knowing that for want of food he would be forced ere the spring of the year to depart, and also assuring himself within that time to get some good draught to be drawn upon him by some of the provincial rebels, who, now being heartbroken, would do anything for their pardons or for a little money, not only rejected his offers, but bid O'Dalley tell him that although he were ever so wary, yet he doubted not before long to have his head sent to him in a bag, willing him to forbear to send any more to him.

While these forces aforesaid were gathering, according to the directions afore recited, the Governor of Kerry, losing no opportunity and forbearing no labour, had the like fortune upon the Knight of Kerry that Sir Samuel Bagnall had upon Tirrell; for, being conducted to his quarter in the night, he killed forty of his men and took from him his whole substance, which consisted of five hundred cows, two hundred garrans, and two months' provision of meal and butter for his soldiers, which small spoil was a great loss to the poor Knight; for thereby he, being disfurnished of all his provision and unable to minister entertainment to his followers, and having no castle whereunto he might safely retreat, was constrained, like a wolf, to shelter himself in waste woods and desolate mountains, until he could work means with Sir Charles to accept his humble submission, which incontinently, upon his defeat, he earnestly solicited, by the means of O'Sulevan More. And surely this service was of good consequence for the settling of Kerry; for Thomas Oge, induced by the example of the Knight, and likewise Donnell O'Sulevan, son to the said O'Sulevan More, all jointly submitted themselves, and Her Majesty's protection was granted them. The former performed as much as was promised; but the latter, in the interim that he should have put in sureties for his loyalty, according to a clause inserted in his protection, in the malice of his heart to our nation, committed a most base and traitorous murder upon a sergeant and ten soldiers going after Sir Charles towards Donkerran, who, not suspecting any false measure at his hands, being protected, were most cruelly butchered by that inhuman perjured rebel. His father, old O'Sulevan, conceived so great discontentment against him for this damnable fact that he threatened to withdraw from him his favour, his blessing, and birthright. But of this sufficient.

CHAPTER XVII.

Sir Charles Wilmot Chief Commander of the forces in the absence of the Lord President—The rebels make three divisions of their forces—Tirrell, afraid, flies the province—The Lord Barry and Sir George Thornton join their forces with Sir Charles Wilmot—A skirmish entertained—A prey taken from the rebels out of the fastness—Divers rebels submitted themselves—William Burke, John O'Connor Kerry, and O'Sulevan Beare with the bonoghs fled out of the province—The rebels' loss in their passage through the County of Cork, and the hard shift they made over the Shannon—The good service done upon the rebels by the Sheriff of the County of Tipperary—Captain Henry Malby slain—Beare, Bantry, and Dorseys spoiled, and the Castles of Ardea and Carrigness rendered—Captain Taffe employed against the rebels in Carberry—The Pope's vicar slain and the rebels defeated—The Cartys of Carberry submit themselves to the Lord President.

THE Lord Barry and Sir George Thornton were now upon their third march towards their rendezvous at Donkerran, there to attend the directions of Sir Charles Wilmot, who in the President's absence (for by this time he was upon his way to Galway) commanded all that army in chief, composed of the garrison of Kerry, and of the garrisons of Bantry, Kinsale, Baltimore, etc., aforementioned, who with great valour and discretion discharged the same. The rebels, understanding by continual advertisement of the great preparations made to rouse and hunt them out of their fastness, thought fit in their councils to divide themselves in three several parts, to the intent that Her Majesty's forces, then united, might likewise be severed and divided in several prosecutions, whereby each party might be the less endangered; for if the English should neglect any one part of them they might harass and spoil the subject, for whose defence a good part of the army must be withdrawn. This resolution being taken, O'Sulevan Beare and William Burke with seven hundred men were appointed to remain in Beare, other four hundred were appointed for Carberry, to be commanded by Sir Owen MacCarty's sons, and the third division, which was five hundred strong, and commanded by Captain Tirrell, were to go with the Lord FitzMaurice into Kerry. But Tirrell, being upon his pretended march for Kerry, fearing to run so hard a fortune, suddenly altered his former determinations; and, notwithstanding that he had lately received a great impress of Spanish money from O'Sulevan Beare, and farther he promised to him 1500 more in good reals of plate and one thousand cows to stay with him but three months longer, resolved with all possible expedition to leave the province, and therefore acquainting the Lord Fitz-Maurice with his intention, without farther consultation, giving a deaf ear to any contrary persuasions, leaving all his carriages, sick men, and other impediments behind him, he set forward[1] on his hasty journey, and never looked back till he came into O'Carrel's country, which is from the mountain of Slewlogher, where he began his march, no less than sixty Irish miles; and this his departure was the same day that our forces should meet at their rendez-

---

[1] Tyrrell, a brave soldier, must have been by this time thoroughly disgusted with the Munster lords.

vous, whose defection from the rest made the work in hand much more easy to be effected.

Our forces under the Lord Barry and Sir George Thornton met with Sir Charles Wilmot upon the seven-and-twentieth of December. The thirtieth we encamped in Glangarrem,[1] on a plot of dry ground (environed with woods and bogs) of so small capacity that most of our guards and sentinels were held either on the bog or in the edge of the wood, and yet there was not so much firm ground together within five miles of that place. Within two miles thereof encamped Donnell O'Sulevan and William Burke with his bonaghts. Before the camp was settled, the rebels entertained a skirmish for an hour's space, and hurt three of our men, whereof Captain Stafford's lieutenant, William Jeffries, was one. The same night they gave us an alarm and poured into our quarter a volley of shot; but, being encountered by our guards adjoining, were repulsed and driven into the wood.

The one-and-thirtieth, a convoy was sent to Donkerran for victuals; and the same day Sir Charles Wilmot sent four hundred of the risings-out under the command of Captain John Barry, and two hundred of the army in list under the command of Thomas Selby, Lieutenant to Captain Francis Slingsby, to beat the fastness where the rebels with their cartel lodged. Their quarter was entered by our men, and their cartel seized, whereupon ensued a bitter fight, maintained without intermission for six hours; nevertheless they kept the prey they had got; the enemy not leaving their pursuit until they came in sight of the camp, for whose relief two regiments

[1] Glengariffe. Not a word of its beauty.

were drawn forth, to give countenance, and Downings, lieutenant to Sir Francis Barkley, was sent with one hundred and twenty choice men to the succour of Barry and Selby, who in the rear were so hotly charged by the rebels that they came to the sword and pike, and the skirmish continued till night parted them. Many were slain on either side, but the greatest loss fell upon the traitors. There were taken from them in that day's service, 2000 cows, 4000 sheep, and 1000 garrans.

Immediately upon this defeat, many of the country that escaped, leaving the rebels, having before lost all their goods, submitted themselves to the Governor and obtained mercy. Hugh MacSwine and Owen Grayne, with eighty of their followers and other of the bownoghs, likewise became suitors for Her Majesty's protection, which, to weaken the adverse party, was also granted; whose revolt, or rather return, so disturbed and distracted William Burke, the chief commander of O'Sulevan's forces, that he endeavoured, by assaulting them on their way to Sir Charles, to resist their submission, wherein some men were lost; and, not prevailing in the same, purposed to follow the steps of Tirrell his forerunner, and therefore wished O'Sulevan Beare either instantly to rise with him or else to shift for himself as well as he could, for a longer stay in those parts could promise him nothing but apparent ruin and destruction. And when the other urged the entertainment that he had given to him and his company beforehand, Burke answered that he had already lost, not that only which of him was received, but whatsoever else he either brought into the province or gained therein, besides the slaughter of many of his followers and near kinsmen, whom he prized and valued [1] (in his affection) above all the King of Spain's treasure; and therefore with extreme passion (as was reported) cursing and damning himself for staying so long in Munster, in all haste with two hundred men (for the rest were either slain or protected) he fled and followed Captain Tirrell into O'Carrel's country. O'Sulevan, finding his estate desperate, that either he must starve in Munster or beg in Ulster, made choice of the less evil, and therefore himself and John O'Connor Kerry kept company with the bonoughs, content to partake with their fortunes till he might get to Tyrone.[2]

As they passed by the skirts of Muskerry they were skirmished with by the sons of Teg MacOwen Carty,[3] where they lost some of their men and most of their carriage. In passing by Liscarcell, John Barry, brother to the Viscount, with eight horsemen and forty foot, charged their rear at the ford of Bellaghan, where he slew and hurt many of them, and of his part one horseman was slain.

When they came to the river Shannon, they, finding the river high and no boats or troughs

[1] A touch of nature and reality. The mutual affection and fidelity of the chief and his chosen followers were indeed very great. Of the chief and his clan that cannot be said, for the clan teemed with malcontents. William Burke was a chieftain without land.

[2] Of O'Sullivan Bere's heroic retreat into the North there is a very animated account in the *Historia Hiberniæ* by his kinsman, Philip O'Sullivan, who derived his information from the men who partook in it.

[3] While he was in rebellion O'Sullivan had committed many spoils and devastations on this lord. But indeed O'Sullivan was attacked by every lord through whose territory he fled. This, observe, was not the retreat of a clan. The clan were now Queen's people under the sons of Sir Owen O'Sullivan. It was the retreat of a foiled chieftain, guarded by his faithful bonoughs or hired warriors.

to pass them over into Connaught, killed many of their horses, and made shift with their hides to make certain little boats, called in Irish *nevogs*, in which they transported their men and baggage. Nevertheless, before all had passed the river, the Sheriff of the county of Tipperary fell upon their rear and slew many of them. Being in Connaught they passed safely through the County of Galway until they came into the Kelly's country, where they were fought with by Sir Thomas Burke, the Earl of Clanricard's brother, and Captain Henry Malby, who were more in number than the rebels. Nevertheless, when they saw that either they must make their way by the sword or perish, they gave a brave charge[1] upon our men, in which Captain Malby was slain, upon whose fall Sir Thomas and his troops, fainting with the loss of many men, studied their safeties by flight, and the rebels with little harm marched into O'Rwyke's[2] country.

The next morning, being the fourth of January, 1602, Sir Charles, coming to seek the enemy in their camp, entered into their quarter without resistance, where he found nothing but hurt and sick men, whose pains and lives by the soldiers were both determined.[3] The Governor sent the Lord

---

[1] The battle was won by O'Sullivan against great odds, mainly through his own valour, skill, and presence of mind. The field of battle was Aughrim.

[2] Brian of the Battle-Axes, referred to in Preface. This lord was not now at ease in his mind. A Queen's O'Rourke had arisen in Leitrim who in the end conquered and expelled him. This Queen's O'Rourke was Cathal, son of the late chieftain and the Lady Mary Burke, sister of Ulick, Earl of Clanricarde. Brian was illegitimate. When he seized upon O'Rourkeland, Cathal was a boy at school, Master White's school, in Limerick.

[3] As Irish history is usually written, this horrible atrocity would be set down to "the English." But observe Wilmot's force con-

Barry with some of his light foot after them, but all in vain, for they flew so swift with the wings of fear that passing by many preys directly in the way they never made so much stay as to molest either the cattle or their keepers.

Hereupon Sir Charles, with the English[1] regiments, overran all Beare and Bantry, destroying all that he could find meet for the relief of his men, so that that country was wholly wasted. He also sent Captain Fleming with his pinnace and certain soldiers into O'Sulevan's island.[2] He took there certain boats and an English bark which O'Sulevan had got

---

sisted mainly of the rising-out of the County of Cork, the 1600 provincials already referred to, under the leading of Lord Barry, and 500 English "inhabitants in Mounster as Undertakers." So in an army of 2100 men less than a fifth are stated to have been English.

Now as to the 500 so-called English "inhabitants of Mounster as Undertakers." The Undertakers had but recently returned to their estates. Therefore they simply had not had time to plant them with English tenants. When the Undertakers first settled in Munster it was years before any of them could get over a few English families. When a great Undertaker had *twelve* such, he seemed to consider that he had done a wonderful feat in the way of transportation and settlement. Now all the Undertakers were assessed each at so many soldiers. They too in times of trouble had to rise-out with their forces. The recently returned Undertakers ·could no more have furnished 500 armed men out of their English tenants than they could fly in the air. Their 500 were nearly all Irish, but being under the direct and immediate control of Englishmen, are written of by Stafford, who could not delay for nice distinctions, as English. Moreover in this he was but following contemporary parlance. The regular soldiers of a Royalist army are always spoken of as English, being under English discipline and the direct control of State-appointed men. The rest of Wilmot's force consisted of the regular companies, which were mostly or altogether Irish.

[1] Observe again the loose use of the word English. So on the other side P. O'Sullivan always calls a Royalist force, "English." And in this very context it was, according to him, an "*Anglus exercitus*" which invaded and devastated Bere. This method has its conveniences, but leads to distracted views about Anglo-Irish history.

[2] Dursey Island.

and kept for his transportation into Spain when he should be forced there. They took also thence certain cows and sheep, which were reserved there as in a sure storehouse, and put the churls to the sword [1] who inhabited therein. The warders of the castles of Ardea and Carrickness, on the sixth of the same month, despairing of their master O'Sulevan's return, rendered both their castles and their lives to the Queen's mercy; so that although he should have *animum revertendi* he had neither place of safety whereto he might retire nor corn or cattle to feed himself, much less to uphold or renew any war against the State.

The sharpness of this winter journey exceedingly weakened our companies; for the mountains of Beare, being at that time quite covered with snow, tasted [2] the strong bodies, whereby many turned sick, and some, unable to endure the extremity, died standing sentinel.

But whilst this service was in prosecution in Beare the President, on his journey towards the Lord Deputy, chanced to meet with some of the country risings-out, to the number of four hundred foot or thereabouts, that came short of the rest that were under the commands of the Lord Barry and Sir George Thornton; and understanding that the son of Sir Owen MacCarty, and Donnogh Reugh, brother to Florence MacCarty, were retired with their crets and

---

[1] This was that terrible massacre already referred by Philip O'S., in which some 300 of his father's tenants, men, women and children, were slaughtered. The island was assailed twice by Carew's people, once during the siege of Dunboy and again now. Philip, who was something of a literary artist, combines the two events into a single picture.

[2] I suggest as an emendation, "wasted the strongest bodies."

followers into the strengths of Carberry, his Lordship commanded Captain Taffe, with the said risings-out, forty of Sir Edward Wingfield's company, and his own troop of horse, to draw into those parts and to endeavour the best service he could upon them, whilst the rest were busied by the Governor of Kerry in Desmond as aforesaid, wherein it pleased God to give him good success, for on the fifth of January his foot, entering their fastness, took a prey of two or three hundred cows and garrans. The rebels, in pursuit of their cattle, gave them so brave a charge that they were disordered, whereby some of them were slain, which Captain Taffe perceiving, being at the head of his horse troop, in the skirt of the fastness, and espying some of their horsemen doing much hurt upon our foot, charged them into the wood, slew four of their horsemen, and put all the rest to rout, wherewith our men, being encouraged, pursued them. Owen MacEggan, the Pope's Apostolic Vicar so often before mentioned, to put fresh heart into his company, with his sword drawn in one hand, and his portius[1] and beads in the other, with one hundred men led by himself, came boldly up to the sword and maintained a hot skirmish until he was slain with a shot, whereupon his men (together with a fresh charge of our horse) were so amazed and terrified, partly by his death and partly by their own danger, that they broke instantly, and, for better expedition throwing away their arms, leaped into the river Bandon, hoping by that means to escape; but that little availed them, for they all

---

Recall how Archer's "portace" and sword were captured by Carew in the battle of Castle Dermot. The portace was a handbag.

for the most part were either killed or drowned in the river. There were slain in this service, besides Owen MacEggan, who was of more worth than all the rest, above one hundred and twenty rebels, and of the provincial rising-out, of our part, a good number lost their lives, and many of Captain Taffe's horses were hurt. We got the arms of 140, and all their horses, cows, sheep, and garrans that were in the country near adjoining. There was also taken a Papist priest, being, as it seemed, a chaplain to Mac-Eggan, whom the President, shortly after, caused to be executed in Cork.

Upon this discomfiture the Cartys, who formerly had been petitioners to the President for protection, but denied, became suitors to Captain Taffe in the like, who not knowing of the good success that the Governor had against the other rebels (according to direction before given him by the President that he should accept their submission after a blow given them if it were humbly sought) granted protection to them and their followers; and, upon the President's return from Galway, Captain Taffe, having them in his company upon the highway, not far from Moyallo, presented them to his Lordship, who, with great show of unfeigned penitence, desired his allowance and acceptation of their submission, who, to gratify the service of Captain Taffe, and to ratify his promise, assented thereto, whereby all Carberry (a very large and spacious country) was wholly reduced to subjection, not one open traitor remaining therein. A principal means of this sudden and universal reduction was the death of that traitorly priest, Owen MacEggan, which doubtless was more beneficial to the State than to have got the head of the most capital rebel in Munster, for the respect that was borne him, by reason of his authority from the Pope, and the credit which he had obtained in Spain, were so great that his power was in a manner absolute over them all, and he only was the cause of their obdurate obstinacy. His dignity, in being the Pope's Vicarius Apostolicus, held them in vassalage to him, and the livings given him in Munster, by the Pope's grant, were to be valued, if he might quietly have enjoyed them, at three thousand pounds per annum. And, farther to engage the Popish clergy of Ireland to him, he had power to dispose at his pleasure of all the spiritual livings in the province of Munster, by which authority, together with the credit he had got with the King of Spain (well testified by the trust committed to him in transporting and disposing of the Spanish money last brought into Ireland), he had obtained in a manner all power, both over the temporality and spirituality of Munster, and to paint him in his true colours, a more malicious traitor against the State and Crown of England never breathed, which well appeared by the barbarous tyranny he exercised upon his own countrymen; for as soon as any prisoners were taken, though of his own country, birth, and religion, yet if they had served the Queen he caused them first, in piety, as he pretended, to be confessed and absolved, and instantly, in his own sight, would he cause them to be murdered, which religious tyranny in him was held for sanctity. The President, upon his return to Cork, employed certain messengers, whom he might trust, into the country to make search in such places as MacEggan usually resided for such books and papers as were belonging to him. Divers books, of school divinity for the most part, were got, all which by the President's gift, fell to my share, and certain papers, amongst which I will only insert three in this present relation ; the first containing large indulgences granted by P. Clement the Eighth, to such of the Irish as should bear arms against God's chosen servant and their anointed Sovereign the Queen's Majesty, the tenor whereof here ensueth : [1]—

[1] See Appendix.

CHAPTER XVIII.

False rumours divulged of the state of Munster—The Lord President sent one thousand foot munitioned and victualled to the Lord Deputy—A letter from Her Majesty to the Lord President concerning the Earl of Clanricard—A letter from John Burke to the Lord President—A letter from John Burke to Sir George Thornton—A certificate from a Popish Bishop in behalf of John Burke.

The President, therefore, as well to debar these stragglers from relief as to prevent all means of succours to O'Sulevan if he should return with new forces, caused all the country of Kerry and Desmond, Beare, Bantry, and Carberry to be left absolutely wasted, constraining all the inhabitants thereof to withdraw their cattle into the east and northern parts of the county of Cork. These things thus effected, his Lordship signified by his letters to the Lords of Her Majesty's Privy Council in England that, although the hearts of the Irish were no less corrupt than heretofore, and that nothing but the sword held over their heads could contain them in subjection, yet would he undertake (God assisting) that no rebellion should arise in the province, except the towns (who grew daily into deeper discontentment by reason of the new standard) should peradventure revolt, which in his judgment was unlikely. About this time it was commonly reported in England by some who had their tongues pointed with slander and their hearts stuffed

with malice that Munster was newly burning with
fresh flames of rebellion, that the Viscount Roche, the
Lord of Cahir, and Cormock MacDermond had entered into open hostility, and that Tirrell was come
again into the province and had taken the prey of
Moyallo from the garrison at noonday. Although the
world may be satisfied concerning these slanderous
reports by that which hath been already delivered, yet
to give more particular satisfaction to all, or to any
that should make question hereof, first the Lord
Roche was never touched with the least spot of disloyalty against Her Majesty, yea such loyal constancy
did he always embrace and practise that in the universal inundation of treasons, when all the province in
general, and his father in particular, combined against
their anointed sovereign, at that time, and ever since,
did he continue himself within the lists of an obedient
subject, so that his Lordship herein was much wronged.
Then for my Lord of Cahir; although it be true
indeed that at first he ran the common fortune of the
rest, and peradventure would do so again if the like
occasion were offered, yet that he ever relapsed since
the President's government is merely false; yea, such
outward obedience hath he professed that he hath
brought to execution some notorious traitors. And as
for Cormock MacDermond, since his submission he
was himself, in person with Sir Charles Wilmot, at
the late service in Glangarue,[1] and lost thirty of his
best men in Her Majesty's service in Carberry with
Captain Taffe. Lastly, for the burning of Moyallo,
there was no rebel that ever durst attempt anything
against that town, or any part of the cattle thereunto
belonging, since the President's first coming into the

[1] Glengariffe.

province, and, to demonstrate the fear that the rebels ever lived in since the siege of Kinsale, I can assure the reader, upon certain knowledge, that all the spoils that the traitors have taken from the subjects, *conjunctim* or *devisim*, do not amount to three hundred cows, but have lived in their strength, spending upon the Spanish wines and their own victuals.

The Lord Deputy, having occasion to employ more forces into Connaught, with the Council of Estate upon the eighteenth of January wrote to the President to pray and require him to spare out of his list of Munster, if he might conveniently do it, one regiment of one thousand foot, with a competent proportion of victuals, which not many days after was accomplished. Also, about this time, the President received a letter from Her Majesty, which, although it concerns the Earl of Clanricard in particular, yet that the reader may inform himself how much that noble gentleman was esteemed (and that worthily) by his sovereign mistress, I think it meet to be related:—

A LETTER FROM HER MAJESTY TO THE LORD PRESIDENT CONCERNING THE EARL OF CLANRICARD.

Your most assured constantly affected Sovereign, E. R.

RIGHT TRUSTY AND WELL-BELOVED,—We greet you well. We need not use many arguments to you when we resolve to recommend either man or matter, seeing you have made so good demonstration of your obedience and entire affection to perform our will and pleasure, much less then the person or causes of this nobleman, our cousin Clanricard,[1] whose carriage

---

[1] Young Clanricarde was a great favourite with the Queen at this moment, as indeed he deserved to be, considering his services. He

here doth challenge our extraordinary good opinion, as his merit there procured your own plentiful testimony of the same; even when all trees did show what fruits they bear: his coming over was to do his duty to us, where he was desirous (as other noblemen have done) to have stayed some time, unless some occasion for our service should necessarily require his return: of which kind, because the one has presented itself, by the going of our deputy into that province, where his possessions lie, and that the weak state of his mother likewise falleth out to be such that (if Almighty God should call her before the same were better settled) many inconveniences might fall to the house by his absence, he is now returned with as much expedition as he can. And therefore we do (as to one of our principal Councillors in that State) recommend him to you to be furthered and assisted in all his occasions, wherein as we know that public trial which he hath made of himself (to the honour of the nobility of that kingdom) whereof so many scandalous rumours have been spread, only to invite our enemies under that opinion of their ill affection, both hath, and will invite you to love him, so we do think that we have missed our marks in George, if he shall not have the best fruits which either your public credit or private friendship may afford, whomsoever we shall recommend as now we do this nobleman (besides his public desert) for many other constant

was very handsome, and thought to resemble the late Earl of Essex. Let the reader remember that, once upon a time, the Queen's officers were hunting him through Connaught like a wolf. Yesterday a wolf, to-day a pillar of the State, perhaps to-morrow a wolf again. Such was life then. Just now at all events the wolf is "our cousin Clanricarde," and even something more, for a melancholy flirtation was on foot, on which the young Earl's friends built high hopes.

professions of his humble and reverent affections towards ourself. Let this therefore suffice for him, and for yourself, of whom we can say no more than heretofore we have done, either of our good opinion of you or of our gracious thanks for all your great and honest services. Given under our Signet at our Palace of Westminster, the seventeenth of December, 1602, in the five-and-fortieth year of our reign.

Now although the present state of this province promised a present reduction and future quiet, yet to make it appear that the false hearts of the superstitious Irish were in no way addicted and inclined thereunto, omitting many instances that I might remember, I will recite only certain particulars concerning John Burke,[1] a gentleman of the county of Limerick, of whom we have spoken before in the beginning of the first book, who much grieved (as it should seem) that their expectations had been frustrated concerning Spanish hopes, this last summer would therefore take a journey to the Court of Spain, as a general agent to solicit the King for supplies against the next spring; and, therefore, suddenly leaving his wife (who was one of Sir George Thornton's daughters) and family, about the middle of December last fled to the rebels' camp, not doubting but from them to be furnished with all necessaries for his employment. At his departure he left certain letters with his wife to be delivered to the President and Sir George Thornton, his father-in-law, declaring his intention for a journey into Spain, but to disguise his treasons he made religion a mask by pretending a

[1] This was the gentleman who *walked* upon his knees when Carew would not see him.

pilgrimage to Saint James of Compostella and Rome; but that his dissembling may the better appear, I will set down the words of his own letters written to the Lord President and Sir George.

A Letter from John Burke to the Lord President.

If you remember, Right Honourable and my very good Lord, the first time I met your Honour how desirous I was to forsake the world and to follow the service of God, from which determination I was, through the weakness of my spirit, restrained by the simple persuasions of certain of my friends; since which time I have been so enamoured with the world that I did not spare to walk in all the ways where he led me, either of envy, malice, deceit, flattery or falsehood, as I doubt not but your Lordship in some degree noted, when through envy and hatred I have, to procure their deaths, accused Lord Burke and others of certain articles of treason, and now being bound to satisfaction I acknowledge mine error in speaking evil of my neighbours. I have as I said by all means to curry favour with the world, so that by seeking to make myself a friend unto the world I was thereby made an enemy unto God, but, being now called to repentance by the especial grace of God, I have vowed to go to the pilgrimage of Rome and Saint James, and do assure your Lordship that I will carry always as faithful a disposition to the State of England (to whom I wish all honour, dignity, and prosperity) as any other of my calling, and do desire your Lordship not to believe anything which should be said to the contrary. I have left the little lands and goods which

I had with my wife, and do desire your Lordship to maintain her in the same until my coming. I would never come amongst these fellows but for fear my friends would persuade your Lordship not to grant me your passport to go. But now, seeing it pleased your Lordship to grant me Her Majesty's protection, I will remove from this company, desiring your Lordship to send me your passport to go this pilgrimage, which I will expect near Cork. And now, taking my leave with your Lordship, I rest,

Your Lordship's loving friend,

JOHN BURKE.

A LETTER FROM JOHN BURKE TO SIR GEORGE THORNTON.

Right worshipful, and my very loving Father, for that I know you would be much troubled in mind to think what should move me to depart thus from my wife, friends, and lands, I thought good to tell you the very truth, which I desire you without any scruple to believe; I have taken upon me to be a pilgrim for the space of two years. First, I must visit Saint Jago in Spain, and thence to Rome. I have sought letters of favour from certain priests in this country to their fellows beyond the seas. You nor my Lord President may not think that I go to procure any mischief to the English State, to which I should be more willing to do good than able to do harm. I do not now speak unto you in the spirit of flattery or fear, falsehood or deceit, or for any worldly policy; I speak before God, and God knoweth that I speak the truth; I do not go with any intent to harm any person, but only to do judgment upon myself for a satisfaction unto God for my sins. The little living I have I do leave with my wife, which and herself do leave to your fatherly care. And so I rest,

Your son,[1]
JOHN BURKE.

Some man peradventure giving credit to these colourable protestations would persuade himself that this professed pilgrimage was the true and only end of his journey, and so should I were not these vizards dismasked, and these frauds detected, by certain letters from sundry priests and Popish clergymen, found and conveyed to the President. I will not trouble the reader with needless transcripts of these several letters; I will only relate one or two, which may apparently convince his deep dissembling, written from a Popish bishop.[2]

If then as in a former letter he took upon him this journey to make himself an expert soldier, whereby he might prove in time a champion and ornament to his country, or if the allegation of the latter may be credited, namely, that he hath business with the King of Spain about affairs of great moment and consequence for the good of this nation, then are his own pretexts of religion, vows, and pilgrimages, devised only for a blind to conceal his traitorous complots. To prevent therefore such mischiefs as might grow unto the State from his solicitations in Spain, the President was content that Sir George Thornton should send a messenger to him, being then in the rebels' camp, to revoke and recall him, if it were possible, from this irreligious expedition, which at last was effected by the persuasions which his mother, wife, and friends used to him.

[1] Son-in-law. [2] See Appendix.

CHAPTER XIX.

The Lord Deputy sent to the Lord President for men and munition, and himself to repair to him—The list of Her Majesty's forces in Munster—Sir Edward Wingfield sent by the Lord President with five hundred foot into Connaught—The Lord of Lixnaw defeated by Captain Boys—The Castle of Kilco taken by Captain Flower—The Castle of Berengarry taken by Sir Charles Wilmot—Sir Charles Wilmot and Sir George Thornton left by the Lord President Joint Commissioners for the government of Munster—A letter sent by the Lord President from the Lord Deputy to the Lords of the Council.

THE Lord Deputy, understanding now in what state the province of Munster stood, directed letters to the President requiring of him that if necessary occasions of present service did not forbid he would send to Athlone, for the war of Connaught, certain foot companies and a proportion of victuals from Limerick, so much as from Her Majesty's store there might conveniently be spared, and withal to repair himself to Dublin, whence he was to take his journey into England. The list of Munster consisted at that time of horse and foot as followeth :—

THE LIST OF MUNSTER AS IT STOOD.
Of Horse.

Lord President	100
Earl of Thomond.	50
Captain William Taffe.	50
	200

Of Foot.

Lord President	200
Earl of Thomond	200
Lord Audley	150
Sir Charles Wilmot	150
Sir Richard Percy	150
Sir Francis Barkley	150
Sir George Thornton	100
Captain Francis Kingsmill	100
Captain George Kingsmill	100
Captain George Flower	100
Captain Charles Coote	100
Captain Gawen Harvy	100
Captain Thomas Boyce	100
Captain Francis Slingsby	100
Captain William Stafford	100
	1900

Although there was never weary mariner in a violent and tempestuous storm more desirous of arriving into his wished harbour, nor a virgin bride, after a lingering and desperate love, more longing for the celebration of her nuptial than the Lord President was to go for England, yet was he content to defer his private affections in regard of the public charge committed to him; and, therefore, he first sent for Sir Charles Wilmot out of Kerry, acquainting only him with that journey, because his purpose was, having beforehand had good experience of his sufficiency, to leave him in special trust with the government in his absence. Then he took order for the satisfying of the Lord Deputy's demands, and therefore appointed Sir Edward Wingfield, with five hundred foot, the three-and-twentieth of February to take his journey into Connaught; and, lastly, having taken order how the other forces should be disposed he took his journey from Cork towards Dublin. About the beginning of February, being newly come to Dublin, he received letters from Sir Charles Wilmot that the Lord of Lixnaw, having assembled some two hundred foot and twenty horse in his fastness near Listall, Captain Thomas Boys, left by Sir Charles to command the garrisons in Kerry, drew upon his quarter in the night, killed eighty of his men, took all his substance of cows, hackneys, garrans, and all his provisions of wheat, oatmeal, and butter; so that, although his company was not all slain, yet were they for ever after unable to assemble together in any number. About the same time also Captain George Flower took the Castle of Kilcow,[1] being a place of great strength, and the only Castle in Carberry that held out in rebellion. Presently after this defeat Captain Boys was advertised that the Lord of Lixnaw's brother, Garret Roe Stack,[2] and some other provincial rebels were in the Castle of Berengarry; whereupon that night he blocked up the castle with a sufficient guard of men, that none should issue forth until the Governor, his colonel, might be acquainted therewith. Sir Charles, receiving intelligence hereof, being then holding the Sessions at Limerick, instantly left the city, and, taking with him by sea two small pieces of ordnance, presented him-

---

[1] Kilcoe.
[2] Recall that Undertaker of small stature and great heart, celebrated formerly by the writer and murdered by Honor ny Brien's gentlemen-in-waiting. The Christian name, cognomen and politics of Garret Roe Stacke show that the Stackes, though an Undertaking family, showed at least a tendency to become Irish.

self before the said castle. The warders, and the rest within, perceiving no possible means of escape, yielded themselves to Her Majesty's mercy. But the advertisement concerning the Lord of Lixnaw himself failed; the remainder were all taken, the principals presently executed, and the rest were pardoned by the Lord Lieutenant at his coming to Cork. The Lord President, having thus left Munster re-established in a firm and universal peace, by the assent of the Lord Deputy, having appointed Sir Charles Wilmot and Sir George Thornton Joint Commissioners for governing the province, prepared himself for England; but before his departure he made an ample relation to the Lord Deputy and Council, in what state he had left his province, and the Lord Deputy and Council having likewise declared to him the present state of the whole kingdom, they gave him large instructions to negotiate with Her Majesty and the Lords touching the affairs of Ireland, which done, the Lord Deputy, upon the six-and-twentieth day of February, took his journey towards Drogheda, to parley with Tyrone and to receive his submission as he promised (and performed), and at his taking leave of the President he delivered to him this letter, directed to the Lords of the Council :—

A LETTER SENT BY THE LORD PRESIDENT FROM THE LORD DEPUTY TO THE LORDS OF THE COUNCIL IN ENGLAND.

May it please your Lordships, although I am unwilling to inform you often of the present state of this kingdom, or of any particular accidents or services, because the one is subject to so much alteration, and the other lightly delivered unto all that are not present, with such uncertainty, and that I am loth to make any project unto your Lordships, either of my requests to you, or my own resolutions here, since so many things fall suddenly out, which may alter the grounds of either; yet since I do write now by one that can so sufficiently supply the defects of a letter, I have presumed at this time to impart unto your Lordships that I think fit to be remembered, or do determine on; most humbly desiring your Lordships that if I err in the one, or hereafter alter the other, you will not impute it to my want of sincerity or constancy, but to the nature of the subject whereof I must treat, or of the matter whereon I work. And first to present unto your Lordships the outward face of the four provinces, and after to guess (as near as I can) at their dispositions. Munster, by the good government and industry of the Lord President, is clear of any force in rebellion, except some few unable to make any forcible head. In Leinster there is not one declared rebel. In Connaught there is none but in O'Rwrke's [1] country. In Ulster, none but Tyrone, and Bryan MacArt, who was never lord of any country, and now doth with a body of loose men and some creaghts continue in Glancomkynes,[2] or near the borders thereof. Cohonoght Macguyre,[3] sometime Lord of Fermanagh, is banished out of the country, who lives with O'Rwrke, and at this time Connor Roe MacGuire is possessed of it by the Queen, and holds it for her. I believe that generally the lords of the countries that are reclaimed desire a peace, though they will be wavering till their

---

[1] O'Rourke's. Here still held out Brian of the Battle Axes and his ally, O'Sullivan Bere, who did some brave feats in the North before he set sail for Spain.

[2] Glenconkeane.

[3] *Recte* Cuconacht, brother of Hugh Maguire, slain by Sir Warham St. Leger.

lands and estates are assured unto them from Her Majesty, and as long as they see a party in rebellion to subsist, that is of a power to ruin them if they continue subjects, or otherwise shall be doubtful of our defence. All that are out do seek for mercy, except O'Rwrke and O'Sulevan, who is now with O'Rwrke; and these are obstinate only out of their diffidence to be safe in any forgiveness. The loose men, and such as are only captains of bonaghts, as Tirrell and Brian MacArt, will nourish the war as long as they see any possibility to subsist, and, like ill humours, have recourse to any part that is unsound. The nobility, towns, and English-Irish are for the most part as weary of the war as any, but unwilling to have it ended, generally for fear that upon a peace will ensue a severe reformation of religion; and in particular, many bordering gentlemen that were made poor by their own faults, or by rebels' incursions, continue their spleen to them now they are become subjects; and having used to help themselves by stealths, did never more use them, nor better prevailed in them, than now that these submittees have laid aside their own defence and betaken themselves to the protection and justice of the State; and many of them have tasted so much sweet in entertainments that they rather desire a war to continue them than a quiet harvest that might arise out of their own honest labour; so that I do find none more pernicious instruments of a new war than some of these. In the meantime Tyrone, while he shall live, will blow every spark of discontent or new hopes that shall lie hid in a corner of the kingdom, and, before he shall be utterly extinguished, make many blaze, and sometimes set on fire or consume the next subjects unto him. I am persuaded that his combination is already broken, and it is apparent that his means to subsist in any power is overthrown; but how long he may live as a woodkern, and what new accidents may fall out while he doth live, I know not. If it be imputed to my fault that notwithstanding Her Majesty's great forces, he doth still live, I beseech your Lordships to remember how securely the banditti of Italy do live, between the power of the King of Spain and the Pope. How many men of all countries of several times have in such sort preserved themselves long from the great power of princes, but especially in this country, where there are so many difficulties to carry an army, in most places so many inaccessible strengths for them to fly unto; and then to be pleased to consider the great work that first I had to break this main rebellion, to defend the kingdom from a dangerous invasion of a mighty foreign prince, with so strong a party in the country, and now the difficulty to root out scattered troops, that had so many inaccessible dens to lurk in, which as they are by nature of extreme strength and peril to be attempted, so it is impossible for any people naturally and by art to make greater use of them; and though with infinite dangers we do beat them out of one, yet is there no possibility for us to follow them with such agility as they will fly to another; and it is most sure that never traitor knew better how to keep his own head than this; nor any subjects have a more dreadful awe to lay violent [1] hands on their sacred prince than these people have to touch the person of their O'Neals, and he that hath as pestilent a judgment, as ever any had to nourish and to spread his own infection, hath

---

[1] This is to excuse himself for not having succeeded in getting the Earl assassinated.

the ancient swelling and desire of liberty in a conquered nation to work upon, their fear to be rooted out, or to have their old faults punished upon all particular discontents, and generally over all the kingdom the fear of a persecution for religion, the debasing of the coin (which is grievous unto all sorts), and a dearth and famine which is already begun, and must of necessity grow shortly to extremity; the least of which alone have been many times sufficient motives to drive the best and most quiet estates into sudden confusion. These will keep all spirits from settling, breed new combinations, and, I fear, even stir the towns themselves to solicit foreign aid with promise to cast themselves into their protection. And although it be true that if it had pleased Her Majesty to have longer continued her army in greater strength I should the better have provided for what these clouds do threaten, and sooner and more easily either have made this country a raised table, wherein she might have written her own laws, or have tied the ill-disposed and rebellious hands till I had surely planted such a government as would have overgrown and killed any weeds that should have risen under it; yet, since the necessity of the State doth so urge a diminution of this great expense, I will not despair to go on with this work through all these difficulties if we be not interrupted by foreign forces, although perchance we may be encountered with some new irruptions, and (by often adventuring) with some disasters, and it may be your Lordships shall sometimes hear of some spoils done upon the subjects, from which it is impossible to preserve them in all places with far greater forces than ever yet were kept in this kingdom. And although it hath been seldom heard that an army hath been carried on with so continual action and enduring without any intermission of winter breathings, and that the difficulties at this time to keep any forces in the place where we must make the war, but especially our horse, are almost beyond any hope to prevent, yet, with the favour of God and Her Majesty's fortune, I do determine myself to draw into the field as soon as I have received Her Majesty's commands by the commissioners whom it hath pleased her to send over, and in the meantime I hope by mine own presence or directions to set every party at work that doth adjoin or may be drawn against any force that now doth remain in rebellion. In which journey the success must be in the hands of God; but I will confidently promise to omit nothing that is possible by us to be done to give the last blow unto the rebellion. But as all pain and anguish impatient of the present doth use change for a remedy, so will it be impossible for us to settle the minds of these people unto a peace, or reduce them unto order, while they feel the smart of these sensible griefs and apparent fears which I have remembered to your Lordships, without some hope of redress or security. Therefore I will presume (how unworthy soever I have been), since it concerns the province Her Majesty hath given me, with all humbleness to lay before your grave judgments some few things which I think necessary to be considered of.

And first, whereas the alteration of the coin and taking away of the exchange in such measure as it was first promised hath bred a general grievance unto men of all qualities, and so many incommodities to all sorts, that it is beyond the judgment of any that I can hear to prevent a confusion in this estate by the continuance thereof, that (at least) it would please your Lordships to put this people in some certain hope that upon the end of the war this new standard should be abolished or eased; and that in the meantime the army may be favourably dealt with in the exchange, since by the last proclamation your Lordships sent over they do conceive their case will be more hard than any others; for, if they have allowed them nothing but indefinitely as much as they shall merely gain out of their entertainments, that will prove nothing to the greater part; for the only possibility to make them to live upon their entertainments will be to allow them exchange for the greatest part thereof, since now they do not only pay excessive prices for all things, but can hardly get anything for this money; and although we have presumed to alter (in show though not in effect) the proclamation in that point, by retaining a power in ourselves to proportion their allowance for exchange, yet was it with a mind to conform our proceedings therein according to your Lordships' next directions, and therefore do humbly desire to know your pleasures therein. For our opinions of the last project it pleased your Lordships to send us, I do humbly leave it to our general letters; only, as for myself, I made overture to the Council in the other you sent directly only to myself; and because I found them generally to concur that it would prove as dangerous as the first, I did not think it fit any otherwise to declare your Lordships' pleasure therein. And whereas it pleased your Lordships in your last letters to command us to deal moderately in the great matter of religion, I had before the receipt of your Lordships' letters presumed to advise such as dealt in it, for a time to hold a more restrained hand therein, and we were both thinking ourselves what course to take in the revocation of what was already done, with least encouragement to them and others, since the fear that this course begun in Dublin would fall upon the rest,[1] was apprehended over all the kingdom. So that I think your Lordships' direction was to great purpose, and the other course might have overthrown the means to our own end of reformation of religion. Not that I think too great preciseness can be used in the reforming of ourselves, the abuses of our own clergy, church-livings, or discipline; nor that the truth of the Gospel can with too great vehemence or industry be set forward in all places, and by all ordinary means most proper unto itself, that was first set forth and spread in meekness; not that I think any corporal prosecution or punishment can be too

---

[1] By law every one should come to church, assist in the Anglican services and listen to the sermons of the Reformed bishops and clergy. The bishops were ceaselessly endeavouring to enforce the law; the State as ceaselessly seeking to restrain the bishops. Sometimes the Queen herself intervened with fierce emphasis, reprimanding the bishops personally. The State, for State reasons, desired that these laws should be a dead letter in Ireland, but the bishops having the law with them, their Spiritual and High Commission Courts for the enforcement of that law, and a great body of Puritan feeling in England upon which to work, could never be got to give over their purpose.

Bingham once set in motion in Connaught one of the laws relating to religion. The incident is so curious and so characteristic of the age, that I take the liberty of telling it. There was a law, unrepealed, against the marriage of ecclesiastics. It was passed in the reign of Philip and Mary, and was still on the Statute Book, for the Queen would not sanction its repeal. Bingham, in want of money for his wars, summoned the Western clergy to appear before his officers and fined such as were married or lived in concubinage. How much he got by this ingenious stroke history does not record. Bingham, it will be suspected from this, was not zealous for Protestantism, and that is the fact. His task was to drive "the Composition of Connaught" over his province, and to that end he used all means possible, even the persecution of married clergymen.

severe for such as shall be found seditious instruments of foreign or inward practices; not that I think it fit that any principal magistrates should be chosen without taking the oath of obedience, nor tolerated in absenting themselves from public divine service, but that we may be advised how we do punish in their bodies or goods any such only for religion as do profess to be faithful subjects to Her Majesty, and against whom the contrary cannot be proved. And since, if the Irish were utterly rooted out, there was much less likelihood that this country could be thereby in any time planted by the English, since they are so far from inhabiting well any part of what they have already;[1] and that more than is likely to be inhabited may be easily chosen out and reserved in such places by the seaside, or upon great rivers, as may be planted to great purpose, for a future absolute reducement of this country, I think it would as much avail the speedy settling of this country as anything that it would please Her Majesty to deal liberally[2] with the Irish lords of countries, or such as are now of great reputation among them, in the distribution of such lands as they have formerly possessed, or the State here can make little use of for Her Majesty. If they continue as they ought to do, and yield the Queen as much commodity as she may otherwise expect, she hath made a good purchase of

[1] This is a strong support of my assertion that the 500 men whom the lately returned Undertakers of Munster brought to the provincial muster were Irish soldiers in the Undertakers' service.

[2] This advice was followed, and yet it was a confession of defeat. The great lords and gentlemen of the North went into rebellion to secure their lands from such shameless confiscation and redistribution amongst court favourites as they had witnessed in the confiscation of MacMahonland, i.e. the county of Monaghan, during the vice-royalty of FitzWilliam.

such subjects for such land. If any of them hereafter be disobedient to her laws, or break forth in rebellion, she may, when they shall be more divided, ruin them more easily for example unto others, and (if it be thought fit) may plant English or other Irish in their countries. For although there ever have been, and hereafter may be, small eruptions in some places which at first may easily be suppressed, yet suffering them to grow to that general head and combination did questionless proceed from great error in the judgment here, and may be easily (as I think) prevented hereafter. And further, it may please Her Majesty to ground her resolution for the time and numbers of the next abatement of the list of her army somewhat upon our poor advice from hence, and to believe that we will not so far corrupt our judgments with any private respects, and without necessity to continue her charge, seeing we do thoroughly conceive how grievous it is unto her estate, and that we may not be precisely tied to an establishment that shall conclude the payments of the treasure, since it hath ever been thought fit to be otherwise till the coming over of the Earl of Essex; and some such extraordinary occasions may fall out that it will be dangerous to attend your Lordships' resolutions; and when it will be safe to diminish the army here, that there may be some other course thought of by some other employment to disburden this country of the idle swordmen, in whom I find an inclination apt enough to be carried elsewhere, either by some of this country of best reputation among them, or in companies as now they stand under English Captains who may be reinforced with the greatest[1] part of the

[1] Observe Mountjoy speaks here of the Irish companies under

Irish; that it may be left to our discretion to make passages and bridges into countries otherwise inaccessible, and to build little piles of stone in such garrisons as shall be thought fittest, to be continual bridles upon the people, by the commodity of which we may at any time draw the greatest part of the army together to make head against any part that shall first break out, and yet reserve the places only with a ward to put in greater forces as occasion shall require, which I am persuaded will prove great pledges upon this country, that upon any urgent cause the Queen may safely draw the greatest part of her army here out of the kingdom to be employed for a time elsewhere, wherein I beseech your Lordships to consider what a strength so many experienced captains and soldiers[1] would be to any

English captains, and says that the greatest part of the Irish swordmen would willingly join the service if a military career might be provided for them so. The root of the troubles was of course the land question, but it was the teeming military caste—the born swordmen, who could not without disgrace dig, plough, or harrow, being as they considered themselves gentlemen, it was, as I say, the presence and the numbers of this caste that enabled angry lords to fight the State.

[1] That course, so evidently statesmanlike, should have been adopted long since. But a vile economy governed the proceedings of the State through all this century. The Tudor Princes were in my opinion, to a great extent, slaves of that powerful bureaucracy which they had set up as a counterpoise to the territorial power, the great feudal families which had formerly oppressed the Crown, and this hungry bureaucracy absorbed the State revenues to such a degree that nothing was left for the execution of great purposes. Owing to the liberality of Parliament, the income of the State during the years which succeeded the Armada was enormous, yet in those years the State did not employ 500 of the Irish military order. In their thousands these swordmen moved about the country, hunting, duelling, dicing, card-playing, and begetting more thousands. "We are willing to work" (as soldiers), was their cry, "but we've got no work to do." Then the angry lords said to them, "Come to us and we will give you work." So the angry lords broke out and prevailed against the State, prevailed until the State in its turn called upon the swordmen to fight

army of new men erected in England against an invasion, or sent abroad in any offensive war. But until these places be built I cannot conceive how Her Majesty (with any safety) can make any great diminution of her army. Lastly, I do humbly desire your Lordships to receive the further explanation of my meaning, and confirmation of my reasons that do induce me unto these propositions; for the Lord President of Munster, who, as he hath been a very worthy actor in the reducement and defence of this kingdom, so do I think him to be the best able to give you thorough account of the present estate and future providence for the preservation thereof; wherein it may please your Lordships to require his opinion of the hazard this kingdom is like to run in, if it should by any mighty power be invaded, and how hard it will be for us in any measure to provide for the present defence, if any such be intended, and withal to go on with the suppression of these that are left in rebellion, so that we must either adventure the kindling of this fire that is almost extinguished, or intending only that, leave the other to exceeding peril. And thus, having remembered to your Lordships the most material points (as I conceive) that are fittest for the present to be considered, I do humbly recommend myself and them to your Lordships' favour. From Her Majesty's castle of Dublin, the six-and-twentieth of February, 1602.

After the Lord Deputy departed, by reason of easterly winds the President was stayed above three

for the Queen, and created armies of Irish soldiers under State-appointed captains. With such armies, with the levies at which the cities were assessed, and the risings out of the territories, the State passed victorious through the storm.

weeks in Dublin, during which time, every day, posts were employed between them, until the twentieth of March, which was the day the Lord President set sail for England. The day following he arrived at Beaumaris. At his coming to Chester he met with the lamentable news of the decease of his good and gracious mistress Queen Elizabeth, for whom, as he had good cause, he extremely mourned.[1] But two days following, being at Lichfield, he assisted the Mayor in the proclaiming of King James, which gave him new life, whom I beseech God long to preserve and continue his posterity for ever over his triumphant monarchy of Great Britain and Ireland.

Although my work be finished, yet, according to the course I have held in the end of the two former books, I may not omit to recount to the reader the most memorable services and incidents which happened in this year 1602; in the catalogue whereof I must first begin with the forces sent into Carberry with the Earl of Thomond. The sending of Sir Charles

[1] The "extremely mourned" and the "new life" are very characteristic. Curiously enough, when Tyrone heard the news of the Queen's death, "he wept." Why did Tyrone weep? It is also a fact related by Gardiner, the Chief Justice, who witnessed the scene, that Tyrone wept when starting on his career as insurgent.

The men of this age thought it no shame to weep in public. A lord of the O'Rourke sept wept for joy in public when he heard that, under "the Composition of Connaught," he was free from all authority but the Queen's, and that the high chief of the O'Rourkes was not to *spend* him or reign over him any more. Sir Turlough Lynagh, the O'Neill, with all Dublin looking on, wept at the departure of Sir John Perrott, the Viceroy.

Between our times and those of which *Pacata Hibernia* treats there is a great gulf fixed. It will need an infinitely more dispassionate treatment of the sixteenth century than has been common hitherto amongst historians, English and Irish, to enable us to understand the strange beings whose outlines we perceive so dimly on the opposite side of that gulf.

Wilmot with his regiment into Kerry. The Lord President's departure from Cork with the army towards Donboy. His long abode at Carew Castle, expecting munition and victuals. The difficulty he had in his approaching towards Donboy. The defeat given to the rebels. The arrival of a Spanish caravel in Beare with letters of comfort, money, and munition from Spain. The siege of Donboy, the winning and razing of it. The President's return to Cork, and Sir Charles Wilmot's into Kerry. The flight of James Archer, the Jesuit, and Connor O'Driscal into Spain. The relapse of Sir Owen MacCarty's sons. The Spanish hostages returned into Spain. The restraint of Cormock, Lord of Muskerry. His escape and reduction. The winning of the castle of Mocrumpe. The defeat of Tirrell and his bonoghs in Muskerry. The sending of Sir Samuel Bagnall with fifteen hundred men to the Lord Deputy. The service done upon the Knight of Kerry. The flight of Tirrell with his bonoghs out of the province. The defeat of the rebels in Glangarne. The flight of William Burke with his bonoghs, O'Sulevan Beare and Connor Kerry out of Munster. The overthrow of the Cartys in Carberry, and the killing of the Pope's Apostolic Vicar, Owen MacEggan. The sending of a regiment with munition and victuals for the service in Connaught. The defeat of the Lord of Lixnaw. The final reduction of Munster. The appointing of Sir Charles Wilmot and Sir George Thornton Joint Commissioners for the government of Munster. And the departure of the Lord President into England.

THE END.

NOTE.
HUGH O'NEILL.

Hugh O'Neill, Earl of Tyrone, the greatest man of action of the Irish race who has appeared in modern times, was the son of Ferdoragh, Baron of Dungannon, son of Lame Con, the O'Neill, and first Earl of Tyrone. Lame Con submitted himself, people and lands to Henry VIII., who re granted to him all Tir-Owen, and the rents and services of divers Ulster lords, of old time subject to the O'Neill. The grant was to himself for life, remainder in *tail male* to his eldest son, Ferdoragh, Baron of Dungannon, by English writers called Matthew. Ferdoragh means "the dark man"—*Fear*, man, *dorcadh*, dark. Ferdoragh was illegitimate, and known to be illegitimate, but illegitimacy counted for little in Ireland, and could have counted for little generally in an age in which Henry VIII. endeavoured to secure the throne of England for his illegitimate son, the Earl of Southampton. Froude says that this was his only illegitimate child. But Froude, as usual, is wrong. Though personally I incline to think that, as kings go, bluff King Hal was not an unusually bad specimen of the species. Lame Con's appearance at Henry's Court curiously coincided with the first step upwards of the famous Cecil. While Lame Con was conversing with his august overlord, not yet his King, for Henry was at the time only *Dominus Hiberniæ*, his sentourage of gallowglasses, harpers, poets, shanachies, priests, etc., waited in the anteroom. With two of the priests young Cecil fell into argument touching the King's claim to be head of the Church, and in the ensuing controversy acquitted himself so well on the King's side that next day he received his first promotion.

Cecil was a supple and time-serving politician, and by no means a statesman. I agree with the estimate which Macaulay has formed of his character.

Lame Con having begotten Ferdoragh and divers other children, married in due form a lady of the House of Campbell, and begot the famous Shane O'Neill, Shane the Proud.

Shane, growing to man's estate, argued thus : " By English law this patent with remainder to my father's bastard son is bad and contrary to all reputable English precedents. By Irish law neither Ferdoragh nor I have a good claim, for we are both youths, and the O'Neillship appanages in lands and tributes and services should go to the next eldest of the blood-royal of Tir-Owen, Turlough Lynagh or another. But at all events I have a better right than Ferdoragh the bastard." Seniority—within the blood-royal—not election as represented in popular works, was the principle of succession laid down by Irish law as governing the devolution of chieftainships.

So Shane very properly rose-out against Ferdoragh and the State, slew Ferdoragh, slew Ferdoragh's eldest son, made himself the O'Neill, and stood out in arms there in the North ready to fight all comers in defence of his alleged rights. He beat the State. He beat down all racalcitrant feudatories. He beat hostile

TURLOUGH LYNAGH.
(The O'Neill, predecessor of Hugh.)

neighbours, and eventually made himself lord of all Ulster. Having achieved that position, he stepped forward and said to Elizabeth, " Peace or war, which you will ? If you say 'peace,' I shall be your loyal servant and beat down for you any recalcitrant lord showing himself anywhere in Ireland." The Queen said "peace," and Sir Henry Sidney, her Viceroy, father of Sir Philip the Paladin, stood gossip for his eldest son, Henry O'Neill.

Now, during all this politic business, the State, it will be observed, was untrue to its trust, false to its own undertakings. Ferdoragh's eldest son having been slain, Tir-Owen, by patent, belonged to his next eldest, Hugh O'Neill, who all this time was being educated in England, in the household of Robert Dudley, Earl of Leicester, at Kenilworth. Possibly Hugh O'Neill could have told us the true story of Amy Robsart had he been so inclined.

When the Queen determined to drag down Shane O'Neill she used the boy Hugh as an instrument. She sent him into Ireland, where, under Walter Earl of Essex and other commanders, he behaved stoutly and loyally, warring against his own kindred. Of course the lad's ultimate object in all this was to secure for himself and his faithful followers the dominions to which he was rightfully entitled under the patent. He had two younger brothers, Cormac, afterwards, Baron of Dungannon, and Art, father of Owen Roe. He had many followers who trusted to him to make their fortune, and Hugh had a very great fortune indeed to dispend amongst faithful followers if only he could recover it. But there was the rub, for the Government was very weak and the forces opposed to him very strong. At this time Hugh married his first wife, an O'Neill lady of high rank and position.

When Shane was slain by the MacDonalds, the State, though it could procure an Act of the Irish Parliament abolishing the O'Neillship and making it high treason for anyone to assume the title, was quite unable to abolish the O'Neillship in fact. All Ulster stood on the election of a new captain, and the captain chosen was not Hugh, who was quite out of it by Irish law, but Turlough Lynagh O'Neill, a most brave, most amiable, but not very wise man.

Meantime the Queen, hard pressed upon by the Irish dynasts, forgetting or ignoring that old grant of Henry VIII. to Lame Con in the first place, remainder to Ferdoragh, remainder to the heirs of Ferdoragh in *tail male*, made a grant to Turlough Lynagh of all the lands previously conveyed to the Baron and his heirs. ' Thus troubles commenced between Turlough Lynagh and the State. Again the Queen, ignoring her grant to Turlough, made another of the same lands to young Hugh O'Neill, setting the young man over all Tir-Owen, that is to say, the modern counties of Londonderry, Tyrone, and Armagh. So there were in fact two O'Neills, both holding by patent the same lands! There were a great many such conflicting patents in Ireland, or conflicting State arrangements with reference to land, from which in due course sprang rebellions, the State sowing such far and wide, and, in due season, reaping for a crop armed men and chieftains out on their keeping. The State being weak, unjust, and corrupt, lived from hand to mouth quite as much as modern constitutional administrations, and solved difficulties as they arose by the issue of Patents or Orders in Council without looking to the past or to the future. So they made Red Hugh the O'Donnell and Lord of all Tirconnall, while one of his tenants maintained in his strong box a patent from the Queen securing all Tirconnall to himself.

If anyone supposes that Queen Elizabeth's great officers of State were very wise, virtuous, and statesmanlike persons, he is much mistaken.

So the Queen set up Hugh O'Neill there in the North as a rival and counter-weight to Turlough, Turlough's patent notwithstanding. From this time forward poor Turlough, oppressed by liquor and manifold injustices and perfidies of the kind which I have mentioned, year by year decayed, while young Hugh O'Neill was waxing stronger and stronger. Old Turlough, really a most noble and upright old chieftain, though given to liquor, now struck an agreement with this strong young Hugh O'Neill, and, under Perrott's supervision, rented to him a considerable portion of Tir-Owen. Hugh, as the weaker party, in order to strengthen himself, divorced his first wife, the purpose of that marriage having been fulfilled, and married the Lady Joan (*Siubhan*) O'Donnell, sister of Red Hugh and daughter of the reigning O'Donnell. Hugh was weak in the North, the Crown could give no help, and so he struck this league with the powerful house of O'Donnell, a league cemented by a marriage. The fact of the divorce is indisputable. He refers to it himself above his own hand in the letter in which he justifies his abduction of Miss Bagenal, mentioning that afterwards his divorced wife had married another man and had borne him children. The Lady Joan O'Donnell could not have been more than sixteen at this time, he himself being more than forty.

By this alliance he became strong in the North and more than a match for Turlough Lynagh. Then he got into trouble with the State, partly because he had hanged a son of Shane, on his own responsibility, mainly because he was strong, At this step in his upward career his child-wife, the lady Joan O'Donnell, died, and he took to himself a third wife out of the pale, Miss Mabel Bagenal. When the Countess Mabel died, he married the sister of one of his Northern lords, Katherine Magennis.

Finally Hugh grew to be virtually captain of the North, and so strong, that though his loyalty was unimpeachable, the State determined to overthrow and destroy him. He on his side, driven thereto by inevitable necessity, waged war upon the State, and the State waged war upon him, but the State on this occasion had met its match. Year after year Hugh rolled back out of Ulster the strongest tide of invasion which the State could urge against him, and indeed, not to put too fine a point upon it, beat the State hip and thigh. He could not capture castles and walled towns, and the castles and walled towns adhering to the State neutralized his victories, but he could and did, with his victorious armies, tramp about Ireland, nowhere meeting an army which could defeat him in the open, though many armies tried. Twice he marched unopposed through Ireland into Munster. We assist here at his second invasion of that province. Had Ulster alone stood by Hugh O'Neill he could never have been beaten, and even though Ulster betrayed him, he did not lay down his arms until he had wrung from the State everything that he wanted when he commenced the war, viz. security for his life, and the free enjoyment of the estates conferred upon him indirectly by Henry VIII. and afterwards directly by Elizabeth.

In his letters to the Privy Council, he always declared that he went into rebellion merely to save his life and his lands, and though he afterwards put forward other aims and objects, savouring of religion, and savouring of patriotism, and savouring of Spain, he most certainly never commenced the war for any other objects than those which I have specified, and which at the time in many letters he set out. He had spies even in the Queen's bedchamber, and knew everything that was intended against him. If Ireland, speaking generally, had not been against him, he would, as Hugh the First, have founded a Catholic Monarchy or have established himself here, himself and his descendants as hereditary lieutenants of the Crown, reviving in the House of O'Neill the powers once enjoyed by the House of Kildare. But Ireland was against him, and though he did all that valour and wisdom could do, he had to end as he began. Why Ireland was against him is a very deep question, about which volumes might be written.

Hugh O'Neill was of medium stature but athletic and powerfully built, with black eyes and a swarthy complexion. In speech he was "plain and blunt," in aspect grave, inclined to sombre, but in social intercourse could unbend and be very agreeable. Sir John Harrington, the witty author of *Nugæ Antiquæ*, no mean judge, celebrates his conversational powers. His letters published in the State Papers prove a literary faculty superior to that of any public man of his time in Ireland. They are not unfrequently very vivid and pictorial. They are not so much ingenious as ingenuous, for it is a fact that this man, whom his enemies represented as so deep and crafty, was not more, but far less, tainted with the prevailing duplicity of the age than his contemporaries. He was, in fact, more plain-dealing than any of them, and I may add that it is an enemy, Sir John Davies, who describes him as " plain and blunt of speech."

He always said and wrote that he had rebelled against Queen Elizabeth only to save his life and lands from those who had conspired to destroy the one and confiscate the other, and there is no ground whatever for supposing that when he did so he was not telling the plain truth.

STANDISH O'GRADY.

APPENDIX.

Instructions given by us the Lord Deputie, and Councell, to our right trustie and welbeloved, Sir George Carew, Knight, Lord President of her Maiesties Councell established in the Province of Mounster, to bee communicated by him to her Maiesties Councell of the same Province, and to be observed by them, and every of them, according as the same are particularly declared in these severall Articles following, dated at Dublin, 7. Martij 1599.

FIRST, the said Lord President shall at all times, when he shall think fit, for the service of the Queenes Majestie, call together all such as bee, or that hereafter shall be appoynted to bee of that Councell: And shall with the advice of such of the Councell as shall bee by these Instructions appoynted to assist him with Councell by Letters and Precepts, commaund all and every person of the said Councell, at all convenient times, to doe such things as shall be meet for the service of the Queenes Majestie in administration of Iustice, & maintenance of the same, amongst all her subjects residing or comming into the parts of the Iurisdiction of the said Commission. And in his commandements and directions, to the sayd Councell, he shall haue such regard to their Estates, Vocations, and other Conditions, as the credits and severall estimations of the same Councellours may be in their due actions and well-doings preserved and maintained, for the furtherance of her Majesties service.

And on thother part, her Majestie willeth, chargeth and commandeth that all and euery of her Majesties said Councellors, shall exhibit and vse to the saide Lord President, all such Honour, reverence and obedience, as to their duties appertaineth, and to the person having the principall place in the Councell is due, and shall receiue, and execute, in such sort all the precepts and commandements, to them to be addressed, in any Processe to be done, or served in her Majesties name, and shall giue at all times, such advice and counsell as appertaineth to the duties of trustie Servants and Councellors to her Majestie, and according to their corporall oath.

And because it shall be convenient that some number shall be continually abiding with the Lord President, or such as shall supply his place, with whom he may consult, in hearing such matters as may bee exhibited unto him, for the better expedition of the same: Wee the sayd Lord Deputie and Councell by these presents doe ordaine, That *William Saxey*, Esquire, Chiefe Iustice, and *James Golde*, second Iustice of the sayd province of Mounster, being of speciall trust appoynted to be of the sayd Councell, shall giue their continuall attendance at the sayd Councell, and shall not depart at any time without the speciall Licence of the sayd Lord President. Likewise —— Clarke of the Councell, shall make his like attendance upon the Lord President and Councell, &c.

And the said Lord President shall have in consideration of his continuall attendance, and great paines to be taken in that Office, the wages and entertainments of one hundred and thirty three pounds sixe shillings eight pence sterling by the yeare, for himselfe: and for that the Countreys aforesaid being in such disorder, and the people in the same in such disobedience as partly they are, whereby it shall be needfull for him to have continually about him some competent number of Souldiers, whereby his decrees and orders justly taken and made, may the more effectually bee executed; It is considered and ordained, that the said Lord President shall have for his guard and retinue, thirtie horsemen and twentie footmen, and two shillings by the day for a petty Captaine, and for a Trumpeter and Guydon two shillings each of them: the entertainment and daily wages of all which Officers and Martiall men, shall runne in the course, and pay appointed for the Queenes Majesties ordinary Garisons, resident in this Realme. Provided always, that the said Lord President, shall at the first entrie, give in the names, of all and every the aforesaid Souldiers, to the Clearke of the Cheque, to bee entred in his booke, and from time to time shall certifie the deaths and alterations of the same to the Lord Deputy, and the Clearke of the Cheque, in convenient time, as the same may reasonably be done: having regard to the distance of the place, and as other Captaines of the army are bound to doe.

Item the said Iustice *Saxey* shall have for his stipend yearely one hundred pounds sterling; and the said *Iames Gold*, assistant or second Iustice, one hundred marks sterling, and the said Clark of the Councell, twenty pounds sterling; all which stipends and wages shall be payed quarterly, by the hands of the Treasurer, at warres, or Vice-treasurer here of this Realme of Ireland: And if the said Iustice, or assistant, and secondary Iustice, shall depart out of the Limits of the Commission aforesaid, without the speciall licence of the said Lord President, or having leave, shall tarry longer out then the time granted, then (without reasonable cause of excuse) the said Lord President shall deduct, and defalke out of their said severall entertainments, so much as the said wages of so many dayes doth amount unto, to the use of her Majestie towards her other charges, to be extraordinarily sustained in the execution of their Commission, at the discretion of the said Lord President.

Item for further reputation and honour of the same Office, the said Lord President shall have continually attending upon him, a Serjeant at Armes, who shall beare the Mace of the Queenes Majesties Armes before him, in such manner as the Serjeant at Armes doth beare the

Appendix.

Mace before the President in Wales; which Serjeant may at all times be sent by the said Lord President and Councell, for the apprehending and bringing in of any disobedient person, receiving of every such person, being of the degree of a Gentleman, so commonly knowen, and having yearely liuelihood by any meanes of tenne pounds, for his arrest ten shillings; and for the arrest of every particular person, six shillings eight pence, and six shillings eight pence for every dayes travell, and not aboue. He shall also haue his dyet in the Household of the said Lord President, and towards his maintainance the ordinary wages of one of the thirtie Horsemen. And forasmuch as there must bee of necessitie one Officer to whom all offenders and malefactors are to bee committed, during the time of their imprisonment: it is thought meet that the said Lord President shall appoint one Porter, to haue charge of the Goale, who shall haue his dyet in the househould of the said Lord President, and bee accounted as one of the twentie Footmen, and receiue the wages due for the same, and also such other profits upon every prisoner, as ensueth, *viz.* for the entry of every prisoner so to him committed, having liuelihood of tenne pounds by the yeare, three shillings four pence, and twelue pence by the day for his dyet, during his abode in prison, and for every other person of inferiour condition, two shillings for his entry, and six pence by the day for his dyet.

Item, The said Lord President and Councell, (if oportunitie may serue) monethly, or once every two moneths at the least, advertise us the Lo. Deputie and Councell here of the State, of the Country within their commission, or oftner if they shall see cause.

And where the said Lo: President and Councell shal haue by their Commission, sufficient authoritie to heare and determine, by their discretions, all manner of complaints, within any part of the province of Mounster, as well guildeable as franchise, yet they shall haue good regard, that except great necessitie, or other matter of conscience, conceived upon the complaint, shall moue, him, they shall not hinder nor impeach the good course and usage of the common Lawes of the Realme, but shall to their power further the execution thereof, nor shall without evident cause, interrupt such Liberties, and Franchises, as haue lawfull commencement, and continuance[1] by the warrants of the Law, other wayes then where any speciall complaint shall be made unto them, of any manifest wrong, or delay of Iustice, done, or used, by the owners, Officers, or Ministers of the said Franchises or Liberties: In which cases; the Lord President and Councell shall examine the said defaults, so alledged, by way of complaint, to be counted in the Franchises, and shall send for the Officers, against whom complaint shall be made: and finding the same to be true, they shall not only heare and determine the particular & principall causes of the parties complaints, but shall also reforme & punish, according to their discretions, the defaults of the said

---

[1] *Scilicet* as well within the walled towns as wherever in the open country our predecessors may haue granted immunities.

owners and Ministers of the said Liberties ; and if the matter shall so serue, upon due information to be made to us, of the abuses of the said Franchises and Liberties, so as the same may be done by order according to the lawes tryed, and upon just causes the Liberties resumed into the Queenes Majesties hands.

Item, where the said Lo : President and Councell shall haue Commission, power, and authoritie, by Letters Patents under the Great Seale of this Realme of Ireland, and of Oyer, Determiner, and Goale deliverie, in as large and ample manner as any such Commission or Authoritie is graunted to any Commissioners for that purpose, within the Realmes of England, or Ireland : Wee the said Lord Deputie and Councell, doe earnestly require and charge the said Lord President and Councell, that hee and they doe diligently and often, severely and justly sit, heare, and determine, by vertue of the same, such causes as shall bee brought before them, in such severall places as best may agree with the necessitie of the cause, and the commoditie of the people.

Item, where also the said Lord President hath full power and authoritie, by Letters patents under the great Seale of this realme, to execute the Martiall law, when necessitie shall require, in as large and ample manner as to any other it hath beene accustomed to bee graunted within this realme of Ireland : The said Lord President shall haue good regard thereunto, that no use be made of the Martiall law, but when meere necessitie shall require ; for the exercise thereof is only to bee allowed, where other ordinarie administration of Iustice cannot take place : foreseeing alwayes, that no person having fiue [1] pound of Freehold, or goods to the value of tenne pound, shall not be tried by the order of the Martiall Lawe to be executed vpon any one person or moe being of greater value in lands or goods, then aboue is expressed, the President in such speciall causes may use his discretion, and thereof, and of the causes that mooved him, shall make us the Lord Deputie and Councell privie.

Item it is, and shall bee lawfull for the Lord President and Councell, or any two of them, whereof the Lord President to bee one, to prosecute and oppresse any rebell, or rebells, with sword and with fire, and for the doing of the same, to leavie in warlike manner and array, and with the same to march, such and so many of the Queenes Subjects, as to his discretion shall seeme convenient ; And if that any Castle, Pile, or House, bee with force kept against them, it shall be lawfull for the said Lord President and Councell, or two of them whereof the Lord President to be one, to bring before any such Castle, Pile, or House, so to bee kept against them, any of the Queenes Majesties Ordnance and great artillery, remaining within the limits of the Commission : And with the same, or by some other meanes or

---

[1] One of the chief complaints against the Queen's Presidents was that they exhibited a strong tendency to extend the sphere of martial law. Sir R. Bingham, President of Connaught, did a great many illegal things of this description.

APPENDIX. 325

Ingine, any such Castle, Pile, or House, to batter, mine, or overthrow, as to their discretions shall seeme best, Streightly charging and commanding all Archbishops, Earles, Bishops, Vicounts, Barons, and Baronets, Knights, Majors, Sheriffs, Iustices, and Ministers of peace, and all other Gentlemen and Commons being her Majesties Subjects to helpe, aid and assist the said Lord President and Councell, in such sort, and at such time, as by the said Lord President and Councell, or two of them, whereof the Lord President to bee one, they shall bee commanded, upon such paines, as for the nature and of the defaults shall bee thought meet, to the said Lo : President and Councell to limit and assesse.

And it is ordered by us the said Lord Deputy and Councell, that if any person complaine to the said Lord President and Councell, and that they shall thinke their Complainants worth the hearing, that the persons so complained upon, shall be sent for by a Letter missive under the Queenes Signet, to appeare before the Lord President and Councel at a day and place by them to be appointed, there to answer to such things as shall bee laid to their charges, and further to be ordered, as shall stand with right, justice, equity and conscience : and for lacke of appearance upon such Letters they shall send foorth Letters of alleagance, Proclamations, or other Processe, to bee made, directed, and awarded by their discretions to the Sheriffe, Constable, or other Minister whereby the partie complained upon may be called to come to his answer as appertaineth, and if by the obstinacy of the partie complained upon, the case so require, to sequester his or their lands or goods, or either of them by their discretions. And furthermore if in case any person or persons having habitation or dwelling by any lands or tenements by lease or otherwise, within the limits of the Commission aforesaid, shall by covin, fraud, or deceit, or otherwise absent himselfe, or goe out of the limits of the said Commission : That then Letters missive signed with the Queenes Signet, shall be delivered at his House, Lands, or Tenements, and the copies of the same shall bee left there, so that by the most likelyhood the same may come to his knowledge being so sent for. And if within a certaine time after limited by their discretion, the person or persons so sent for, will make default of apparance : the said Lord President and Councell, or any two of them, whereof the Lord President to bee one, shall as well proceede to other Processe, as to the hearing and determining of the matter or cause in variance, according to the Lawes, Statutes, Ordinances made therein, or otherwise at their discretions.

And if in case any Letters missive, be sent and addressed from the Lord President and Councel, to any person or persons, of what estate, or degree soever they be, to appeare before them at a day appointed, the same Letters being delivered to him or them, or otherwise left at his or their house, as is above specifyed, the said Lord President and Councel, or any two of them, whereof the Lord President to bee one, shall cause him or them so contemning or disobeying, to be punished by imprisonment, and reasonable fine, or shall other wayes proceed according to their discretions. In which sayd causes, if any of the parties commit any resistance, or disobedience, either of their appearance, or contrary to the Commaundements, direction, decree or determination, made, or to be made, and decreed by the said Lord President and Councell; That then the said Lord President and Councell, or any two of them, whereof the Lord President to be one, shall or may command the Sherife, Major, Serjeant at Armes, Constable, Bailife, or other Officer or Minister, to whom it shall appertaine, to attach every person so offending, contemning, or disobeying, and to send him or them to the Lord Deputie in ward, together with Certificate of his contempt or disobedience, or else by their discretions to cause the parties so attached, to bee committed to ward, there to remaine in safe custodie, untill the time that the pleasure of us the Lord Deputie and Councell be knowen in the premisses, or that the same person or persons, assent, fulfill, and agree to the determination of the said Lord President and Councell, or any two of them, whereof the Lo: President to be one.

And the said Lord President and Councell shall haue full power and authoritie, by these presents, diligently to heare and determine, and trie, all, and all manner of extortions, maintenance, imbracery and oppressions, Conspiracies, rescues, escapes, corruptions, falsehoods, and all manner evill doings, defaults, misdemeanours of all Sheriffes, Iustices of peace, Majors, Soveraignes, Portriffes, Bailiffes, Stewards, Lieftenants, Excheators, Coroners, Goalers, Clarkes, and other Officers and Ministers of Iustice, and other Deputies, as well within all the Counties and Countries within the Province of Mounster, as within the supposed Liberties of Typperarij and Kerrij,[1] and in all Cities & other townes corporate, within the limits of their said Commission, of what degree soever they be, and punish the same according to the quality and quantity of their said offences, by their discretions, leaving neverthelesse, to the Lords and owners of all lawfull Liberties, such profits, as they lawfully claime.

And it shall be lawfull for the said Lord President, and Councell, or any three of them, whereof the Lord President to bee one, to conceaue, make, and caused to be proclaimed, in her Highnesse name, any thing or matter tending to the better order of her Majesties Subjects, within the precincts of their Commission, and the repressing of malefactors and misorders, after such tenour and forme, as they shall thinke convenient, and to punish the Offenders then according to their discretions.

---

[1] Kerry had been a Palatinate of the Earl of Desmond. He alone was supposed to execute justice there. The greater part of Tipperary was at this time a Palatinate under the government of the Earl of Ormonde. It is not generally known that Ormonde, *i.e.* East Munster, was Tipperary. So the Earl of Ormonde was Captain of Tipperary. Consequently again as the Earl was Royalist and his people loyal to him, the Queen in her Southern wars had Tipperary as a strong ally.

And also wee the said Lord Deputie and Councell have thought meete, that the said Lord President and Councell, or any three of them whereof the said Lord President to bee one, shall and may compound upon reasonable causes by their discretion, with any person, for all forfeitures, growing, or comming, or that shall grow, or come, as well by all and singular penall Statutes, as also of obligations and Recognizances, taken, made, or acknowledged, before the said L: President and Councell, or any of them, within the limits of their authorities and Commission for apparance, or for the peace or good abearing, or by reason of any speciall Statute whatsoever, then made or to be made, And shall also have authority, to cesse reasonable fines for any offences, whereof any person shall happen to bee convicted, before the said Lord President and Councell and such Summes of mony, as shall grow or come, by reason of any such compositions or Fines, they shall cause it to bee entred into a booke, subscribed with the hands of the said Lord President and Councell, or two of them at the least, whereof the Lord President to bee one: To the end the Queenes Majestie may be answered of the same accordingly: And also upon such compositions made of Fine or Fines, set as aforesaid, shall have authority to cancell or make voyde all such Obligations and Bonds.

And also the said Lord President shall cause, as much as in him lyeth, all Writts or Processes, sent or to bee sent, to any person or persons inhabiting, or being within the precinct of his Commission out of the Kings Bench, Chauncerie, or Exchequer, or any other Court of Record, diligently to bee observed, and effectually to bee obeyed, according to the tenor of the same. And if hee shall find negligence, slacknesse, or willfull omission, in any Officer or other Minister to whom the delivery or serving of such Processe doth appertaine: Hee shall punish the same severely according to the greatnesse and qualitie of the offence.

And it shall bee lawfull for the said Lord President and Councell, or any three of them, whereof the Lord President to bee one, after examination in the causes necessary, upon vehement suspition and presumption of any great offence in any partie committed against the Queenes Majestie, to put the said partie so suspected to tortures,[1] as they thinke convenient, and as the cause shall require : and also to respitt Iudgement of death upon any person convicted or attainted before him and that Councell, for any treason, murder, or any other felony: Or after Iudgement given to stay execution untill such time as hee shall certifie us the Lord Deputie and Councell of his doings, and consideration of the same, and receive answere from us thereof: Provided alwayes, that the same certificate bee made to us the Lo: Deputie and Councell within the space of 21 dayes after such thing is done.

---

[1] I don't find that torture was much used in these times, though it certainly was used. I suspect the public opinion of the country was against it.

APPENDIX.

Also if any Inquest within the precinct of their Commission, within Liberties or without, being sworne and charged upon triall of any fellonie, murder, or any like offender whatsoever hee bee, having good and pregnant evidence for sufficient proofe of the matter whereof the said offendor shall be accused, indicted or arraigned, doe utterly acquite such offendor contrary to the said evidence, that then the said Lord President and Councell, or any two of them, whereof the Lord President to bee one, shall examine such perjuries as well by deposition of witnesses, as by all other kinde of proofes by their discretions; and if the said Inquest bee convicted before the said Lord President and Councell, or three of them at the least, whereof the Lord President to be one, the said Lord President, and Councell may and shall proceed to the punishment of such offence by fine, imprisonment, or wearing of papers, or standing on the pillorie, as by their discretions shall seeme meet.

Also, wee the said Lord Deputie and Councell, doe earnestly require, and straightly charge the said Lord President and Councell, that they at all times, and in all places, where any great assembly shall bee made before them, doe perswade the people by all good meanes and wayes to them seeming good, and especially by their owne examples, in observing all Orders for Divine Service, and other things appertaining to Christian Religion, and to embrace, follow, and devoutly to obserue the Order and Service of the Church, established in the Realme by Parliament, or otherwayes by lawfull authoritie, and earnestly to call upon and admonish all Bishops and Ordinaries, within the precinct of their Commission, diligently, fervently, and often to doe the same. And if the Lord President and Councell, shall finde them negligent and unwilling, or unable to doe the same, That then they shall advertise the Lord Deputie and Councell thereof, and they shall call earnestly upon the Bishops, severely to proceed according to the censuring of the church, against all notorious Advowterers, and such as without lawfull divorce, doe leaue their Wiues, or whilest that their lawfull Wife liveth doe marry any other, and the Sentence pronounced by the Bishop or Ordinarie upon the offendor: The said Lo: President and Councell shall endeavour themselues to the uttermost that they conveniently may, to cause the same Sentence to bee put in execution according to the Lawes; And if they shall finde the Ordinaries slacke or remisse in this duetie, and not doing according to his Office, they shall punish, or cause to bee punished, the same Bishop or Ordinary, according to their discretions.

Also the Lord President and Councell shall examine the decay of all parish Churches, and through whose defaults the same be decayed, and to proceede to the procuring or informing of such as ought to repaire any Church or Churches, with all convenient speed, according to their discretions: And in cases where her Majestie shall bee (after due and advised inquisition) found by reason of her possessions bound to repaire the same Churches, In those cases advertisement shall bee given to us the Lord Deputie, &c. Or if they shall know of any that shall spoyle, rob, or deface any Church, they shall with all sincerity proceed to the punishment of the Offendors, according to the Lawes, Statutes, and Ordinances of this Realme, or according to their discretions: They shall assist and defend all Arch-Bishops, Bishops, and all other ecclesiastical Ministers in the ministry of their function, and in the quiet possessing of their Landes, rents, services, and hereditaments and shall punish the with-holders, intruders, and usurpers of the same, according to their discretions, and the quality of the offence. They shall also giue earnest charge for the observation of all Lawes, and Statutes, or Ordinances made, or to be made for the benefit of the Common-wealth, and punishment of malefactors, and especially the Statute for Hue and crie, for Night-watches, and for Weights and Measures, to be diligently considered, and severely put in execution.

Also the said Lord President shall haue and retaine, one Chaplin or Minister, that shall and can preach, and reade the Homilies, who shall bee allowed his Dyet in the Houshold of the sayd Lord President, and shall receiue his entertainment to bee payd out of the Fines growing in that Province, to whom the Lo: President shall cause due reverence to be given, in respect of the Office that he shall haue for the Service of God.

Also the said Lo: Deputie and Councell will, that the sayd Lord President and Councell, or two of them at least, whereof the Lord President to bee one, shall endeavour themselues to execute as well all and all manner Statutes of this Realme, Proclamations, and to doe and execute all other Lawes and Statutes of this Realme, and other Ordinances, as to punish the transgressors of the same, according to the said Statutes, Ordinances, and Proclamations: And to leavie or cause to be leavied all and all manner of forfeitures contained in the same, according to the order limitted by the sayd Lawes: And if cause so require, shall compound for reasonable causes for all and singular such forfeitures and paines by their discretions; Having therein regarde not to diminish the fines specially limited by the Lawes, without great necessitie of the poverty of the parties to be ioyned with repentance and disposition of amendment in the partie, for otherwise it is perillous to giue example in weakening the iust terror of good Lawes.

Also the Lord President and Councell or two of them whereof the Lord President to be one, shall and may assesse and taxe Costs and dammages, as well to the Plaintiffe as to the Defendant, and shall awarde Executions for their doings, Decrees and Orders: And shall punish the Breakers of the same, being parties therevnto by their discretions.

And the said Lord President and Councell, shall immediately upon their repair to some convenient place, where they meane to reside within the Limits of their Commission, appointing two sufficient men to bee Clearkes or Attornies to that Councell, for the making of Bils, Answers, and Processes for all manner of Subiects, and therein not multiply such officers, lest also they be occasion to multiply unnecessary suites, and some trusty wise persons to examine witnesses betweene partie and partie, which of necessitie would be chosen with good advice, foreseeing expressly and charitably, that no excessiue fees be by any of them taken of the Subiects, but that their fees bee assessed by the Lord President and Councell, and the same faire written upon a Table, and fixed upon some publike place where the same may be seene, and understood of all Suitors, and that in the beginning the Fees may appeare, and be meane and reasonable; So as in no wise the prosecution of releefe by way of Iustice bee not so chargeable as the poor oppressed sort bee thereby discouraged to make their complaints.[1]

And because it shall be convenient, that a Register bee daily kept for all the doings, orders, decrees and proceedings, which from time to time shall passe by the said Lo. President and Councell : The Lord Deputie and Councells pleasure is, that the Clarke of the sayd Councell for the time being, have reasonable allowance for the same of the parties having an interest thereby, shall diligently execute and performe this charge without any further expences then shall bee specially directed unto him by the said Lord President to be sustained by her Majesties Subjects, for enteries of Actes and Orders, &c.

Also the said Lord Deputie and Councell haue thought it convenient, that there shall bee one honest and sufficient man appointed to bee Clarke and receiver of the Fines, at the nomination of the sayd Lord President, who shall diligently and orderly keepe a Booke of all such Fines as shall be taxed upon any person; the fine to bee alwayes entred by the hand of the Lord President, and shall haue full power to send out Processe for any person, upon whom any such fine shalbe so seased, and to receiue all such fines, and in every Michaelmas Terme, thereof to make a true and perfect account before the Barons and other Officers of the Queenes Majesties Exchequer for the time being, to the end we may be assertained what fines haue bin acquired to the Queenes Majestie, and how the same haue been imployed. Provided alwayes, and it shall be lawfull for the said Lord President and Councell, to imploy of the said Fines, reasonable summes for reward of Messengers, and repairing the Queenes castles and houses, and in building and reedifying Goales within each Countie, in the precinct of their Commission, where by Lawes of the Realme no other persons are thereto bound and chargeable : and also for furnishing of necessary utensils for the houshold, as to the said L. President and Councell, or to any two of them, whereof the Lord

---

[1] The Queen always represented herself as the defender of the poor. Her Irish officers in their despatches usually take care to mention that they were acting in the interests of the poor and oppressed. This, at all events, was the theory of the State, put forward on all occasions, no doubt acted up to in a measure. The "Four Masters" describing Perrot's surrender of the Presidency of Munster, inform us that the poor and the oppressed lamented at his departure.

President to bee one, shall seeme needful and convenient. In all which the said Lord President shall haue regard to moderate those allowances, as of the Fines assessed and levied, the Queenes Maiestie may be answered some reasonable yeerely Sommes towards her great chardges in maintaining of this Councell, the same being to the Crowne of England a new chardge, and any warrantment signed by the said Lord President, or any one of the Councell for any such Somme or Soms, shall be a sufficient dischardge to the said Clearke our Receiver of the said Fines for the issuing of the said Sommes. And the said Clearke or Receiver shall haue full power for the sending out of Processe against any person upon whom any such Fine shall be cessed, and to haue his Processe gratis from the Clearke of the Signet, and hee to haue his diet in the house of the said Lord President, and to bee accounted one of the number of his Horsemen, and to receiue the wages, and entertainement due for the same.

Also the said Lord Deputie and Councell haue thought meete there shall be a continuall housholde kept within the precinct and limits of the Commission aforesaid in such place, as to the Lord President shall seeme most convenient; All servants necessary for which houshold shall be at the Nomination of the said Lord President; In which house, each Councellor bound to continuall attendance, and attending shall bee allowed their diets, and the clearke of the Councell, and every other Councellor, being either sent for or comming for any needful busines, for the Queene, or countrey shall be allowed during their aboad there their diet. And for the more honourable porte of the said Houshold, there shall be allowed unto the said Lord President and Councell after the rate of ten pounds sterling by the weeke, to bee imployed upon the Table chardges of the said Household, halfe yeerely to bee received at the hands of the Vice-treasurer, and generall Receiuer of the Queenes Maiesties revenewes of this Realme, for payment of which there shall remaine in the hands of the said Vice-treasurer (who is also Treasurer for the Warres), a Warrant dormant, whereby the said Vice-treasurer shall be authorized to pay to the said Lord President, one halfe yeeres allowance alwayes before hand towards the making his necessary provision, out of the revenew: Or if he shall not haue sufficient Treasure, then out of any other Treasure, the said Lord President shall nominate and appoint one discreete and sufficient man of his servants to bee Steward, or clearke of the same Houshold, who shall weekely write and summe the chardges thereof, and the same also shall hee weekely present to the Lord President and Councell, to be considered.

And because her Maiestie meaneth principally to benefit her Subiects, not onely with the fruites of Iustice, but with the delivery of them from all unnecessary burdens: The Lord President and Councell shall foresee, that no manner of extraordinary or excessiue charge bee put and layed upon any person against their Wils and Agreements, by finding or sustaining of any Horsman, or Footman, or Horse-boy, or Horse belonging to the said Lord President, or any of the said Councell, or any belonging to them. And in the like manner shall see that the Subiects bee not oppressed with the like by any other, contrary to the Lawes of the Realme for such causes provided.[1]

Item, considering the Queenes Maiestie hath title and right to no small quantity of possessions, within Mounster, as well of auncient revenew of the Crowne, and of other Seigniories devolued to the Crowne; And also of the dissolved Monasteries and other Houses of religion, the which are not duely answered to her Maiestie as reason would; The said Lord President and Councell shall from time to time imploy their Labours by all their good discretions, to procure that her Maiesties Officers or Farmors appointed for that purpose, may peaceably and fully from time to time possesse and receiue the profits of the same.

The Oath to bee ministred by the Lord President to such as shall be admitted to bee of the Councell of Mounster, being not already sworne of her Majesties Privie Councell in Ireland, as well the oath provided in the Statute for swearing of Officers, as also this heereunder written, *viz.*

You shall sweare to the uttermost of your power, will, and cunning, you shall be true and faithfull to the Queenes Majestie our Soveraigne Lady, and to her Heires and Successors.

You shall not know nor heare any thing that may in any wise be prejudiciall to her Highnes, or the Commonwealth, peace and quiet of this her highnesse Realme, but you shall with all diligence reveale and disclose the same to her Highnesse, or to such other person or persons of her Majesties Privie Councell in Ireland, as you shall thinke may and will soonest convey and bring it to her Highnesse knowledge.

You shall serue her Maiestie truely and faithfully in the roome and place of her Maiesties Councell in Mounster.

You shall in all things that bee moved, treated, and debated in any Councell, faithfully and truely declare your mind and opinion according to your heart and conscience: In no wise forbearing so to doe for any respect of Favour, Meade, Dreade, Displeasure, or corruption.

Yee shall faithfully and uprightly to the best of your power, cause Iustice to bee duely and indifferently ministered to the Queenes Maiesties Subiects, that shall haue cause to sue for the same, according to equity and order of Lawes.

Finally, you shall bee vigilant, diligent, and circumspect in all your doings and proceedings, touching the Queenes Maiestie and her affaires.

All which points and Articles before expressed, with all other Articles signed with the hands of the Lord Deputie and Councell of

---

[1] Coigne and Lyvery were such inveterate evils in Ireland that it was almost impossible to root them out. The words mean "man's meat and horse meat." The State indeed was a chief offender. The Queen regarded as her most certain prerogative the right to quarter horse and foot upon the country. When the gentlemen of a county would not yield to pay her rent she applied this form of pressure.

APPENDIX.

this Realme, and delivered to mee the Lord President of her Highnesse Councell established in these parts: You shall faithfully obserue, keepe, and fulfill to the uttermost of your Power, Wit, Will, and cunning, so helpe you God, and the contents of this Booke.

The names of the Councellors to bee Assistant to the Lord President of Mounster, as they are directed under the hand of the Lord Deputie.

The Earle of Ormond.
The Earle of Kildare.
The Earle of Thomond.
The Vice-Co: Barry.
The Lord Audley.
The Bishop of Corke.
The Bishop of Limer.
Sir Nicholas Welsh.
Justice Saxey.

Sir Francis Barkley.
Sir George Thornton.
Justice Golde.
The Queenes Sergeant.
The Q. Attorney generall.
The Q. Solicitor.
Sir Charles Wilmot.
Garret Comerford, Esq.
Hugh Cuffe, Esquire.

Adam Dublin.
Thom. Midens.
George Cary.
Rich. Wingfield.
Anth. St. leger.
George Bourcher.
Geof. Fenton.
Fra. Stafford.

HER MAJESTIES LETTERS PATENTS, FOR JAMES FITS GERALD, TO BEE EARLE OF DESMOND.

ELIZABETH Dei Gratia, Angliæ, Franciæ, & Hiberniæ Regina, fidei Defensor, &c. Archiepiscopis, Ducibus, Marchionibus, Comitibus, Vicecomitibus, Episcopis, Baronibus, Iusticiarijs prepositis, Ballivis, Ministris, & omnibus alijs fidelibus suis salutem. Cum non ita pridem Gerot nuper Comes Desmondæ, Cuius proavos ob præclaras suas erga Rempublicam res gestas, progenitores nostri Regij Comitum titulo ornarunt, infandi in nobis Coronamq ; nostram perduellionis attinctus generis sanguinisq ; sui nobilitatem vitiaverit, totumq ; illud dignitatis nomen penitus aboleverit. Ea tamen semper fuit nostra ad clementiam propensitas atque ad ignoscendum Regia facilitas, vt in totaimperij nostri moderation in hujusmodi proditor' posteros, non modo, non summo jure vsi sumus, sed etiam eos (meritis suis non obstantibus) ijsdem quibus reliquos subditos nostros favoribus & præmijs affecerimus. Eaque de causa nos sumptibus nostris properijs, Iacobum fits Gerald filium prefati Gerot natu maximum aluimus, omniq ; apparatus & educationis genere homine tam nobili orto non indigno institui curavimus : Non ferentes delictata mala meriti patris, in bono indolis filio castigari. Et quoniam idem Iacobus ita vere virtutis & nobilitatis insignijs preditus est, vt merito illum & nobis & Coronæ nostræ omni fidelitate inseruitur, ac Patriæ suæ summo futurum ornamento aperemus, si honoribus dignitatisq; titulis per patrem nuper amissis insigniretur. Sciatis igitur, quod nos de gratia nostra speciali, ac ex certa scientia & mero motu nostro, prefatum Iacobum fits Gerald in Comitem Desmoniæ, in Regno nostro Hiberniæ ereximus, perfecimus, & creavimus ; Ac per presentes erigimus, perficimus, & creamus ; Et ei nomen, statum, stilum, titulum, honorem et dignitatem Comitis Desmoniæ, Loco & suffragio, in Parliamentis nostris in prædicto Regno nostro Hiberniæ, tenendum, sicut & eodem modo quo prædictus Gerot jam ultimus Comes, aliquo tempore ante attincturam suam prædictam, habuit, seu habere debuit, seu consuevit, Cum omnibus alijs & singulis preheminencijs, honoribus, ceterisq; quibuscuncq ; huius modi, statui, & dignitati Comitis Desmoniæ, temporibus retroactis pertinent' seu spectant', damus & concedimus, per presentes : Ipsumq ; statu stilo honore & dignitate Comitis Desmoniæ per Cincturam gladij insignimus & realiter nobilitamus. Habendum & tenendum nomen, statum, titulum, honorem & Dignitatem Comitis Desmoniæ predict'. Cum omnibus & singulis preheminencijs, honoribus, suffragijs, & ceteris premissis quibuscunq ; præfato Iacobo fits Gerald, & Heredibus masculis de corpore suo legitime procreatis, & procreandis, imperpetum. Quoniam autem Comitis Dignitat', convenire, putamus, vt qui ejusdem dignitat' à patre, aut alio parente successionem proximam expectet, aliquo inferioris dignitatis titulo decoretur, proinde de vberiori gratia nostra volumus, & concedimus, pro nobis Heredibus & Successoribus nostris, quòd quilibet Heres masculus de corpore dicti Iacobi fits Gerald legitime, procreat', qui successionem in dict' Comitate velut proximiore gradu expectet, & pro Hered' apparente, juxta tenorem huius concessionis nostræ habeatur, Baro de Inchequin in Comitatu Corke, in dicto Regno nostro Hibernæ durante ejus vita, qui prædict' dignitat' Com' obtinet perpetuis futuris temporibus vocetur & appelletur, ac nomine, stilo, statu dignitat' & preheminencijs Baronis de Inchequin, eodem pro tempore gaudeat & vtetur. Et hoc absq ; fine, seu feodo, solvend' in hamperio nostro seu alibi, ad vsum nostrum quoquo modo, Eo quod expressa mentio de certitudine premissorum, sive eorum alicuis, aut de alijs donis siue concessionibus per nos seu per aliquem Progenitorum nostrorum, præfato Iacobo fits Gerald, ante hæc tempora fact' in presentibus minime fact' existit, aut aliquo Statuto, Actu, Ordinatione, Provisione, siue Restrictione, in Contrarium inde antehac habit' fact' edict' ordidat', sine provisa, haud aliqua alia re causa vel materia quacunq ; in aliquo non obstante. In cujus rei Testimonium has Literas nostras fieri fecimus Patentes Teste me ipsa apud Oatlands, primo die Octobris Anno Regni nostri Quadragesimo secundo.

Peripsam Reginam.

APPENDIX. 335

THE COPIE OF THE PROCLAMATION FOR PUBLISHING THE NEW MONEY FOR IRELAND.

The Queenes most excellent Majestie finding by the Records of both her Realmes of England and Ireland, that in the times of divers of her Progenitors, Kings, of England and Ireland, it hath beene accustomed as a thing by them found convenient for good of the loyall Subjects of both Realmes; that there should bee a difference betweene the Standerds of the monies allowed to bee currant, in each of her said Realmes; and knowing by many Lawes of this her Realme of England; and namely by one made in the third yeare, and another in the nineteenth yeare of Her Majesties Grandfather of famous memory King *Henry* the seventh, that the transportation of monies of the Coyne and Standard of England, into that his Realme of Ireland is severely forbidden under great penalties; perceiving also by experience in some part heretofore, but more fully and apparently now of late yeares, since the last rebellions (which haue caused Her Majestie to send great summes of money into that Realme for the paiment of her Armie, & for other services) that a great part of such monies into that Realme sent, doe either come into the hands of the Rebels, by divers slights and cunnings of theirs, who by the use and meanes thereof, trafficking in forraine Countries, doe releeue themselues with such warlicke provisions as they need; as with Powder, Lead, Match, Armour and Weapons of all sorts, and with Wines, Cloath, and other necessaries; without which they could not possibly so long subsist in their treasonable courses, and bring so huge Calamities to the rest of her good Subjects, and waste the whole Realme; or else the said sterling monies, aswell in respect of their goodnesse, being better then the monies of other Countries, is also for want of merchandize wherein to employ them; which that Countrey now specially since the Rebellion doth not yeeld, are partly by Merchants Strangers, and partly by the naturall Merchants of the Countrey (vsing trade in forraine Countries) transported from thence into the said Countries, to the inestimable losse and impoverishment aswell of that Realme of Ireland, as also chiefely of this Her Majesties Realme of England : Hath therefore in Her Majesties princely wisedome, entered into consideration with the advice of her Privie Councell, how these great inconveniences might be avoyded; and found after long and serious debating, that the readiest way to prevent the same, is to reduce the State of her Monies and Coynes, to the ancient course of her Progenitors, that is, to a difference in finenes, betweene the monies of this Realme of England, and that her Realme of Ireland : And for that purpose hath caused great quantities of moneys, according to the ancient Standard, which was in use for this Realme in the dayes of Her Majesties Father, Brother, and Sister, to bee coyned here into severall peeces of shillings, sixpences, and peeces of threepence, stamped with Her Highnesse Armes crowned and inscription of her vsuall stile, on the one side, and on the other with the Harpe crowned, being the Armes of that her Kingdome of Ireland with the insription, *Posui deum Adjutorem meum*, and also certaine peeces of small moneyes of meere Copper of pence, halfepence, and farthings, for the use of the poorer sort, stamped on each side as the other: And the same moneyes so coyned hath sent into her said Realme of Ireland, there to bee established as the lawfull and current moneys of that Realme, and so to bee uttered and issued as well to the Armies and Officers in payments to them, as also to all other her subjects of that Realme and others there abiding, or thither resorting for trifficke, and intercourse of buying, selling, and all other manner of trading amongst themselues; which sayd Coynes, as well of Silver of three ounces fine, as also of meere Copper for small Moneys, her Majestie doeth hereby publish and make knowen to all men, to be from thenceforth, immediately after the publishing of this Proclamation, her Coyne of Moneys established and authorised to bee lawfull and currant within that her Realme of Ireland, and proper to that Kingdome, and doeth expressely will and command the same to bee so used, reputed, and taken of all her subjects of that Realme, and of all others conversing there; And doth expressely charge and command, that they nor any of them, shall not after the day of the publishing heereof, refuse, reject, or denie to receiue in payment of Wages, Fees, Stipend, or in payment of debts, or in Bargaine, or for any other matter of Trade, Commerce or dealing betweene Man and Man, any of the said Moneys of either kind, either mixt of Siluer, or pure Copper, but that they shall receiue and accept the same at such values and rates as they are coyned for, *viz.* shillings for shillings, pieces of sixpence for sixpence and so of all other the severall kinds of that Coyne respectiuely; Denouncing hereby to all such as shall be found wilfully, and obstinately to refuse the said Moneys of this New Standerd, being tendered unto them in payments, or in any dealings betweene partie and partie, that they shall for that their contempt, receiue such punishment, as by her Majesties Prerogatiue Royall may be inflicted upon persons contemning publique Orders established for the universall good of that her Realme: And to the end the said Moneys may the better haue their due course and passage among her Majesties subjects of that Realme, and the good intended to both the Realmes, the more speedily take place: Her Majestie doth hereby also publish and make knowne that her pleasure is, that after the day of this present Proclamation, all other Moneys heretofore established, tollerated, or used as lawfull or currant Moneyes within that Kingdome, shall bee decryed, anulled, and called downe, and no other Moneyes, of what Coyne, Nature, Mixture, Allay or Finenesse, now used in that Realme of Ireland, bee they either Moneys of her Majesties owne Coyne and stampe, currant here in her Realme of England, or if any her Predecessors, or of any forraine Realmes permitted heretofore to be currant there, shall be any longer currant within her Realme of Ireland nor offered, nor received by any person there inhabitating, or there conversing in any manner of dealing amongst men, but that all such moneys be from that day forward held and esteemed for Bullion onely, meet to bee moulten downe and

APPENDIX. 337

brought into her Majesties Mint, or Exchange, there as heretofore is expressed; although this open and publike notification of her Majesties pleasure, bee and ought to be to all her Subjects, and others being in that her Realme, a sufficient declaration and warning, as well of the authorizing of the New Moneys of the New Standerd, now appoynted to be currant, and also the calling downe, and decrying of all other Moneys whatsoever, from any use there either publique or private: Yet her Highnesse being a Prince, that in her gracious disposition, doth ever affect to make all her Actions cleare and allowable, in their owne nature rather then in the power of supreame authoritie, intending in this cause to giue to all persons such satisfaction as is reasonable. And in the dayes of Her Progenitors, when such Moneys were in use, was not offered, doth likewise heereby make knowne, that shee hath established an Exchange to bee had and maintained in convenient places, in both her kingdoms of England and Ireland; as namely in Ireland, at *Dublin, Corke, Galway,* and *Carrigfergus;* and in England at *London, Bristow* and at *Chester,* at which places shall bee from henceforth continually resident, Officers of her appoyntment and in other places also of both the Realmes, where it shall bee found convenient for the ease of her Subjects; At which places, and by which Officers, all her subjects of either her Realmes of England and Ireland, and all others resorting into her said Realme of Ireland, in trade and Merchandise, and otherwise, shall and may, from time to time, exchange and commute, as well Moneys currant of England, into Moneys of this new Standerd of Ireland; as also Moneys of this Standerd of Ireland into Moneys of the Standerd of England, at their pleasure, in a manner as is hereafter expressed.

First, all persons being either Her Majesties Subjects, or the Subjects of any Prince or State, in amity with Her Majestie, who shall bring to any place of Exchang within Ireland any monies of the Coyne of her Realme of England, or of the Coynes of any forraine Countries, or any plate or bullion, being of the Standard of England, or better, desiring to receiue for the same in England, now is currant of England, shall receiue from the Officer in Ireland a bill directed to such place of Exchange in England, where the partie shall desire to haue his payment: By which bill hee shall receiue of the Officer in England, not onely monies of England, valew for valew, by tale or by weight, of the Monies, Plate, or Bullion delivered in Ireland, but also an overplus of sixe pence English money upon every twentie shillings English, by him delivered, by tale, or of eighteene pence English upon every pound weight of such Monies, Plate, or Bullion delivered by the partie by weight; and after the same rate for more or lesse, in quantity or number, delivered by weight or tale.

Item, all persons being Her Majesties Subjects, or the Subjects of any Prince or State in amity with Her Majestie, which shall haue in their hands any quantity or summe of the monies of this new Coyne appointed for Her Majesties Realme of Ireland, and shall be desirous to receiue for the same in England, monies currant of England, and

VOL. II. Z

thereupon shall deliver to any of Her Majesties Officers of the Exchange in Ireland, such summes of money as hee is desirous so to exchange, hee shall receiue of the said Officers in Ireland, a bill directed to such place of Exchange in England, as shall bee desired by the deliverer, by which Bill hee shall recline of the Officer in England, to whom the same is directed, the like summe of monies of England by tale, as by the Bill it shall appeare, he shall haue delivered in Ireland wanting onely twelue pence in the pound : So as for every twentie shillings of the new Coyne of Ireland, delivered in Ireland, hee shall haue in England nineteene shillings currant monie of England, and after the same rate for more or lesse in quantity delivered in Ireland.

Item, if any such person having in his hands, within the Realme of Ireland monies currant of England, shall be desirous to exchange the same there for monies now appointed to be currant in Ireland ; the Officers of the exchange there to whom hee shall bring any summe of English money to bee exchanged, shall deliver to him for every twentie shillings of English money received, one and twenty shillings of the Coyne of Ireland, and after that rate for more or lesse in quantitie received.

Item, if any person being her Majesties Subject, or otherwise, having cause to resort into the Realme of Ireland, shall be desirous to exchange monies currant of England into monies currant of Ireland for his use there, and shall deliver to that end any English monies, to any of Her Majesties Officers of exchange here in England, the said Officers shall deliver unto the said person, a bill directed to such place of Exchange in Ireland, as the deliverer shall require, by which Bill the Officer of the Exchange in Ireland receiving the same, shall deliver to the Bringer thereof for every twenty shillings English, delivered in England, one and twentie shillings of the new Coyne of Ireland, in Ireland, and after the same rate for more or lesse in quantity delivered.

And whereas there are at this present, divers old Coynes of base allay within that Her Majesties Realme of Ireland, vsed and passed in payments betweene men, which being now decryed, adnulled, and called downe, Her Majestie doth thinke fit, to haue the same brought in and reduced to one vniforme Coyne of this new Standard ; Her Highnesse is therefore pleased that every person who shall haue in his hands any quantity of such base Coyne, and shall bring in the same to any of her Officers of her Exchange there in Ireland, that the Officer receiving the same, shall deliver to the Bringer, money for money, or valew for valew, of the monies of this new Standard, now appointed to bee currant in Ireland,

And forasmuch as this notorious inconvenience aforesaid, cannot bee prevented, without there bee a due observation of such Lawes of this Realme of England, as heretofore haue beene made, restrayning the transporting of the monies currant in England into that Realme of Ireland, in *Specie*, wherein great disorder hath beene of late yeares committed, and thereby great inconveniences ensued ; Her Majestie doth straightly charge and command, all Magistrates and Officers, to whom it shall appertaine, to see severe execution of such Lawes as doe prohibit the transportation of her Coyne of England into Ireland; and namely one Statute made in the nineteenth yeare of the raigne of Her Majesties Grandfather of famous memory King *Henry* the seventh. Her Majesties purpose being (by this Proclamation) to admonish all her Subjects of both her Realmes, and all others trading in her Realme of Ireland, that they shall from henceforth forbeare all transportation of monies of England into Ireland, for that Her Majestie will cause the former Lawes (prohibiting the said transportation of money) to be so straightly looked into and executed, as the penalties thereof shall fall heavy upon the Offenders against the same without any hope of remission.

THE COPIE OF CERTAINE ARTICLES CONTAINED IN THE INDENTURES, BETWEENE HER MAJESTIE, AND SIR GEORGE CARY, TREASURER OF IRELAND, TOUCHING THE EXCHANGE ESTABLISHED UPON THE ALTERATION OF MONIES.

Item, the said Sir *George Cary* doth covenant, &c. That hee shall and will maintaine for the better exercise of the said Exchange, according to her Majesties princely meaning, three Officers at the least within the Cities of London, Bristoll and Westchester, or so many, and in such convenient places as hee shall thinke meete discreete persons to be there continually residing by themselues, or their sufficient deputies to attend the said Exchange, and to performe the same according to the establishment. And other officers also in other parts of this her Majesties Realme of England (if cause shall require) and likewise to place and maintetain at fower severall port Townes within her Majesties Realme of Ireland, *viz.* Dublin, Corke, Galway, and Carrigfergus, or at such of them as shall bee found requisit other officers who shall be there continually resident by themselues, or their sufficient deputies to attend her Majesties subjects for the exchange of their monies according to the establishment; and if cause shall require, others officers also or under ministers in other places of the said Realme of Ireland, for the ease of her Majesties subjects.

Item, the said Sir *George Carie* doth covenant, &c. to discharge and acquite her Majestie of all Fees, Allowances, and wages, needfull for any of the sayd Officers, or Vnder-ministers aboue mentioned, and them to maintaine, entertaine, and wage at his owne costs and charges, for and in consideration of a summe of two thousand pounds of the Moneys of this new Standerd of Ireland, mentioned in another Article of this Indenture, to bee by her Majestie allowed unto him for the Fee of himselfe, and all other Officers necessarie to bee had and used for and about this Exchange, as well in *England* as in *Ireland*; The sayd allowance of two thousand pound *per annum*, to take beginning, and to bee due unto him, from the first day of *May* now next ensuing the date hereof, and to continue during the time of the Exchange : And the Queenes Majestie our said Soveraigne Lady, doth covenant and agree to and with the sayd Sir *George Carey*, that hee as   of her Highnesse sayd Exchange, shall haue full power, authoritie, and libertie, to make choyce of all Officers, and under-officers, needfull to bee had and imployed, for, and about the exercise and maintenance of his Exchange, as well within this her Highnesse Realme of *England*, as in *Ireland*, and them and every of them to nominate and place, and to them to assigne such Fees and entertainments as hee shall thinke convenient, and all and every the sayd Officers to remooue, alter, or displace, as often as to him shall be thought good, and others in their places and roomes to substitute without any interruption of her Highnesse, in or concerning the same.

Item, our said Soveraigne Lady doth covenant and agree, to and with the sayd Sir *George Carey*, and by these presents doth giue him power and authoritie, in and for performance of one breach of her Highnesse Proclamation aboue specified, whereby all persons are invited to bring in all manner of sterling Moneys, or if any other Standards, or like finenesse, or better, into her Exchange in *Ireland*, that hee the sayd Sir *George Carey*, shall and may allow to all bringers in of such Money, Plate, or Bullion, aboue the just and true value thereof, the summe of eighteene pence currant money of *England*, upon every pound weight, or sixpence upon every twentie shillings by tale ; the same to bee taken, defaulked, and allowed by the sayd Sir *George Carey*, out of such profits as doe arise unto her Highnesse upon this Exchange.

And our Soveraign Lady doeth covenant and agree, to and with the sayd Sir *George Carey*, and by these presents doeth warrant and authorize him, that to all her subjects of her Realmes of *England* and *Ireland*, and to all Strangers, Merchants, or others, being subjects of such Princes or States as are in amitie with her Highnesse, which shall bring to any place, for the Exchange appoynted within the Realme of *Ireland*, any Moneyes of this new Standerd of *Ireland*, and desire to receiue for the same, moneyes currant of *England* heere within this Realme of England, That the sayd Sir *George Carey*, may deliver unto them and every of them here in England, moneys currant of this her Realme, by tale, for tale, *viz.* twentie shillings sterling, for every twentie shillings of her new Coyne, detaining only, and rebating to her Highnesse use, twelue pence sterling upon every twentie shillings so to bee delivered for twentie shillings of her sayd new Coyne, and after the same rate for more or lesse in quantitie.

Item, our sayd Soveraigne Lady doeth covenant and agree, &c. That hee shall and may to all persons which within her Highnesse realme of Ireland, shall at any of the places for the Exchange appoynted, deliver to him or his Deputies, the value of twenty shillings sterling, in money, plate, or bullion, and desire to receiue for the same, moneys Irish of this new coyne, for every value of twenty shillings, the summe of one and twenty shillings eight pence Irish by tale, and after the same rate for more or lesse in quantitie.

APPENDIX. 341

And our Soveraigne Ladie, &c. That hee or his Assignes shall or may to all and every persons, which at any of the places for the Exchange appoynted, heere within this Realme of England, shall deliver any Moneys, Plate, or Bullion of the Standerd of England, to the end to receiue for the same, within the Realme of Ireland, moneyes of the new Coyne of that Realme, pay, or deliver vnto them for the value of euery twenty shillings sterling, one and twenty shillings Irish by the tale, and after that rate for more or lesse in quantitie.

Item, our said Soveraigne Lady, &c. That hee shall and may, to all and every persons, bringing into any place for the exchange appointed in Ireland, monies of base allay, heretofore currant, or now vsed within the Realme, deliver by himselfe or his deputies, like quantities by weight of the monies of this new Coyne, as he or his deputies shall receiue of any such old base monies by weight.

Item, our said Soveraigne Lady doth, &c. That she wil allow unto said Sir *Geo. Cary*, or his Assignes for the charges of transportation of the monies of this new Coyne, from her Tower of London into her Majesties said Realme of Ireland, as well to the Citie of Dublin, as to any other places where Exchanges are to be established, or payments to bee made for her service, after the rate of twentie pounds of this new Standard, upon every thousand pound of the same coyne, the same to bee allowed unto him upon his account, as her Majesties Treasurer at warres in Ireland.

Item, our said Soveraigne Lady doth, &c. That whensoever and as often as any of the monies of this new Standard of Ireland, after their first uttering, in payment to her Highnesse Armie there, being being brought back againe to the Exchange to be converted in sterling, or otherwise shall by her Majesties commandement bee uttered againe for her Highnesse service in payment of her Armie, or otherwise: That so often her Highnesse will allow to the said Sir *George Cary* or his Assignes, after the rate of ten pounds of this new Standard, upon every thousand pounds of the same coyne by tale, the same to bee allowed unto him, upon his account as Treasurer of her Highnesse warres in Ireland.

Item, our said Soveraigne Lady doth, &c. That shee will allow unto the said Sir *George Cary* for all such summes of money, as shall by her Highnesse from time to time, bee sent or delivered out of her Exchequer, for the furnishing & maintenance of this Exchange after the rate of   upon every thousand pounds by tale. The said Sir *George Cary* taking upon him the charges and expence, of conveying her Majesties said Treasure unto the places where the same shall bee vsed for the exchange.

Item, our said Soveraigne Lady doth, &c. That all hazard and danger hapning in the transportation of this her majesties monies, out of her Realme of England into Ireland, either by wrecke of Sea or tempest, or by violence of enemies, shall bee at the only perill of our said Soveraigne Lady her Heires and Successors, as heretofore it hath beene in like cases; the said Sir *George Cary* making proofe, that hee his deputies or Assignes, having charge of the said transportation, haue vsed all such care, heed, and diligence, for the safe conveyance thereof, as they would or might haue done for the assurance of their own goods, or as heedful provident men use to doe for the safetie of their goods in like adventures.

Item, our sayd Soveraigne Lady doth, &c. That shee shall and will from time to time, furnish and deliver to the said Sir *George Cary*, or his Assignes, all such summes of money as shall be requisite and needful for Exchanging, and converting of this new Irish Coyne into moneys of the Standerd of England according to her Majesties Proclamation, after the rate of one fourth part at the least, of such quantities of this Irish moneys, as her Majestie shall cause to be coyned from time to time, or after a greater rate (if it shall appeare by experience) that a greater portion then a fourth part of the same shal be returned to the Exchange.

Item, our sayd Soveraigne Ladie doth, &c. That if at any time heereafter her Majestie shall thinke good to cease the Exchange, and not to continue the converting of Irish moneys into sterling, and that it shall happen, that at such time there shall bee remaining in the hands of the sayd Sir *George Cary* any quantities of Irish Monies, great or small, not issued for her Majesties service, that in such case her Highnesse will accept, and allow unto the said Sir *George Cary* upon his account all such summes of money at such rate, and valew as the same were delivered unto him, to bee issued in payment for her service.

And further, her Majestie doth covenant, &c. That for the defraying of all Wages, Fees, and Stipends, as well to him the said Sir *George Cary* as   of the Exchanges, as also to all other Officers needfull to bee established for the exercise of the same, either within the Realme of England or in Ireland, wheresoever her Highnesse doth, and will, allow unto the said Sir *George Cary* the summe of two thousand pounds of the monies of this new Standard, by the yeare to bee taken unto him and stayed in his owne hands out of such profits, as upon the exchange doth arise unto her Majestie : The said allowance of two thousand pounds *per annum*, to take beginning the first day of May now next ensuing the date hereof, and to continue during all the time that the Exchange shall be upheld.

A LETTER FROM TYRONE, JAMES FITS THOMAS, FLORENCE MAC CARTY, AND MAC DONOGH TO THE POPE.

Sanctissime Pater, cum superioribus annis Dei summi nutu & voluntate excitati ad recuperandum Hoc Regnum ab Anglorum gravissimo jugo, qui & Religionem & regionem vi & tyrannide multis seculis occuparere, id nunc tandem post multa pericula exantlata, pro majore parte excussimus, sanctitati vestræ exponimus, quod prima nobis &

præcipua fuit cura perpetuoq ; erit, statum ecclesiæ, hic fere extinctum in integrum restituere & collapsum rediutegrare, ita apud nos judicantes nostrarum partium esse, vitam ipsam omnemque subtantiam nostram in eo augendo impendere, id quod libentiori animo præstare conamur (ut non dicamus cogimur) quia nisi tempestive communi malo in utroque statu occurseriaus nobiscum deterius longe actum fuisset quam Turcæ solent agere, cum sibi subditis Christianis adeo ut vel fugæ esset consulend' vel hic mors obeunda. Rebus itaque in angustias has redactis, ad quem majore spe jureque accedere cujusque opem implorare possumus, ac debemus, quàm ad te Pater spirituum in terris, ut filijs spiritualibus miserè adhuc afflictis jugoque longe graviore & crudeliore quàm Pharaonico attritis adsis. Quod nos speramus à pietate tua consecuturos exemplo omnium afflictorum, qui ad sedem tuam in talibus ærumnis accedentes opem atque desideratiorem exitum fuerunt consecuti. Ad te igitur communem omnium afflictorum, præsertim fidei causa laborantium pium & benevolum Patrem, tanquam ad unicum nostrum refugium & tutissimum asylum confugimus, fusisque lachrimis humiliter petimus, ut nostros gemitus audiat, vota suscipiat, ac postulatus concedat, ut eorum ora obstruantur franganturque vires qui oderunt Sion, ac impediunt diruta Ierusalem denuo reædificari Mænia, ubi si nobis credere dignetur tua Sanctitas ; Nunquam antecessores nostri ex tempore quo Regnum hoc in manus Anglorum devenerat, adjutores fuerant quàm nos sumus ad fidem à nostro Apostolo Sancto Patricio, traditam suscipiendum ad eamque (proh dolor) in his partibus fere extinctam hactenus & pene sepultam excusso jam pro parte Anglorum jugo exsuscitandam, promovendam augendam, & amplificandam ; Quia nihil aliud in his votis habemus quàm videre Dei gloriam & fidei orthodoxæ propugnationem : annuere itaque dignetur vestra sanctitas nostris petitionibus, qui spretis honoribus & commodis quibuscunque diem ulteriorem vivere non desideramus, quàm videre Dei Ecclesiam toto orbe florentem : petimus autem inprimis, ut ad majora fidei incrementa illis sedibus vacantibus in hoc Regno ij qui vita moribus & literatura sunt conspicui, quique in negotio fidei promovendo plurimum nobiscum laborant præficiantur quosque nobiscum Reverendissimus Corcagen' ac Cloanen' Episcopus nominavit ac commendavit tanquam idonei Pastores ad Dei gregem verbo et exemplo instruendum, ne indignis qui sine ordine & fortasse summâ cum authoritate & ambitione sese animarum curæ ingererent, nisi occurreretur aditus pateat. Quod ut petamus movemur propter summam animarum jacturam, quam ob Pastorum paucitatem in vtraque Monioniæ provincia qui undecim Episcopatus sub Metropoli Cassilensi complectitur : excipimus enim Reverend' Corcagen' & Cloaneum qui senio & labore jam pene est confectus, nostri potiuntur, & hoc eo confidentius petimus, quia qui electi consecrati, & ad nos dimissi fuerunt à vestra sacrosancta sede ad vacuas hijs in partibus sedes occupandas a nobis pro viribus in ijsdem Dei gracia defendantur, ut gregibus sibi Commissis tuto invigilare queant. Insuper desideramus ut quemadmodum felicis recordationis Pius Quintus, Pontifex Maximus contra Reginam Angliæ ejusque fautores Bullam excommunicationis ediderat; Necnon Gregorious 13. eandem continuaverat, ac vim habere in bello Giraldinarum indicavit: similem quoque sententiam ad hoc bellum promovendum, & ad felicem exitum deducendum, Sanctitas vestra emittere dignetur ac generatim sanctitati vestræ affectu quo possumus maximo regnum hoc vestrum à te solo post Deum dependens nosque humiles tuos subditos una cum procuratoribus præsentium latoribus quos pro nobis & nostro nomine deputamus, quique fuse & veraciter omnia quæ in hoc bello gessimus adjuti eorum opera & doctrina viva voce aperient plenius. Deprecantes ut Sancta vestra indubiam illis fidem dignetur adhibere eidem committimus & commendamus.—Dat' in Castris nostris Catholicis 30. Martij 1600.

Sanctitatis vestræ Obedientissimi
filij & fidelissimi subditi,
ONEALE. JAMES DESMOND.
MAC CARTIE MORE.
DERMOND MAC CARTIE, alias
MACDONOGH.

POPE CLEMENT THE EIGHTH'S INDULGENCE TO THE IRISH WHO WERE IN REBELLION.

CLEMENS P. 8. Vniversis, & singulis venerabilibus fratribus, Archiepiscopis, Episcopis, & Prelatis, nec non dilectis filijs, Principibus, Comitibus, Baronibus, ac populis Regni Hiberniæ salutem, et Apostolicam Benedictionem: cum jam diu, sicut accepimus, vos Romanorum Pontificum Prædecessorum nostrorum, ac nostris & Apostolicæ sedis Cohortationibus adducti, ad vestram libertatem recuperandam, eamq; adversus Hereticos tuendam & conservandem, bonæ memoriæ Iacobo Giraldino (qui duru servitutis jugu vobis ab Anglis sanctæ ecclesiæ desertoribus impositum, summo animi ardore depellere dum vixit pro viribus procuravit) Deinde Iohanni Giraldino ejusdem Iacobi Consobrino, & novissime dilecto filio nobili viro Hugoni principi Onel, dicto Comiti Tironensi, Baroni Dungenaniæ, et Capitaneo generali Exercitus Catholici in Hibernià conjunctis animis et viribus presto fueritis, ac opem et auxiliu prestiteritis: ipsiq; Duces & eorum Milites, nostrum Domini exercitum illis assistentes progressu temporis plurima egregia facinora contra hostes viriliter pugnare perstiterint, et in posterum præstare parati sunt; Nos, ut vos, ac Dux, et Milites prædicti alacrius in expeditionem hanc contra dictos Hereticos opem in posterum etiam præstare studeatis, spiritualibus gratijs et favoribus vos prosequi volentes, corundû Prædecessorum nostrorû exemplo adducti, ac de Omnipotentis Dei misericordiâ ac beatorum Petri et Pauli Apostolorum ejus authoritate confisi, vobis omnibus & singulis qui prædictum Hugonem Tyronensem ducem ejusq exercitum Catholicæ fidei assertores & propugnators sequimini, acillis vos adjunxeritis, aut Consilio, Favore, Commeatibus, armis, alijsq bellicis rebus seu quacung ratione eis in hac expeditione operam dederitis, ipsiq Hugoni Duci ejusq exercitus Militibus vniversis & singulis, si verè pœnitentes & confessi, ac etiam, si fieri poterit, sacra Communione refert fueritis plenariam omnium peccatorum suorum veniam & remissionem, ac eandem que proficiscentibus ad bellum contra Turcas, & ad recuperationem Terræ sanctæ per Romanos Pontifices concedi solita est, misericorditer in Domini concedimus, non obstantibus, si opus sit, nostris Decretis de non concedendis indulgentijs ad instare, ac susceptionis Indulgentiarum occasione anni Iubilæi alijsg constitutionibus et ordinationibus Apostolicis cæterisg contrarijs quibuscung. Verúm quia difficile foret præsentes nostras ad omnium quorum interest noticiam pervenire volumus, ut earum exemplis etiam impressis manu alicujus Notarij publici subscriptis ac Sigillo personæ in dignitat' Ecclesiastica Constitutæ munitis eadem fides ubig habeatur quæ ijsdem præsentibus haberetur. Datum Romæ apud Sanctum Petrum, sub annulo Piscatoris, die decimo octavo Aprilis, 1600. Pontificatus nostri, Anno Nono.

Subscrip.

The second, which was found among MacEggan's papers, was a letter written from the Holy Father Pope Clement the Eighth, to Hugh O'Neale, Earl of Tyrone, to exhort him and all his adherents to persevere, for the defence of the Catholic cause, in their unnatural rebellion; from the original whereof this following copy is extracted:—

A LETTER FROM POPE CLEMENT THE EIGHTH TO TYRONE AND THE IRISH REBELS, ANIMATING THEM TO PERSEVERE IN REBELLION.

DILECTE Fili Nobilis vir. Salutem et Apostolicam benedictionem cognovimus ex literis nobilitatis tuæ & ex hijs quæ dilectus filius Petrus Lombardus Civis nostræ præpositus Cameracensis nobis coram exposuit sacrum fœdus, quod tu & quamplures Principes & proceres, & Nobiles primarij regni istius Dei benignitate iniistis charitatis glutino Colligatum conservari & augeri quodqúe eiusdem Domini exercitum ope & virtute prospere à nobis pluries pugnatum est adversus Anglos Ecclesie & fidei desertores magnam ex his voluptatem in Domini cepimus, ipsig Patri miserecordiar' Deo gratias egimus, qui adhuc in regno istoreliquit sibi multa millia virorum qui non curvaverint genua sua ante Baal. Hi enim impias hæreses, & prophanas no vitates non sunt sequnti, imo eas detestati fortiter pugnant, pro hæreditate maiorum suorum, pro fidei salute, integritate et unitate cum ecclesia retinenda, quæ una est Catholica et Apostolica extra quam non est salus; laudamus egregiam pietatem et fortitudinem tuamfili & principum, et cæterorum omnium qui tecum juncti ac federati nulla pro Dei gloria pericula recusant, seg majoribus suis qui bellicæ virtutis & Catholicæ Religionis studio, ac laude imprimis floruerunt dignos nepotes & justos Successores ostendunt et palam profitentur: conservate filij hanc menteĉ, conseruate vnionem, et consensionem vestram, & Deus Omnipotens, Deus Pacis & Concordiæ erit vobiscum, & pugnabit pro vobis, & quemadmodum fecit prosternet inimicos suos ante faciem nostram ; Nos autem qui Nobilitatem tuam & vos omnes avitæ fidei & gloriæ imitatores paternæ, a manus & gerimus in visceribus Iesu Christi, non cessamus Deum orare nostrum pro vestra felicitate & salute, vestrig soliciti sumus & erimus semper quantum cum Deo poterimus, atque ubi opus fuerit scribemus efficaciter ad Reges & Principes Catholicos filios nostros ut vobis & causæ vestræ omni ope suffragentur: Cogitamus etiam propediem mittere ad vos peculiarem Nuntium nostrú, & huius sanctæ sodalitiæ, in qua Deo authore meritis licet imparibus præsidemus vestrum, pium, prudentem, zelo Dei predict' et nobis probatu, qui nostri erga nos honoris testis sit vobis; omnibus in rebus ubi usus venerit adjumento sit ad salutarem & necessariam Vnionem vestram conservandam, ac Catholicam fidem propagandam, ac omnia denique pro sui muneris Officio, officianda, quibus Dei honor & cultus in regno isto augeatur. Interea placuit has nostras literas ad vos præmittere testes amoris nostri, in vos et Regnum istud, et ut vos omnes tanquam filios nostros in Christo dilectos paterno affectu consolaremur ; ipsum veró Petrum Lombardum, quem Nobilitas sua oratorem & negotiorum gestorem constituit apud nos, et jam libenter audivimus, et deinceps audiemus, tibi veró et cæteris qui tibi unanimes pro fidei Catholicæ propugnatione adhærent, nostram & Apostolicam benedictionem benignè impartimur ; Denig precamur ut Angelos emittat in circuitu vestro, & pios conatus vestros sua cœlesti gratia dirigat vosg dextra suæ potentiæ perpetuo tueatur. Datum Romæ apud Sanctum Petrum, sub Annulo Piscatoris, die 20. Ianuarij, Anno 1601. Pontificatus nostri anno 9.

SILVIUS ANTONIANUS CARDINALIS.

Dilecto Filio Nobili viro Vgoni
Principi Nœlio, Exercitus
Catholici in Hibernia Duci,
& Capitaneo Generali.

The third is an instrument here immediately following, comprehending the prescript form of the Pope's Bull, usually granted in the presentation to spiritual dignities, together with the oath to the Pope's supremacy, and of the Articles of Faith, whereunto the Popish Clergy are enjoined to subscribe: All which things being not so familiar in this land (thanked be God) as in former ages, and many no doubt desirous to be made acquainted with the particulars thereof, although it may seem somewhat tedious, by reason of the prolixity, yet have I thought good in this place to transcribe the same *verbatim* according to the original:—

POPE CLEMENT THE EIGHTH'S BULL FOR THE GRANTING OF SPIRITUAL LIVINGS TO OWEN MACEGGAN.

CLEMENS Episcopus servus servorum Dei : Dormitio episcopo Corrag' salutem & Apostolicam benedictionem ; Romani pontificis providentiam circumspecta Ecclesijs & Monasterijs singulis, quæ vacationis incommoda deplorare noscuntur: vt gubernatorum vtilium fulciantur

Appendix.

præsidio prospicit diligenter, & personis Ecclesiasticis qui huslibet, vt in suis opportunitatibus, Congruum suscipiant relevamen subvetionis auxilio, prout decens est, providet opportunè. Cum itag ficut accepimus Monasterium Abbatia nuncupatum loci de Namona sancti Benedicti, vel alterius ordinis, Corrag' Dioc'. certo modo vacaverit, & vacet ad præsens, licet quidam Larcus schismaticus authoritate pretensæ Reginæ Angliæ, jam à multis annis citra Monasterium illiusque fractus redditus, & proventus vsurpaverit, & in suos damnabiles vsus converterit, & adhuc & convertit: Nos volentes tam eidem Monasterio, de gubernatore vtili, & idoneo perquem circumspectè regi, & salubriter dirigi valeat, quum dilecto filio Eugenio MacEggan dictæ Dioc' Bacchalaureo in theologia, et magistro in artibus apud nos de literarum scientia, vitæ ac morum honestate alijsg probitatis, ac virtutum meritis multipliciter commendato, vt commodius sustentari valeat de alicuius subventionis auxilio providere ipsumque Eugenium præmissorum suorum meritorum intuitu favore prosequi gratioso, & à quibusvis excommunicationis suspensionib' & interdictis; alijsque Ecclesiasticis sententijs censuris à jure, vel ab homine quavis occasione vel causa latis, si quibus quomodolibet accomodatus existat ad effectu præsentium duntaxat consequedum harum serió absolventes, & absolutum fore consentes, nec non verum & vltimum dicti Monasterij vacationis modum, etsi illo quævis reservatio generalis, & in corpore juris clausa resultet, præsentibus pro expresso habentes fraternitati tuæ per Apostolica scripta mandamus ostendamus, si per diligentem examinationem dictam Eugeniique idoneam repereris ad ipsum Monasterium in commendam obtinendum, super quo conscientiam tuam oneramus, Monasterium prædict' quæ cura & conventu curet, ac cujus & illi forsan annexorum fructuum redditus, & proventus centum & quinquaginta marcharum sterlingorium, secundum communem estimationem valorem annun, vt dictus Eugenius asserit non excedunt quovismodo, & excujuscunque persona seu per liberam cessionem cujusuis de illius regimine & administratione in Romana curia, vel extra eam, & coram notario publico et testibus fide dignis sponte factam vacat, et si illius provisio ad sedem eandem specialiter vel generaliter pertineat, et super eodem regimine administratione inter aliquos bis habita, cujus statum etiam præsentibus haberi volumus pro expresso penderit indecisa Domini de tempore dat', presentium eidem Monasterio de Abbate prouisum, aut illud alteri commendatum canonicè non existat, cum annexis hujusmodi ac omnibus juribus, & pertinentijs suis eidem Eugenio quatenus illud commendari consueuerit per eum quoad vincrit, tenendum, regendum, gubernandum, ita quòd liceat eidem Eugenio debitis & consuetis ipsius Monasterij supportatis oneribus, ac tertia parte illius fructuum redituum & proventuum restaurationem ipsius fabricæ, seu ornamentorum emptionem, vel fulcimentum, aut pauperum alimoniam, prout major suaserit aut exegerit necessitas omnibus alijs deductis annis singulis impertita; de residuis illius fructibus, reditibus, & proventibus disponere & ordinare, sicuti ipsius Monasterij Abbates qui pro tempore fuerant, de illis disponere & ordinare potuerunt, seu & debuerunt, alienatione tamen quorumcung bonorum immobilium, & preciosorum mobilium dicti monasterij sibi pœnitus interdicta authoritate nostra commendes curam ipsius Monasterij, ac hujusmodi regimen & administratione eidem Eugenio in spiritualibus & in temporalibus plenariè committendo. Ac illi in adipiscenda possessione, seu quasi regimini & administratione, bonorum Monasterij hujusmodi assistendo facias sibi à dilectis filijs, vassalis, & alijs subditis ejusdem monasterij consueta servitia, & jura sibi ab eis debitas integrè exhiberi contradictores authoritatis nostræ predicta appellatione postposita compescendo : Non obstantibus fœlicis recordationis Bonifacij, P. 8. predecessoris nostri & alijs apostolicis constitutionibus, ac monasterij & ordinis prædict' etiam juramento confirmatione apostolica, vel quavis firmitate alia roboratis statutis & consuetudinibus contrarijs quibuscung. Aut si vassalis & alijs subditis prefatis, vel quibusvis alijs communiter, vel divisim ab endem sit sede indultum quod interdici, suspendi & excommunicari non possint per literas apostolicas, non facientes plenam & expressam, ac de verbo in verbum de indubitato hujusmodi mentione. Volumus autem quod propter commendam monasterij hujusmodi monasterium predictum in spiritualibus, non lædatur & in temporalibus detrimenta non sustineat, sed illius congruè supportentur onera consueta, vtque postquam dictus Eugenius repertus fuerit idoneus, & antequam dictum monasterium ei commendetur fidem Catholicam iuxta articulos pridem a dicta sede propositos, in manibus tuis juxta vnam profiteri omnino teneatur, alioquin presens gratia, & omnia que inde sequentur nulla sint, tuque aliter commendans a collatione beneficiorum suspensus sis eo ipso, sicque suspensus remaneas donec relaxationem suspensionis hujusmodi à sede predicta merueris obtinere, ac quod antequam dictus Eugenius regimini, & administrationi predictis se in aliquo misceat in eisdem manibus tuis nostro & Romanæ Ecclesiæ nomine fidelitatis debitæ solitum prestet iuramentum iuxta altera formis presentibus adnotatur, ac professionis quam idem Eugenius faciet, et iuramenti quod prestabit formas huiusmodi ; nobis de verbo ad verbum per eius patentes literas suo sigillo immunitas per proprium munitium quantociùs destinare procures. Et insuper si dictus Eugenius ad hoc repertus idoneus fuerit, vt prefertur, ei nunc perinde irritum decernimus, & mano si serius super his à quoquam quavis authoritate, scienter vel ignoranter attentari contigerit, ac si die dat' presentium eidem Eugenio ad id reperto idoneo monasterium predictum cum interpositione decreti huiusmodi mandavimus commendari : Forma autem iuramenti hec est. Ego Eugenius Abbas Monasterij, Abbatiæ nuncupati loci de Namona sancti Benedicti, vel alterius ordinis Corragen' dioc' ab hac hora ni antea fidelis ero obediens beato Petro sanctæque Apostolicæ Romanæ Ecclesiæ, & Domino nostro Domino Clementi Papæ octavo eiusque successoribus canonice intrantibus : Non ero in consilio aut consensu vel facto ut vitam perdant aut membrum, seu capiantur aut in eos violenter manus quomodolibet ingerantur vel injuriæ aliquæ inferatur quovis quesito colore ; cosilium verò quod mihi credituri sunt per se aut Nuntios seu literas ad eorum damnum me sciente nemini pendam.

Appendix.

Papatum Romanum & regale sancti Petri adjutor eis ero ad retinendum & defendendum contra omnium hominum legatum Apostolice sedis in eundo & redeundo, honorifice tractabo & in suis necessitatibus adiuvabo. Iura, honores, privilegia & authoritatem Romanæ ecclesiæ Domini nostri Papæ et successorum suorum conservare et defendere, augere et promovere curabo. Nec ero in cousilio vel facto seu in tractatu in quibus contra ipsum dominum nostrum vel eandem Romanam Ecclesiam aliqua sinistra seu prejudicialia personarum nostri honoris status et potestatis eoru machinentur, et si talia à quibuscung tractari novero, vel procurari impediam, hoc pro posse et quanto citus potero comode significabo eidem domino nostro vel alteri per quem ad ipsius notitiam possit per venire Regulus sanctorum patrum decreta, ordinationes, sententias, provisiones, reseruationes, et mandata apostolica totis viribus observabo, et faciam ab alijs obseruari. Hereticos, Schismaticos, et rebelles domino nostro, vel successoribus predictis pro posse persequar, et impugnabo, vocatus ad Synodum veniam nisi propeditus fuero Canonica præpeditione; possessiones vero ad mensam meam pertinentes, non vendam, neg donabo, neg impignorabo, neg de nouo infeudabo, vel aliquo modo alienabo, & cum consensu conventus Monasterii mei inconsulto Romano Pontifice, sic me Deus adiuvet & hæc sancta Dei evangelia. Forma vero professionis fidei talis est. Ego Eugenius firma fide credo & profiteor omnia, & singula quæ continentur in Symbolo fidei, qua sancta Romana Ecclesia utitur, viz.

Credo in unum Deum Patrem Omnipotentem factorem Cœli & terræ visibilium omnium et in visibilium, et in unum Dominum Iesum Christum filium Dei unigenitum, et ex Patre natu ante omnia, secula, Deum de Deo, Lumen de lumine, deum verum de Deo vero genitum non factum, consubstantialem Patri, per quem omnia facta sunt, qui proper nos homines, et propter nostram salutem descendit de cœlis, et incarnatus est de spiritu sancto ex Maria Virgine, et homo factus est, crucifixus etiam pro nobis sub Pontio Pilato, passus et sepultus est, et resurrexit tertio die secundum Scripturas, et ascendit in Cœlum, sedet ad dextram Patris, et iterum venturus est cum gloria judicare viuos et mortuos, uius regni non erit finis; et in spiritum sanctum dominum & vnificantem, qui ex patre, filiog procedit, qui cum patre & filio simul adoratur, et conglorificatur, qui locutus est per Prophetas, et unam sancta Catholicam et Apostolicam ecclesiam; Confiteor unum Baptisma in remissionem peccatorum, et expecto resurrectionem mortuorum, et vitam venturi sæculi, Amen; Apostolicas et Ecclesiasticas Traditiones reliquasg ejusdem Ecclesiæ observationes et constitutiones firmissime admitto et complector. Ite sacram Scripturam iuxta eum sensum quem tenuit et tenet sancta Mater Ecclesia, cuius est judicare de vero sensu et interpretatione sacrarum Scripturaru admitto, nec eam unqua nisi juxta unanime consensum patrum accipiam et interpretabor; profiteor quog vere et propriè septem esse Sacramenta novæ Legis à Iesu Christo Domino nostro instituta, atque ad salutem humani generis licet non omnia singulis necessaria, viz.

Baptismum, Confirmationem, Eucharistiam, Pœnitentiam, extremam Vnctionem, Ordinem & Matrimonium; illag gratiam conferre, ex his Baptismum, Confirmationem & Ordinem sine sacrilegio reiterari non posse. Receptos quoque & approbatos Ecclesiæ Catholicæ Ritus in supradictorum omnium Sacramentorum solemni administratione recipio, & admitto omnia & singula quæ de peccato originali, et de Iustificatione in sacro sancta Tridentina Synodo definita, et declarata fuerunt amplector, et recipio; profiteor pariter in Missa offerri Deo verum proprium & propitiatorium Sacrificium pro vivis & defunctis, atque in Sanctissimo Eucharistiæ Sacramento esse verè realiter & substantialiter Corpus & Sanguinem vna cum Anima & Divinitate Domini nostri Iesu Christi fierique conversionem totius substantiæ Panis et Corporis et totius substantiæ Vini in sanguinem, quam conversionem Catholica Ecclesia Transubstantiationem appellat. Fateor ut sub altera tantum specie totum atque integrum Christum verumg Sacramentum sumi constanter teneo purgatorium esse animasq ibi detentas fidelium suffragijs iuvari, similiter et sanctos unà cum Christo regnantes venerandos atg invocandos esse cosg orationes Deo pro nobis offerre, atg eoru reliquias esse venerandos; firmissimè assero imagines Christi et Deiparæ semper Virginis, nec non aliorum Santoru habendas et retinendas esse ac eis debitum honorem & venerationem esse impartiendum, Indulgentiarum etiam potestatem Christo in Ecclesia relictam fuisse, illarumg usum Christiano populo vnanimi salutarem esse affirmo sanctam Catholicam et Apostolicam Romanam Ecclesiam omnium Ecclesiarum Matrem et magnam agnosco; Romano Pontifici beati Petri Apostolorum principis successori ac Iesu Christi Vicario veram obedientiam spondeo ac Iuro. Cætera item omnia à sacris Canonibus & Œcumenicis Consilijs, ac præcipuè a Sacrosanctâ Tridentina Synodo tradita, definita, & declarata indubitanter recipio; profiteor simulque contraria omnia atque Hæreses quascung ab Ecclesia damnatas & anathematizatas, ego pariter damno rejicio & anathematizo. Hanc veram Catholicam Fidem extra quam nemo salvus esse potest, quam in præsenti sponte profiteor, & veraciter teneo eandem integram et inviolatam, usg ad extremum vitæ spiritum constantissimè Deo adjutante retinere, & confiteri atg à meis subditis, vel illis quorum cura in munere meo spectabit, teneri, doceri, & prædicari quantum in me erit curaturum. Ego idem Eugenius spondeo, voueo, et juro, sic me Deus adjuvet, et hæc sancta Dei Evangelia. Dat' Romæ apud Sanctum Petrum Anno Incarnationis Domini, 1595. Pridie Calend. Novemb' pontificatus nostri Anno quarto.

Let the understanding reader now cease to marvel that the Bishop of Rome doth strive and struggle to depose Princes and to animate and encourage subjects to heathenish and inhuman murders and rebellions, since he dareth (like the ancient giants) to attempt and assault Heaven itself and to displant and displace from the Throne of his Majesty Christ Jesus himself, who is God to be blessed for evermore. What is it else but to make the precepts and traditions of men equivalent with the doctrine and commandments of God? What is it else but to usurp an absolute and universal power and authority over the flock of Christ, as his Lieutenant and Vicar, for the warrant whereof he hath no commission, nor was he called thereunto as Aaron was? Lastly, what is it else but to remove and pull down the Son of God from his triumphant glory, where he sitteth at the right hand of his Father, and where he must abide, the holy Apostle bearing witness, till all his enemies be subdued under his feet, and to bring back his glorified body and deified soul, at the beck and word of every hedge-priest, into their sacrilegious Sacrament of the altar; surely a man need go no farther for testimony, seeing the Antichristian lowing of this profane Bull doth lively delineate and plainly demonstrate that purple harlot who hath made all nations drunk with the dregs of her fornication, having seated herself upon the seven hills of Rome. I should be over troublesome to the reader to shake up all the trumpery and rake in all the dirt conveyed in his Bull's belly; yet one thing more I cannot pass over in silence, namely, forasmuch as the Pope perceiveth that his kingdom cannot long stand, but that Babel must fall, and Antichrist must be consumed with the breath of the Lord's mouth, therefore with prudent care and politic circumspection he suffereth none to be initiated into his holy Sacrament of orders, nor preferred to any ecclesiastical promotion, but he is first bound by his hand, word, and corporal oath to maintain and defend the pomp, honour, privileges, prerogatives, and doctrines of the See of Rome, especially and namely such as are contradictorily repugnant to the written word of God; and that they shall persecute and impugn all those (whether prince or people) that shall be adjudged heretics or schismatics in the Pope's consistory: Consider, therefore, I beseech thee, gentle reader, whether any priest that taketh this oath (for they all take it) can be accounted a good subject to the Crown of England; but to proceed.

Many of the traitors being put to the sword, the strangers banished, and the provincials protected, as you have heard, there were still remaining in action in Munster (left for example to perdition) Fitz-Maurice, the Lord of Lixnaw; John FitzThomas, the brother of James, the late titulary Earl; the Knight of the Glyn, and Thomas Oge Geraldine, all of whom, with their forces joined, were not able to make two hundred men, lurking about the mountain of Slewlugher and in the fastness of Clanmorriss.

A CERTIFICATE FROM A POPISH BISHOP ON BEHALF OF JOHN BURKE.

Nos Mallachias Dei et Apostolicæ Sedis gratia Duacensis in Hibernia Episcopus, notum facimus Catholico ac invictissimo Hispaniarum Regi Phillipo, Domino Matheo de Oviedo, Archiepiscopo Dublinensi, et Metropolitano Hiberniæ: Omnibusç Christi fidelibus, tam spiritualibus, sive regularibus, quam secularibus personis ac si proprio nomine nominara Horum Latorem Iohannem Burk, Nobile præstant' virtutis virum propugnatore Hæreticæ pravitatis acerrimu, refugium, ac defensor religiosarum personarum esse, & ob id versari inter Anglos veræ fidei desertores, in maximo vitæ, & bonorum que hereditario jure non sine multorum præcertim Catholicorum commendo, & vtilitate adhuc possidet, terras petere alienas eo animi decreto vt aliquando in propriam reversus patriam, et patriæ miles et decus esse possit.

Proinde vos omnes pietatis et veræ religionis amatores, Catholicum Regem Philippum, Dominum Matheum supra dictos cæterosq cujuscung nationu conditionisue sitis, quos vna fides vnum baptisma, vnus spiritus adjunxit. Oramus, obsecramus, & obet est amur in Christi visceribus, vt cum prædictum Iohannem Burke, omni fide, omni auxilio, omni favoure, dignissimum Catholicum, de repub' optimo meritum, accipiatis, benigneque tractetis. In cujus rei fidem & testimonium, Sigillum ac Chirographium apposui, &c.

MALACHIAS DUAC' EPISCOPUS.

Another, that calleth himself Friar Simon de S. Sto., hath these words, writing to the said supposed Archbishop of Dublin :—

A CERTIFICATE FROM A POPISH PRIEST ON BEHALF OF JOHN BURKE.

NOTUM tibi facio, vt hoc invictissimo Regi notum facere cures harum Latorem Iohannem Burke, relictis bonis paternis te adire, quo illi ad Regem aditum præbens sui temporis opportunitatem, ad peragenda negotia maximi ponderis & momenti, quæ vnanimis hujus regionis saluti conducuut, &c.

INDEX TO NAMES AND PLACES.

A.

ABBOT, the Blind, Chief of the Low Burkes, i., 189.
Andrada, Captain Juan de Albomozy, ii., 46.
Anias, John, ii., 187.
Aquila, Don Juan de, i., 260, 277, 295 sqq.; ii., 45, 71 sqq., 101 sqq., 136, 217, 247.
Archer, James, the Jesuit, i., 20; ii. 186, 213.
Ardart Castle, i., 116.
Ardea, ii., 183, 185.
Arlogh, i., 158.
Asketon, i., 70, 97.
Awdley, Lord, i., 177.
Awneby, v. Owneboy, river.

B.

BAGNALL, Sir Samuel, ii., 197, 210, 222, 261, 266.
Ballitrarsny, Castle, i., 62.
Baltimore Haven, ii., 215.
Bandon, river, i., 291, note.
Bantry, Abbey of, ii., 152.
Barkley, Sir Francis, i., 111, 126, 161, 255.
Barkley, Sir John, i. 191, 299.
Barrett, William, i., 38.
Barry, John (Sheriff of Cork), i., 169.
Barry, Lord, i., 10 sq.
Bearhaven, ii., 214 sqq.

Beaumaris, i., 3.
Bingham, George, ii., 208.
Blarney Castle, ii., 223 sqq.
Blunt, Captain George, ii., 97 sqq.
Blunt, Sir Charles, i., 3.
Bonratty Castle, i., 66.
Borehero, Don Diego, i. 281.
Boyle, i., 131, 135.
Brien, Honore ny, i., 116.
Brochero, Don Diego, i., 248.
Brough Castle, i., 32.
Burke, John, i., 62; ii., 295.
Burke, Lord, i., 96.
Burke, Redmond, i., 36, 47, 63, note, 140, 151, 168, 192; ii., 51, 64.
Burke, Theobald ne Long, i., 153.
Burke, Walter, i., 189.
Burke, William, i., 77, note, 84; ii., 119, 280, 282.
Burkes, the, i., 60.
Butler (clan), i., 16, note, 24, note.
Butler, James Goldie, i., 53 sq., 112; ii., 226.
Butler, Sir Edmund, i., 24.

C.

CAHIR Castle, i., 2, 53, 112.
Cahir, Lord of, i., 2; ii., 292.
Caracena, Earl of, 113 sq., 123.
Carberry, ii., 86.
Carew Castle, ii., 159, 177.
Carrickfoyle Castle, i., 91; ii, 42.
Carriguess, ii., 171.

VOL. II. A a

Cashel, Archbishop of, *v.* sub MacGrath, Miler, ii., 21.
Castlehaven, ii., 216.
Castlelishin, i., 78.
Castlemange, i., 126, 134, 143.
Cecil, Mr. Secretary, i., 262.
Clanricard, Earl of, i., 154 ; ii., 28, 58, 293.
Clear, Cape, ii., 116.
Cloghan Castle, ii., 271.
Clonmel, i., 157.
Collins, Dominic, ii., 186, 202.
Comerford, Geralt, ii., 139.
Comerford, Justice, i., 113.
Condon, MacHawghe, i., 38.
Corgroge Castle, i., 97.
Cork, i., 259 *sq.*
Cormocke, Oge Carty, i., 35 ; ii., 231.
Crook Haven, i., 274.

D.

DENNY, Sir Edward, i., 102.
Dermot, Maol, i., 87, note.
Desmond, titular Earl of, *v.* sub FitzThomas, James.
Dingle Castle, i., 147.
Donboy, ii., 118 *sqq.*, 152 *sqq.*, 190 *sqq.*, 207, 220.
Don John, *v.* Aquila, Don Juan de.
Down Manus, ii., 176.
Downings, the, ii., 209.
Dublin, Archbishop of, i., 167, 228, 245, 291 ; ii., 104.
Duhallow, i., 114, note.
Dursea Island, ii., 127.

F.

FERRERS, Donnoll, i., 238.
FitzEdmonds, John, i., 39.
FitzGerald, James, i., 126 *sq.*
FitzGerald, Lady Ellis, i., 160.
FitzGerald, Lady Joan, i., 161.
FitzGerald, Lady Margaret, i., 160.
FitzGerald, Thomas Oge, i., 134, 143, 183, 241 ; ii., 277.

FitzGerald, William, i., 108.
FitzGibbon, John, i., 106.
FitzMaurice, Lord, i., 102.
FitzMorris, ii., 169.
FitzNicholas, Garrett, i., 111.
FitzThomas, James, i., 9, 27, note, 43, 56, 63, 67, 73, 86, 100, 103, 114, 118, 167, 204 *sqq.*, 228, 236 ; ii., 221.
FitzThomas, John, i., 35 ; ii., 220.
Flower, Capt., i., 29 *sq.*, 91, 189, 290 ; ii., 270, 301.
Franquesa, Secretary, ii., 106.

G.

GALDIE, James, i., 53 *sq.*
Glancomkynes, ii., 303.
Glancoyne Castle, i., 126.
Glangarrem, ii., 281.
Glynn, the, i., 82, 88.
Græme, Captain, i., 122.
Græme, Sir Richard, ii., 56 *sqq.*
Grayne, Owen, ii., 282.
Grome, Owen, i., 58.
Godolphin, Sir William, ii., 71.

H.

HARVEY, Capt. Gawen, i., 52.
Harvey, Captain Roger, ii., 86, 115, 129, 241, 270.
Hasey, Oliver, i., 221.
Haulbowlin, ii., 91.
Herbert, Sir William, i., 102, note, 103.
Hopton, Master, ii., 21.
Hotho (Howthe) Head, i., 3.
Hugh Roe, *v.* O'Donnell.

I.

INNYSHARKIN, Island of, ii., 129.

K.

KERRY, Knight of, i., 108, 114, 146 ; ii., 170, 277.
Kilcoo, i., 117 ; ii., 301.

INDEX TO NAMES AND PLACES. 355

Kilcrey Abbey, ii. 225, 230.
Kilmallock, i., 97, 121.
Kilveuny Castle, i., 207.
Kingsmill, Captain George, ii., 197.
Kinsale, i., 280; ii., 23 *sqq.*; Battle of, 54 *sqq.*, 136, 273 *sqq.*
Kirton, Lieutenant, ii., 199.
Knight of the Valley, i., 83; ii., 14.
Knockrobbin, i., 298.

L.

LACY, Pierre, i., 47, 103, 114, 122.
Lambart, Sir Oliver, ii., 56.
Leamcon, Castle, ii., 209.
Leighlin, i., 275.
Leitrim Barony, i., 47.
Lerma, Duke of, ii., 103, 107.
Letterlinless Castle, ii., 210.
Levison, Sir Richard, ii., 21, 43.
Limerick, i., 190.
Limerick, Mayor of, i., 164.
Liscaghan i., 95, 97.
Listoell Castle, i., 126, 144.
Lixnaw, i., 101, 145; ii., 188, 301.
Lixnaw, Lord, i., 108.
Loghguire, i., 37, 58.
Love, Capt. Thomas, i., 274.

M.

MACART, Brian, ii., 303 *sq.*
MacAwly, i., 114, 161, 201, 228; ii., 138.
MacCarty, Dermond Moyle, i. 247, 253; ii., 18, 172, 211.
MacCarty, Donell, i., 9, 64, 109; ii. 169.
MacCarty, Donogh Moyle, i., 234; ii., 214.
MacCarty, Finnin, ii., 214.
MacCarty, Florence, i., 9, 29 *sq.*, 38 *sq.*, 50, 63, 86, 98, 103, 109, 118, 134 *sqq.*, 150, 169, 197, 228, 231 *sqq.*, 290.
MacCarty More, i., 9, 234.
MacCarty Reugh, Sir Owen, ii., 42, 172.

MacCormock, Donough, i., 229.
MacCormock, Teg, ii., 222.
MacCraghe, Dermond, i., 158.
MacDermond, Teg, i., 253.
MacDermond, Cormock, i., 118, 240 *sqq.*, 299; ii., 13, 18, 224, 258 *sqq.*, 292.
MacDonoghs, the, ii., 13.
MacEggan, Owen, ii., 185, 207, 211, 219, 229, 287 *sq.*
MacGarret, Morris, ii., 138.
MacGoghagan, Richard, ii., 178, 185, 202.
Macguyre, Cohonoght, ii., 303.
MacHubbard, William, ii., 137.
MacMaghon, Brian MacHugh Oge, ii., 54.
MacMaghon, Teg Reugh, ii., 178.
MacOwen, i., 114.
MacOwen Carty, Teg, ii., 283.
MacOwen, Dermond, i., 253 *sq.*
MacRedmond, John, i., 105.
MacShane, Garret, i., 106.
MacSorley, James, ii., 95.
MacSwine, Hugh, ii., 282.
MacSwiny ne Doa, ii., 13.
MacTeg, Owen, ii., 267.
Magrath, Miler, i., 55, note, 67, 130, 160.
Malby, Captain, ii., 284.
Mangart, mountain, ii., 171.
Mayne, Castle of, i., 111.
Mellaghlen Moore, ii., 201.
Mocrumpe Castle, ii., 231.
Mordant, Capt. Nicolas, i., 91.
Moroghe ny Moe O'Flaherty, i., 85.
Mountgarret, Lord, i., 25.
Mountjoy, Lord, i., 3.
Moyallo, i., 163 *sqq.*
Munster rebels (letter to O'Donnell), i., 80.
Muskerry, Quirk, i., 157.

N.

NORRIS, Sir Thomas, i., 3.
Nugent, i., 59.

O.

O'Boyle, ii. 13.
O'Brien, Teg, i., 189, 197.
O'Carroll, i., 137.
O'Connor, Carbry, i., 31.
O'Connor, Dermoud, i., 30, 43, 51, 67, 73, 78.
O'Connor Kerry, i., 94; ii., 241.
O'Crowleys, i., 112; ii., 151.
O'Dogan, Dermond, i., 204.
O'Dogherty, ii., 13.
O'Donnell, i., 76, 162, 246 sq., 291; ii., 9 sqq., 15, 45, 64, 114, 216, 266.
O'Driscall, Connor, ii., 127, 213.
O'Driscall, Finnin, ii., 41.
O'Driscalls, the, ii., 40.
O'Dwyer, Dermot, i., 35.
O'Healy, John, ii., 232.
O'Keefe, i., 114.
O'Kelly, ii , 13.
O'Lerys, i., 139.
O'Lough, Owen, ii., 267.
O'Lyne, Maghon Oge, ii., 259.
O'Maghon, Moyle Mo, i., 253.
O'Mahonies, the, i., 112, note.
O'More, Owny MacRory, i., 17 sqq., 71.
O'More, Rory Ogue, i., 17, note.
O'Mulreyan's country, i., 63.
O'Neale, Hugh, v. Tyrone.
O'Neil, Con, i., 32.
O'Norscy, Teg, ii., 151.
Ormonde, Earl of, i., 16.
O'Rourke, Teigue, i., 192; ii., 284, 303.
O'Sullivan Bere, Donnell, ii., 19, note, 41, 47, 118 sqq., 152 sq., 215, 260 sq., 277, 280 sqq., 304.
O'Sullivan, Dermond, ii., 168.
O'Sullivan, Donnell, ii., 170.
O'Sullivan More, i., 65, 104, 124; ii., 168.
O'Sullivan, Owen, i., 234; ii., 150.
Owen, Richard, ii., 93.
Owneboy, river, i., 30, 291.
Owneboy, Abbey of, ii., 12.
Oyster Haven, i., 300.

P.

Parke, Castle Ny, i., 302; ii., 22, 26, 90.
Pelham, Sir William, i., 94.
Power, Sir Henry, i., 13, 30, 33.
Power, Thomas, i., 27.
Powers (Poores), the, i., 68.

R.

Racarkneltagh, ii., 158.
Rathmore Castle, i., 97.
Ratho Abbey, i., 149.
Rathowin Castle, i., 102.
Rincorran Castle, ii., 1 sqq.
Roche, Viscount, i., 2; ii., 292.

S.

Saint John, Sir Oliver, ii., 3 sqq.
Saint Lawrence, Sir Christopher, ii., 10, 51.
St. Ledger, Sir Warham, i., 13, 30 33.
Sarsfield, Dominick, ii., 258.
Saxey, Chief Justice, ii., 228.
Sheehy, Clan, i., 51.
Shelton, Thomas, i., 244.
Sinnet, Patrick, ii., 113.
Slewgort Mountain, 92, 207.
Sligo, O'Connor, ii., 14.
Slingsby, Captain, i., 208 sqq.; ii., 192.
Soto, Pedro Lopez de, ii., 129 sqq., 241.
Spain, King of, ii., 108, 120.
Spittle, the, i., 302.
Stack, Garret Roe, ii., 301.
Stacke, Maurice, i., 95, 116.
Stanley, Sir William, ii., 94.
Sugan Earl, v. sub FitzThomas, James.

T.

Taffe, Captain, ii., 53, 230, 287.
Taylor, Thomas, ii., 202.

Thomond, Earl of, i., 18; ii., 21 *sqq.*, 81, 148 *sqq.*, 175.
Thornton, Sir George, i., 206; ii., 295 *sqq.*
Timoleg, Abbey of, ii., 173.
Tirrell, Richard, i., 48; ii., 153, 175, 206 *sqq.*, 260 *sq.*, 266 *sqq.*, 276, 280.
Tralee, i., 102.
Tyrone, Earl of, i., 198, 234, 236, 249, 291; ii., 9 *sqq.*, 45 *sqq.*, 60, 69, 142 *sq.*, 303 *sq.*, 316, note.

V.

VEADOR, Spanish, ii., 128 *sq.*

W.

WHIDDY, the, ii., 153, 171, 209.
White Knight, i., 105, 119, 205 *sqq.*, 239.
Wilmot, Sir Charles, i., 101, 107, 286; ii., 152, 171, 212, 260, 279, 284.
Wingfield, ii., 300.

Y.

YBARRA, Estevan de, Secretary, ii., 105.

Z.

ZUBIAUR, Pedro, ii., 64, 725.

www.ingramcontent.com/pod-product-compliance
Lightning Source LLC
Chambersburg PA
CBHW032033220426
43664CB00006B/458